Justice, Democracy and the Right to Justification

CRITICAL POWERS

Series Editors:
Bert van den Brink (University of Utrecht),
Antony Simon Laden (University of Illinois, Chicago),
Peter Niesen (University of Hamburg) and
David Owen (University of Southampton).

Critical Powers is dedicated to constructing dialogues around innovative and original work in social and political theory. The ambition of the series is to be pluralist in welcoming work from different philosophical traditions and theoretical orientations, ranging from abstract conceptual argument to concrete policy-relevant engagements, and encouraging dialogue across the diverse approaches that populate the field of social and political theory. All the volumes in the series are structured as dialogues in which a lead essay is greeted with a series of responses before a reply by the lead essayist. Such dialogues spark debate, foster understanding, encourage innovation and perform the drama of thought in a way that engages a wide audience of scholars and students.

Forthcoming titles include:

On Global Citizenship, James Tully
Autonomy Gaps, Joel Anderson
Rogue Theodicy - Politics and Power in the Shadow of Justice,
Glen Newey

Justice, Democracy and the Right to Justification

Rainer Forst in Dialogue

Rainer Forst

B L O O M S B U R Y

LONDON • NEW DELHI • NEW YORK • SYDNEY

Bloomsbury Academic

An imprint of Bloomsbury Publishing Plc

50 Bedford Square	1385 Broadway
London	New York
WC1B 3DP	NY 10018
UK	USA

www.bloomsbury.com

Bloomsbury is a registered trade mark of Bloomsbury Publishing Plc

First published 2014

© Rainer Forst and contributors, 2014

British Library Cataloguing-in-Publication Data
A catalogue record for this book is available from the British Library.

ISBN: PB: 978-1-7809-3999-5
HB: 978-1-7809-3239-2
ePDF: 978-1-7809-3286-6
ePub: 978-1-7809-3285-9

Library of Congress Cataloging-in-Publication Data
A catalog record for this book is available from the Library of Congress

Typeset by Deanta Global Publishing Services, Chennai, India
Printed and bound in India

Contents

List of Contributors

Amy Allen is professor of philosophy and women's and gender studies, and Parents Distinguished Research Professor in the Humanities, at Dartmouth College, where she has taught since 1997. Prof Allen is co-editor-in-chief of *Constellations,* series editor of the Columbia University Press series *New Directions in Critical Theory*, and executive co-director of the Society for Phenomenology and Existential Philosophy (SPEP). Her most recent book is *The Politics of Ourselves* (New York: Columbia University Press, 2008).

Simon Caney is professor in political theory, university lecturer, director of the Centre for the Study of Social Justice, and fellow and tutor in politics, Magdalen College. His most recent book is *Climate Ethics: Essential Readings* (New York: Oxford University Press, 2010) co-edited with Stephen Gardiner, Dale Jamieson and Henry Shue.

Eva Erman is associate professor in the Department of Government at Uppsala University and chief editor of *Ethics & Global Politics*. Her most recent book is *Political Equality in Transnational Democracy* (New York: Palgrave Macmillan, 2013) co-edited with Sofia Näsström.

Rainer Forst is professor of political theory and philosophy at the Goethe University in Frankfurt am Main. He serves as co-director of the Research Cluster 'The Formation of Normative Orders' and the Research Centre 'Justitia Amplificata' in Frankfurt. He is an associate editor of *Ethics*. In 2012, he received the Gottfried Wilhelm Leibniz Prize, the highest honour awarded to German researchers. His most recent books are *Toleration in Conflict* (Cambridge University Press, 2013) and *Justification and Critique* (Polity, 2013).

Anthony Laden is professor of philosophy, and chair, of the Department of Philosophy at the University of Illinois, Chicago. His most recent book is *Reasoning: A Social Picture* (Oxford University Press, 2012).

Kevin Olson is associate professor in political science at the University of California, Irvine. His most recent book is the edited work *Adding Insult to Injury: Nancy Fraser Debates Her Critics* (London: Verso, 2008).

Andrea Sangiovanni is senior lecturer in philosophy at King's College, London. His book *Domains of Justice* is forthcoming with Harvard University Press.

Series Editor's Foreword

Morality, Politics and the Right to Justification

Rainer Forst's lead essay for this volume 'Two Pictures of Justice' exemplifies the theoretical stance that he has been developing since his first book *Contexts of Justice* in its rejection of what Iris Young called 'the distributive paradigm' that has been largely dominant within 'analytic' political philosophy over the past 40 years. Contrasting this picture of justice – which foregrounds the question of who gets what – with a picture that is focused on the question of how you are treated, your standing in intersubjective structures and relationships, Forst argues for the primacy of the second picture in which justice concerns relations between agents that are structured by power. The distributive picture, Forst contends, misleads us in a variety of respects, notably concerning the relationship between morality and justice, particularly the differentiation of humanitarian obligations and duties of justice, and most fundamentally by failing to connect justice and the subjects of justice in a way that acknowledges their standing as agents of justice.

It is perhaps unsurprising that behind the seemingly simple contrast between the two pictures to which Forst attends in this lead essay are a range of debates in moral and political philosophy on which he has developed a distinctive and sophisticated position that is most fully developed in his recent collection *The Right to Justification* – and because many of these responses to Forst's essay focus on its foundations and implications rather than simply the contrast that it draws, it may be helpful to briefly sketch how his wider view animates and drives the argument presented here.

In his work, Forst has developed a Kantian form of practical philosophy whose heart is a conception of human beings as rational subjects who are agents of justification. Practical reason, on Forst's account, is most fundamentally the capacity to offer appropriate kinds of justifying reasons in response to practical questions, where 'appropriateness' is specified by the kind of practical context in question considered as a context of justification. Forst develops this account in characterizing the relationship between reason and morality as one in which the categorical validity of moral norms is to be understood as grounded in their reciprocal and general justification across all human beings. Crucially, for Forst, only reasons that cannot be reasonably – reciprocally and generally – rejected can ground moral norms, where this entails that each and every human being is entitled to raise objections to the claim of any given norm (including those of reciprocity and generality themselves which must be recursively justified). Moral persons, that is, have a *right to justification* and *a duty of justification* as members of the universal moral community.

In contrast to the moral context, political contexts are not universal in this way (although a political context may, as a contingent matter, encompass all human beings). Rather a social context is political when it involves an *order of justification* comprised of the norms and institutions through which some set of persons govern their social relationships to one another. Political contexts thus fundamentally concern relations of rule and the relative standing of persons in relation to one another with respect to relations of rule. The political point of justice, for Forst, as an overarching virtue of such orders of justification is as an emancipatory demand directed at arbitrary rule, where 'arbitrariness' is specified in terms of relations of (formal or informal) rule that cannot be generally and reciprocally justified to those subject to these relations. Thus, the first question of justice is power, the power relationships to which persons are subject and the powers of justification that they enjoy in shaping and contesting structures and relations of rule.

This political conception of justice entails that the first task of justice consists in the construction of a *basic structure of justification* (what Forst calls 'fundamental justice') in which all subject to the order of justification have an equal right to justification (expressed as a qualified veto right) concerning the rule to which they are subject (only then can they experience themselves as both authors and subjects of political rule, as rulers and ruled). The establishment of a basic structure of justification then allows for the development of a *justified basic structure* (what Forst terms 'maximal or full justice'). It is a notable feature of this constructivist conception of justice that it is both substantive in being grounded ultimately in the moral right to justification and procedural in that justified norms of justice are specified through a democratic procedure. However, it is also pertinent to note that, in contrast to the Anglo-American debate about whether justice is confined to states or extends to a global community, Forst's conception of justice tracks contexts and relations of rule in various forms that they take – subnational, national, supranational, transnational, global. Justice, on his conception, is not tied to a particular type of political institution (e.g. the state) but it is tied to political structures and relations of rule (in contrast to those who automatically equate the scope of justice and of morality) and claims of justice, as opposed to claims of, for example, humanitarian aid, can arise wherever the structures and relations of rule in question are not reciprocally and generally justified to those subject to them. This distinctive feature of Forst's account is acutely relevant for the contexts of plural and multilevel governance of the contemporary world.

David Owen

Part One

Lead Essay

1

Two Pictures of Justice

Rainer Forst

Professor of Political Theory and Philosophy
Goethe University Frankfurt, Germany

1. At various times, human beings have made depictions of justice. She appears as the goddess *Diké* or *Justitia*, sometimes with, sometimes without a blindfold, though invariably with the sword and symbols of even-handedness and non-partisanship; one need only think, for example, of Lorenzetti's 'Allegory of Good Government' in the Palazzo Pubblico in Siena. Mostly she is depicted as beautiful and sublime, yet at other times also as hard and cruel, as in Klimt's famous paintings for Vienna University (which were destroyed during the war).

Studying such representations is a fascinating enterprise.[1] However, the understanding of 'picture' which informs my remarks is a different, linguistic, one. In his *Philosophical Investigations*, Wittgenstein writes: 'A *picture* held us captive. And we could not get outside it, for it lay in our language and language seemed to repeat it to us inexorably.'[2] A picture of this kind shapes our language in a particular way, brings together the various usages of a word and thus constitutes its 'grammar'. But such pictures can also point our understanding in the wrong direction,

---

[1] O. R. Kissel, *Die Justitia: Reflexionen über ein Symbol und seine Darstellung in der bildenden Kunst.* Munich: Beck, 1984; D. E. Curtis and J. Resnik, 'Images of Justice', *Yale Law Journal* 96, (1987), 1727–72.

[2] L. Wittgenstein, *Philosophical Investigations*, trans. by G. E. M. Anscombe. Oxford: Basil Blackwell, 1968, p. 48 (§115); on this, see H. F. Pitkin, *Wittgenstein and Justice*. Berkeley: University of California Press, 1972, pp. 91f., 287ff. An interesting application of the idea of 'being held captive by an aspect' can be found in D. Owen, 'Criticism and Captivity: On Genealogy and Critical Theory', *European Journal of Philosophy* 10(2), (2002), 216–30.

much as, in viewing the famous picture puzzle of a duck and a rabbit, one can see only one aspect at a time,[3] or as our thinking is held captive by particular examples that lead us to false generalizations.[4]

In what follows, I would like to discuss two ways of thinking about justice, one of which I want to argue inadmissibly limits and simplifies our understanding of justice, and indeed leads it in a wrong direction. I prefer to regard these two competing notions of justice as 'pictures' because they bring together a wealth of conceptions and images, and not only of justice, but also in particular of injustice. The latter seems to be the more concrete, immediate phenomenon, being associated with stories and images of the oppressed, the wretched and the downtrodden. Thus a 'picture of justice' stands for a very general and at the same time 'thick' and concrete way of thinking about justice and injustice.

2. The picture that holds our thinking concerning social or distributive justice 'captive' is the result of a particular interpretation of the ancient principle *suum cuique* – 'To each (or from each) his own' – which has been central to our understanding of justice since Plato and is interpreted in such a way that the primary issue is what goods individuals justly receive or deserve – in other words, who 'gets' what. This then leads either to comparisons between people's sets of goods, and thus to relative conclusions, or to the question of whether individuals have 'enough' of the essential goods, regardless of comparative considerations. Granted, these goods- and distribution-centred, *recipient-oriented* points of view have their merits, for distributive justice is, of course, concerned with the goods individuals can appropriately claim. Nevertheless, this picture obscures essential aspects of justice. In the first place, the question of how the goods to be distributed come into existence is neglected in a purely goods-focused view; hence, issues of production and its just organization are largely ignored. Furthermore, there is the second problem that the *political* question of who determines the structures of production and distribution and in what ways is disregarded or downplayed, as though

---

[3] Wittgenstein, *Philosophical Investigations*, p. 194.
[4] 'A main cause of philosophical disease – a one-sided diet: one nourishes one's thinking with only one kind of example'. Ibid., p. 155 (§593).

a great distribution machine – a neutral 'distributor'[5] – could exist that only needs to be programmed correctly using the right 'metric' of justice.[6] But, according to the picture of justice I propose, it is essential that there should not be such a machine, because it would mean that justice could no longer be understood as a political accomplishment of the subjects themselves but would turn them into passive recipients of goods – not of justice. This way of thinking also neglects, in the third place, the fact that justified claims to goods do not simply 'exist' but can be arrived at only through discourse in the context of corresponding procedures of justification in which – and this is the *fundamental requirement of justice* – all can in principle participate as free and equal individuals (as I will argue below on the basis of a discourse-theoretical interpretation of the alternative picture of justice).

Finally, in the fourth place, the goods-fixated view of justice also largely leaves the question of injustice out of account; for, by concentrating on overcoming deficiencies in the distribution of goods, someone who suffers want as a result of a natural catastrophe is equivalent to someone who suffers want as a result of economic or political exploitation. Although it is correct that help is required in both cases, according to my understanding of the grammar of justice, in the one case it is required as an act of *moral solidarity*, in the other as an act of *justice* conditioned by the nature of one's involvement in relations of exploitation and injustice and the specific wrong in question.[7] Hence, there are different grounds for action as well as different kinds of action which are required. Ignoring this difference can lead to a

---

[5] In a telling phrase of Gerald A. Cohen, 'Afterword to Chapters One and Two', in ibid., *On the Currency of Egalitarian Justice and Other Essays in Political Philosophy*, ed. by M. Otsuka. Princeton: Princeton University Press, 2011, p. 61.

[6] For the first two points, see esp. I. M. Young, *Justice and the Politics of Difference*. Princeton: Princeton University Press, 1990; and my 'Radical Justice: On Iris Marion Young's Critique of the Distributive Paradigm', *Constellations* 14(2), (2007c), 260–5. Young's decision to call the criticized paradigm 'distributive' often leads to the misunderstanding that she was concerned with 'political' rather than 'social' or distributive justice, which is not the case.

[7] Here a whole series of cases would have to be distinguished: direct participation in or (joint) causation of injustice; indirect participation in injustice by profiting from it without oneself actively contributing to relations of exploitation; and the ('natural') duty to put an end to unjust relations, even if one does not benefit from them but possesses the means to overcome them.

situation where – in a dialectic of morality, as it were[8] – what is actually a requirement of justice is seen as an act of generous assistance or 'aid'. A critique of such a dialectic can already be found in Kant:

> Having the resources to practice such benevolence as depends on the goods of fortune is, for the most part, a result of certain human beings favoured through the injustice of the government, which introduces an inequality of wealth that makes others need their beneficence. Under such circumstances, does a rich man's help to the needy, on which he so readily prides himself as something meritorious, really deserve to be called beneficence at all?[9]

For all of these reasons, it is especially important when dealing with questions of distributive justice to recognize the *political* point of justice and to liberate oneself from a one-sided picture fixated on quantities of goods (or on a measure of well-being to be produced by them). On a second, fuller and more apt picture, by contrast, justice must be geared to *intersubjective relations and structures,* not to *subjective* or *putatively objective states* of the provision of goods or of well-being. Only in this way, by taking into consideration the *first question of justice* – namely, the question of the justifiability of social relations and, correspondingly, how much 'justification power' individuals or groups have in a political context – can a radical, critical conception of justice be developed, one which gets at the roots of relations of injustice. In short, the basic question of justice is not *what you have* but *how you are treated.*[10]

3. What might justify one in speaking of a misleading or 'false' as opposed to a more 'apt' picture of justice, given that the goods- or recipient-centred notion can appeal to the time-honoured principle

---

[8] See my *The Right to Justification: Elements of a Constructivist Theory of Justice,* trans. by J. Flynn. New York: Columbia University Press, 2012, ch. 11.

[9] I. Kant, *The Metaphysics of Morals,* ed. and trans. by M. J. Gregor. Cambridge: Cambridge University Press, 2009, p. 203.

[10] Derek Parfit's distinction between a 'telic' and a 'deontic' egalitarian view captures important aspects of these different ways of thinking about justice, and it is interesting to note that – without commenting explicitly on this – he uses the term justice only in connection with the deontic view. See his 'Equality or Priority?', in M. Clayton and A. Williams (eds), *The Ideal of Equality.* Houndsmill: Macmillan, 2002, p. 90.

of *suum cuique*? Is there, in contrast to this, a more original, deeper meaning of justice which the alternative picture captures more fully? In my opinion there is. Consider the very concept of justice. That concept possesses a core meaning to which the essential contrasting concept is that of *arbitrariness*,[11] understood in a social and political but not a metaphysical sense – that is, assuming the form of arbitrary rule by individuals or by a part of the community (e.g. a class) over others, or of the acceptance of social contingencies which lead to social subordination and domination and are rationalized as an unalterable fate, even though they are nothing of that sort. A metaphysical conception of arbitrariness in the context of social justice would go further and aim to eradicate or compensate for all differences between persons giving them an advantage over others due to brute luck, regardless of whether these differences lead to social domination.[12] This goes too far according to the second picture of justice; justice must remain a human task aiming at non-domination, not one for the gods aiming at a world free from natural or historical contingency. Arbitrariness as domination is a human vice of injustice, contingency generally is a fact of life.

The term 'domination' is important in this context, for it signifies the arbitrary rule of some over others – that is, rule without proper reasons and justifications and (possibly) without proper structures of justification existing in the first place,[13] and when people engage in struggles against injustice, they are combating forms of domination

---

[11] See also John Rawls's definition in *A Theory of Justice*, rev. edn. Cambridge, MA: Harvard University Press, 1999a, p. 5.

[12] Without being able to go into details here, I concur with the critiques of 'luck egalitarianism' by E. Anderson, 'What is the Point of Equality?', *Ethics* 109(2), (1999), 287–337; and S. Scheffler, 'What is Egalitarianism?', in ibid., *Equality and Tradition: Questions of Value in Moral and Political Theory*. Oxford: Oxford University Press, 2010, pp. 175–207. As both of them show, luck egalitarianism is a cousin of libertarianism in that it accepts the results of free choice (or 'option luck') as just, while 'victims' of 'misfortune' are seen as (passive and needy) recipients of compensation. I do not think, however, that the major difference between these views is to be located in the concept of equality; rather, it stems from two very different ways of thinking about justice.

[13] I explain the difference between such a discourse-theoretical understanding of domination and a neo-republican one based on freedom of choice in my 'A Kantian Republican Conception of Justice as Non-Domination', in A. Niederberger and P. Schink (eds), *Republican Democracy*. Edinburgh: Edinburgh University Press, 2013b.

of this kind. The basic impulse that opposes injustice is not primarily one of wanting something, or more of something, but is instead that of not wanting to be dominated, harassed or overruled in one's claim to a *basic right to justification*.[14] This *moral* right expresses the demand that no political or social relations should exist that cannot be adequately justified towards those involved. This constitutes the profoundly *political* essence of justice, which is not captured, but is suppressed, by the recipient-focused interpretations of the principle *suum cuique*. The core issue of justice is who determines who receives what, that is, the question answered in Plato in terms of the ideas of the supreme good and the philosopher king.[15] In my picture, the demand for justice is an emancipatory one; reflexively speaking, it rests on the claim to be respected as a subject of justification, that is, to be respected in one's dignity as a being who offers and demands justifications.[16] The person who lacks certain goods should not be regarded as the primary victim of injustice but instead the one who does not 'count' when it comes to deciding about the process of producing and allocating of goods.

4. One can cut different paths through contemporary discussions of justice. However, the one opened up by the question of the two pictures of justice is especially instructive, for from this perspective certain conventional adversaries unexpectedly find themselves in the same boat.

An example is provided by the recent debate concerning equality. By this is actually meant two points of discussion: on the one hand, the question '*Equality of what?*' – of resources, welfare or capabilities[17] – and,

---

[14] I explain this more fully in Forst, *The Right to Justification*.

[15] On this, see Pitkin's critique of Plato's apolitical notion of justice in *Wittgenstein and Justice*, p. 306: 'A distribution imposed by fiat from above, on creatures with no claim of their own, programmed to accept as their own what the system assigns, cannot really illustrate the problems of justice but only avoid them.'

[16] On the notion of dignity, see R. Forst, *Justification and Critique: Towards a Critical Theory of Politics*. Cambridge: Polity, 2013b, ch. 4.

[17] See, especially, G. A. Cohen, 'Equality of What?: On Welfare, Goods, and Capabilities', in M. Nussbaum, and A. Sen (eds), *The Quality of Life*. Oxford: Oxford University Press, 1993, pp. 9–29; R. Dworkin, *Sovereign Virtue: The Theory and Practice of Equality*. Cambridge, MA: Harvard University Press, 2000, part I; H. Brighouse and I. Robeyns (eds), *Measuring Justice: Primary Goods and Capabilities*. Cambridge: Cambridge University Press, 2010.

on the other, the question '*Why equality at all?*'. From the perspective of the difference between the two pictures of justice, however, it becomes apparent that both the advocates and the opponents of equality frequently operate with the same understanding, and this often finds expression in a specific image, that of the mother who has to divide up a cake and asks herself how this should be done.[18] Egalitarians argue for the primacy of the equal distribution of goods, according to which other arguments for legitimate unequal distributions – for instance, ones based on need, merit or prior claims – then have to be treated as special reasons. Alternatively, an egalitarian calculus of need satisfaction – a measure of welfare – is posited which serves as the goal of distribution.[19] However, in the process the questions of how the cake was produced and, even more importantly, of who gets to play the role of the mother, remain largely unthematized. Yet that is the primary question of justice. Attempts are made to answer it in terms of the distribution of a 'good' of 'power'.[20] But no such 'good' exists as something to be distributed; on the contrary, power comes about in a different way – namely, through processes of recognition without a prior distributive authority.[21]

5. Analogous problems are encountered on the side of the critics of equality. In Harry Frankfurt's view, for example, the defenders of egalitarian conceptions of justice cannot be concerned with the value of

---

[18] See, for example, E. Tugendhat, *Vorlesungen über Ethik*. Frankfurt am Main: Suhrkamp, 1993, pp. 373f; W. Hinsch, *Gerechtfertigte Ungleichheiten*. Berlin: de Gruyter, 2002, pp. 169f.; S. Gosepath, *Gleiche Gerechtigkeit*. Frankfurt am Main: Suhrkamp, 2004, pp. 250ff. The cake example, though without the mother, can also be found in I. Berlin, 'Equality', in ibid., *Concepts and Categories*. Harmondsworth: Penguin, 1981, p. 84. See also Rawls in *A Theory of Justice*, p. 74.

[19] For a paradigmatic expression, see R. Arneson, 'Luck and Equality', *Proceedings of the Aristotelian Society*, supp. vol., (2001), 73–90; and 'Luck Egalitarianism: An Interpretation and Defense', *Philosophical Topics* 32(1/2), (2004), 1–20.

[20] Tugendhat, *Vorlesungen*, p. 379; Gosepath, *Gleiche Gerechtigkeit*, p. 90.

[21] Young, *Justice and the Politics of Difference*; J. Habermas, *Between Facts and Norms: Contributions to a Discourse Theory of Law and Democracy*, trans. by W. Rehg. Cambridge, MA: MIT Press, 1996a. On the importance of the issue of power for questions of justice, see also I. Shapiro, *Democratic Justice*. New Haven: Yale University Press, 1999. The fact that no general 'good' of power exists does not mean that the resources necessary to generate power cannot be the object of distributions. I try to show that power should be situated in the space of justifications in 'Noumenal Power' (Normative Orders Working Paper 2/2013d.).

equality at all; for if you ask them what is so bad about inequality, they respond by pointing to the negative consequences of life in a society of inequality, in particular to the fact that certain people lack goods which are important for living a satisfactory life.[22] What is bad about such a life is supposed to be that the people in question lack essential goods, not that others are better off.[23]

So-called 'sufficientarians'[24] have taken up these arguments and argue that 'at least the especially important, elementary standards of justice are of a nonrelational kind,'[25] and that justice is concerned with creating 'conditions of life befitting human beings' that can be measured according to 'absolute standards of fulfilment', not according to what others have. On this view, a universal conception of the goods 'necessary for a good life' should be produced with reference to particular lists of basic goods or capabilities.

These approaches are also vulnerable to serious objections. For Frankfurt's assertion that the pivotal issue is not how much others have but only whether I have 'enough' is valid *only when* conditions of background justice pertain, that is, only when others have not previously taken advantage of me. Otherwise it could not be reconciled with my dignity as a being who is in principle worthy of equal moral respect (a standard that Frankfurt emphasizes). Hence we must look for reasons for such background justice elsewhere.

But, in addition, the idea of 'having enough' or 'getting enough' does not get at the essence of justice, that is, the prevention of social domination. Justice is always a 'relational' matter; it does not first inquire into subjective or objective *states of affairs* but into *relations between human beings* and what they owe to each other given these relations. In particular, we do not explain the requirements of justice on the model of morally required aid in specific situations of want or need; instead

[22] H. Frankfurt, 'Equality as a Moral Ideal', in ibid., *The Importance of What We Care About*. Cambridge: Cambridge University Press, 1988, pp. 143–58; and 'Equality and Respect', in ibid., *Necessity, Volition, and Love*. Cambridge: Cambridge University Press, 1999, pp. 146–54.

[23] Thus also J. Raz, *The Morality of Freedom*. Oxford: Clarendon Press, 1986, ch. 9.

[24] R. Crisp, 'Equality, Priority, and Compassion', *Ethics* 113(4), (2003), 745–63.

[25] A. Krebs, 'Einleitung: Die neue Egalitarismuskritik im Überblick', in ibid. (ed.), *Gleichheit oder Gerechtigkeit*. Frankfurt am Main: Suhrkamp, 2000, pp. 17f.

they come into play in situations where what is at stake are relations between human beings that are fundamentally in need of justification, where those involved are connected by political relations of rule or by social relations of cooperation in the production and distribution of goods – or, as is often the case, by relations of 'negative cooperation', of coercion or domination (whether by legal, economic or political means). It makes a huge difference whether someone is *deprived of* certain goods and opportunities unjustly and without justification or whether he or she *lacks* certain goods for whatever reason (e.g. as a result of a natural catastrophe, as mentioned above). By losing sight of the former context, one misses or conceals the problem of justice as well as that of injustice. Justice requires that those involved in a context of (positive or negative) cooperation should be respected as equals. That means that they should enjoy equal rights to take part in the social and political *order of justification* in which the conditions under which goods are produced and distributed are determined. The state-mandated assignment of goods in accordance with 'absolute' standards that abstract from the real context of justice or injustice is far from doing justice to the 'dignity' of the individual who seeks justice.

6. But what exactly is supposed to be wrong with taking a sufficiently nuanced theory of *basic capabilities* as the basis for a theory of justice that would put an end to discussions concerning basic goods, resources, welfare, etc.? Isn't justice after all concerned with the satisfaction of the basic claim to be able to live an autonomous good life? Isn't a theory that disregards the results of distribution blind, indeed blinder than any depiction of *Justitia*? Martha Nussbaum argues thus in her study *Frontiers of Justice* against Rawls and for a 'minimal level of justice' in accordance with a list of basic capabilities and faculties that must be secured.[26] A results-oriented view of justice knows the correct outcome and then looks for the necessary procedure leading to it in the best way possible (in Rawls's terms, 'imperfect procedural justice').[27] The

---

[26] M. Nussbaum, *Frontiers of Justice: Disability, Nationality, Species Membership.* Cambridge, MA: Harvard University Press, 2006, p. 74.

[27] Rawls, *A Theory of Justice*, pp. 74f.

procedures themselves are secondary. Against the Rawlsian idea of 'pure procedural justice', in which the acceptability of the result depends on the quality of the procedure, Nussbaum argues as follows:

> Defenders of outcome-oriented views are likely to feel that procedural views put the cart before the horse: for surely what matters for justice is the quality of life for people, and we are ultimately going to reject any procedure, however elegant, if it doesn't give us an outcome that squares well with our intuitions about dignity and fairness. . . . it seems to the outcome-oriented theorist as if a cook has a fancy, sophisticated pasta-maker, and assures her guests that the pasta made in this machine will be by definition good, since it is the best machine on the market.[28]

Here, too, the pictures are revealing. The idea of a 'machine' signals an exclusive orientation to results: 'The capabilities approach goes straight to the content of the outcome, looks at it, and asks whether it seems compatible with a life in accordance with human . . . dignity.'[29] Justice is an instrument that produces something, and the result counts, not the internal workings of the machine. But this misses the political point of justice. Political and social justice is a matter of how a context of political rule and social cooperation is constituted; and the first question in this regard is how individuals are involved in political and social relations generally and in the production of material and immaterial goods in particular, so that a result is just only if it is produced under conditions that can be accepted by all, that is, conditions of non-domination.[30] From a relational point of view, it might be a 'good' thing

---

[28] Nussbaum, *Frontiers*, p. 82.

[29] Ibid., p. 87.

[30] The meaning of 'cooperation' in this context should not be understood in such a way that it prescribes certain stereotypical or economistic ideals of the ability to cooperate and excludes persons who, for example, are not yet or are no longer able to participate in the 'normal' labour market. What is meant is a form of social cooperation in a wider sense of sharing a social and political order. Nussbaum, *Frontiers*, p. 121, correctly stresses the need for such a broad concept of cooperation. In contrast to her, however, I do not think that this extension is a matter of benevolence (ibid., p. 122) because the claim to non-domination also holds for those who are denied the opportunity of full social membership and participation within a basic structure due to a disability – a participation which should also be defined in reciprocal and general terms in the light of their abilities. The terms of cooperation must be determined in a discursive manner. A community of justification is not a community of 'mutual advantage' in the narrow sense.

if a great Leviathan were to hand out manna as an all-purpose good (by comparison with a situation of dire need), but that would have little to do with political and social justice. Were a dictatorship to ensure that basic capabilities were largely assured, that would indeed be 'better' by certain standards than a destitute democracy, but it would not be more just. Justice is not a criterion for universal levels of goods or for all efforts to overcome privation but for quite specific ones, namely, those which eliminate arbitrary rule – that is, domination and exploitation. The primary demand of justice is not that human beings should obtain certain goods but that they should be agents equipped with equal rights within a social context – whether national or transnational[31] – who can raise specific claims to goods on this basis.

7. A number of theories are ambivalent with respect to the two pictures of justice and contain aspects of both.[32] Amartya Sen's interpretation of the idea of justice is an example. He makes a different distinction between two basic ways of reasoning about justice from the one I suggest. Whereas in his view 'transcendental institutionalism' concentrates on an ideal of perfect justice and on institutions rather than on actual behaviours of persons, 'realization-focused comparison', the approach which Sen favours, emphasizes comparative assessments of states of affairs and of 'the kind of lives that people can actually lead'.[33] Against ideal theories, Sen argues that comparative assessments of the quality of life and the justice of a society can be made even when there

---

[31] See my discussion of transnational contexts of justice in *The Right to Justification*, Part III.

[32] In the German version of this chapter, I discussed Axel Honneth's theory of recognition as likewise ambivalent in this sense; see 'Zwei Bilder der Gerechtigkeit', in R. Forst, *Kritik der Rechtfertigungsverhältnisse: Perspektiven einer kritischen Theorie der Politik*. Berlin: Suhrkamp, 2011, pp. 47–51. However, given that this analysis did not refer to the new, more complex approach developed in A. Honneth, *Das Recht der Freiheit: Grundriß einer demokratischen Sittlichkeit*. Frankfurt am Main: Suhrkamp, 2011, I have not included it in the English version.

[33] A. Sen, *The Idea of Justice*. London: Allen Lane, 2009b, pp. 7, 10. I cannot discuss here the issue of whether Sen correctly interprets Rawls's theory as a model of 'transcendental institutionalism'. Briefly, I do not see Rawls as focusing exclusively on institutions rather than persons and their lives, and, since Rawls leaves open such basic institutional questions as whether the well-ordered society has a written constitution or whether there will be a private right of ownership of means of production, I believe one should instead speak of 'institutional agnosticism' in Rawls.

is disagreement over 'perfect' justice, and he proposes the capability approach as explaining the 'material of justice' and an account of public reason as the medium of judgment.

If we compare Sen's distinction with the one between the two pictures, it becomes apparent that the relational and structure-oriented picture of justice which I favour does not pursue an abstract 'ideal theory' but enquires instead into the social relations of rule or domination that exist and need to be transformed into justifiable relations. Also, the relational picture does not just take institutions into account but also social relations in a more comprehensive sense, though it sees institutions as essential for realizing justice. Finally, the second picture of justice shares with Sen the critique of a 'goods-centred'[34] view when it comes to the material of justice.

Still, despite these parallels, the approach favoured by Sen, viewed from a relational or structure-oriented perspective on justice, neglects important considerations of justice – namely, the question of *injustice*, the question of *obligations*, the question of *principles* and the question of *institutions* of justice. With regard to injustice, as explained above, how asymmetries of capabilities, if we take that as the material of justice, actually came about makes an essential difference. Are they the result of deliberate action, of structures that benefit some rather than others and are upheld deliberatively, or are they the result of circumstances the responsibility for which cannot be ascertained? For any theory that, like Sen's, aims to eradicate or at least reduce concrete forms of injustice, it is essential to have a clear focus on these injustices and their historical and structural background. To be sure, a lack of basic capabilities due to hunger or bad health needs to be overcome whatever story is told about how it arose; but for a theory of *justice* it is essential to ask the genealogical question. Sen is aware of that point when, for example, he asserts that 'there is a real difference between some people dying of starvation due to circumstances beyond anyone's control and those people being starved to death through the design of those wanting

---

[34] See especially his critique of Rawls, as developed in A. Sen, *Inequality Reexamined*. Cambridge, MA: Harvard University Press, 1992, pp. 79–85.

to bring about that outcome'.[35] But because the capability approach is primarily focused on outcomes, its ability to integrate such distinctions into its basic framework is limited.

This has implications for its account of *obligations*. Justice, according to the relational view, enquires into the relations between persons in order to ascertain responsibilities of justice, ranging from those who wilfully committed an injustice, to those who merely benefit, up to those who are only involved insofar as they have the means to change things for the better. According to the second picture, locating these responsibilities in the right way is *itself* a demand of justice. Sen, however, has a more consequentialist conception of obligation, one based on capacities and powers of effective action.[36] Although he accepts the Kantian distinction between perfect and imperfect obligations,[37] the thrust of his argument about power-based obligations of justice is that they are conceived as imperfect obligations directed at certain outcomes.

Sen defends the thesis of a plurality of valid *principles* of justice, be they principles of need, contribution or utility, as expressed in the example of the distribution of a flute among children who have different types of claims to it.[38] Moreover, he makes a strong case for the possibility of judgments of justice within the framework of public reason even in the absence of any consensus on perfect justice. Yet, at this point, the argument for a 'plural grounding'[39] of judgments of justice and for a 'plurality of robust and impartial reasons'[40] in a given case is too strong, for it leads to an essential vagueness and contestedness as to the issue of trumping principles of justice. This is not just the case when it comes to an equivalent of the Rawlsian first principle of justice; with regard to that, Sen affirms that the capability perspective cannot provide any such principle.[41] But also with respect to judgments of social justice – such as priorities among capabilities and among persons with different

[35] Sen, *The Idea of Justice*, p. 23.
[36] Ibid., pp. 205, 271.
[37] Ibid., pp. 372ff.
[38] Ibid., pp. 12f., 201, 396f.
[39] Ibid., p. 2.
[40] Ibid., p. 205.
[41] Ibid., p. 299.

deficiencies in capabilities – Sen's approach does not provide any general principles of assessment.

As far as the question of *institutions* is concerned, Sen's critique of 'transcendental institutionalism' leaves little room for a positive theory of institutions. Yet institutions represent essential expressions of social life and they are the primary objects of assessment when it comes to issues of social justice. Individual actions are also important objects of assessment in this regard, though often as part of institutional structures. Most importantly, institutions serve as the guarantors for the realization of principles of equal respect, especially in the guise of institutions of discursive justification. Institutions give expression to these principles, and how institutions work can violate them, not just with respect to outcomes, but also and especially when it comes to processes. Sen is alert to the challenge posed by a process-oriented picture of justice to his view, and that is why he suggests the notion of 'comprehensive outcomes' rather than mere 'culmination outcomes', for the former take procedural issues into account.[42] From the perspective of comprehensive outcomes, it is important how a result came about – who participated in a decision, which interests were taken into account, which considerations were decisive, what kind of possibilities there were for contestation, to mention just a few. All of these questions reflect criteria for the justice of institutions, and thus any comprehensive theory must take them into account. But, as Sen admits, the capability approach 'cannot pay adequate attention to fairness and equity involved in procedures that have relevance to the idea of justice'.[43] I would go even further and suggest that the approach, since it focuses on outcomes and states of affairs, is not only incapable of generating an account of fairness by its own means, but it also needs to accept the priority of the process aspects when it comes to the question of justice.[44] For

---

[42] Ibid., p. 22. See also his 'Consequential Evaluation and Practical Reason', *Journal of Philosophy* 97(9), (2000), 477–502.

[43] Sen, *The Idea of Justice*, p. 295.

[44] This is reflected in Sen's stress on democracy as the basic institution of political justice – an argument that is not used, however, as the basis for a relational and structural, higher-order conception of democratic justice (which I will elaborate on below).

justice is about who determines (and with what justification) the basic structure of society as well as its essential institutional workings; and if we want to rule out the great benevolent Leviathan mentioned above as realizing justice by distributing means of well-being, we need to argue for the priority of principles of equal respect, participation and non-domination within the basic structure of a society or across polities in a transnational context. Conceptually speaking, it is one thing to argue for a better distribution and realization of basic capabilities by way of a theory of social *development* and progress, yet it is another thing to argue for a comprehensive conception of social and political *justice*. If we focus primarily on realizations, then important aspects of (in)justice will be overlooked.[45] The most important of all principles of distribution, therefore, is the one which determines who has the authority to decide about who receives a good like the flute (in Sen's example) in the first place.

8. Here I would like to offer a brief discussion of Rawls's theory of justice. Since Robert Nozick's influential critique, Rawls's theory is generally interpreted as belonging to the first, allocative-distributive and recipient-oriented understanding of justice. Nozick criticizes Rawls's principles of justice as 'end-state principles' which correspond to pre-given patterns that illegitimately constrain the liberty of market participants.[46] But Rawls's theory is also regarded from an entirely different perspective such as that of Thomas Pogge, which is far removed from libertarian theories, as a 'purely recipient-oriented approach', because it concentrates on comparisons between distributive results as regards basic goods which correspond to certain higher-level interests of persons in such goods.[47] This assessment has a certain justification, given the importance of primary goods in Rawls's theory.

---

[45] In section 10, I will come back to the question of capabilities and a possible place for them within the relational picture of justice.

[46] R. Nozick, *Anarchy, State, and Utopia*. New York: Basic, 1974, pp. 149ff. Young, *Justice and the Politics of Difference*, p. 28, is in agreement with Nozick in criticizing end-state theories (to which in her view the Rawlsian belongs).

[47] T. Pogge, 'The Incoherence Between Rawls's Theories of Justice', *Fordham Law Review* 72(5), (2004), p. 1739.

Nevertheless, in my view, Rawls does not share the first but the second picture of justice, the one which accords priority to social structures and relations and the social status of the individual. Let me explain this briefly.

In the first place, the Kantian character of Rawls's theory implies that the autonomy of free and equal persons, which is at the normative heart of the approach, is not the autonomy of individuals who are primarily conceived as recipients of goods which they would need in order to lead a 'good life'. It is rather the constructive autonomy of free and equal subjects of justification which manifests itself in the fact that the persons are able to regard the principles of justice as morally self-given; hence, the citizens view the social basic structure which is grounded in this way as the social expression of their self-determination.[48] The essential conception of autonomy is the autonomy to actively determine the basic structure, not the autonomy to enjoy its goods (even though this is also important). The emphasis on public reason in the later works underscores this because public reason represents the medium of discursive justification in which an autonomous conception of justice is grounded that all can accept as free and equal: 'In affirming the political doctrine as a whole we, as citizens, are ourselves autonomous, politically speaking.'[49]

An important implication of the Kantian background of the theory consists in the fact that its central concern is to exclude the aspects of the social world 'that seem arbitrary from a moral point of view' both in justifying the principles and in the institutions of the basic structure.[50] In this way differences in natural endowments and social inequalities should not lead to advantages that cannot be legitimized, especially towards the worst off. This is a criterion for social relations between citizens of a 'well-ordered society', not primarily a criterion for determining the amounts of goods to which everyone can lay

[48] Rawls, *A Theory of Justice*, §40.
[49] J. Rawls, *Political Liberalism*. New York: Columbia University Press, 1993, p. 98.
[50] Rawls, *A Theory of Justice*, p. 14.

claim.[51] That the pivotal issue here is the absence of relations of unjustifiable social rule – hence, expressed in a different language, *non-domination* – is in my view the most appropriate interpretation of this idea of avoiding social arbitrariness.

This leads to the most important concept in this regard, one which marks the difference from libertarianism most clearly – namely that of social cooperation. Rawls's conception of 'procedural justice' is geared to social relations and structures such that it leads to a system of social cooperation which expresses the 'sociability of human beings' in such a way that they complement each other in productive ways and participate in a context of cooperation which includes all as politically and socially autonomous members – think of the picture of the orchestra employed by Rawls.[52] It is particularly significant in this regard how Rawls contrasts his conception of justice as fairness with a conception of 'allocative justice':

> The problem of distributive justice in justice as fairness is always this: How are the institutions of the basic structure to be regulated as one unified scheme of institutions so that a fair, efficient, and productive system of social cooperation can be maintained over time, from one generation to the next? Contrast this with the very different problem of how a given bundle of commodities is to be distributed, or allocated, among various individuals whose particular needs, desires, and preferences are known to us, and who have not cooperated in any way to produce those commodities. This second problem is that of allocative justice. . . . We reject the idea of allocative justice as incompatible with the fundamental idea by which justice as fairness is organised. . . . Citizens are seen as cooperating to produce the social resources on which their claims are made. In a well-ordered society . . . the distribution of income and wealth illustrates what we may call pure background procedural justice. The basic structure is

---

51 See also Scheffler, 'What is Egalitarianism?', pp. 195f.
52 Rawls, *A Theory of Justice*, pp. 458ff. On the notion of cooperation, see fn. 30 above.

arranged so that when everyone follows the publicly recognised rules of cooperation, and honours the claims the rules specify, the particular distributions of goods that result are acceptable as just . . . whatever these distributions turn out to be.[53]

The overriding issue within such a context of production and distribution is who the individuals 'are', and not primarily what they receive according to an independent yardstick. The decisive point is that the institutions function in accordance with generally justified principles, such as the difference principle, and do not involve any social privileges, and that they do not lead to the creation and cementing of groups which are largely excluded from the system of cooperation and permanently depend on allocative transfers of goods. This is also what underlies Rawls's emphatic criticism of the capitalist welfare state model, because this, in contrast to a 'property-owning democracy', does not ensure that the ownership of wealth and capital is sufficiently dispersed and as a result cannot prevent 'a small part of society from controlling the economy, and indirectly, political life as well'.[54] Here I cannot explore further to what extent Rawls's theory sufficiently accommodates the principle that social asymmetries are in need of justification and provides for corresponding institutional practices of justification. The remarks below show how a discourse-theoretical conception differs in fundamental ways from the Rawlsian conception.

9. Let us review the essential points made thus far from a constructive perspective. I have defined justice as the human virtue and moral-political imperative to oppose relations of arbitrary rule or domination. Domination is rule 'without justification', and it is assumed that a just social order is one to which free and equal persons could give their assent – not just their counterfactual assent but assent based

---

[53] J. Rawls, *Justice as Fairness: A Restatement*, ed. by E. Kelly. Cambridge, MA: Harvard University Press, 2001, p. 50.
[54] Ibid., p. 139.

on institutionalized justification procedures. This is a *recursive* implication of the fact that what is at stake in political and social justice is norms of an institutional basic structure which lays claim to reciprocal and general validity. Thus a *supreme principle* holds within such a framework – namely, the *principle of general and reciprocal justification* – which states that every claim to goods, rights or liberties must be justified in a reciprocal and general manner, where one side may not simply project its reasons onto the other but has to justify itself discursively.

According to this principle, as I remarked above, each member of a context of justice has a fundamental *right to justification*, that is, a right to be offered appropriate reasons for the norms of justice that are supposed to hold generally. Respect for this right is a universal requirement, and the moral equality expressed by it provides the foundation for farther-reaching claims to political and social justice.[55] Every further norm of justice is relational in the sense that it must be constructed via a procedure of reciprocal-general justification. Then, requirements of justice are not moral acts of assistance but obligatory acts within a social system of rule and cooperation.

The decisive criteria of justice, therefore, are those of reciprocity and generality, notwithstanding the plurality of goods and normative viewpoints concerning the distribution of educational opportunities, health care goods, etc. These criteria serve to filter out unacceptable claims to privilege, for the intrinsic social dynamic of justice is always geared in the first instance to the question: Which positions of advantage are not justifiable towards those who do not enjoy these advantages but are nevertheless supposed to recognize them?

This brings us to the central insight for the problem of political and social justice – namely that *the first question of justice is the question of power*. For justice is not only a matter of which goods, for which reasons

---

[55] Having this right does not depend on a particular capacity to exercise it; it is a right of persons in a deontological sense. Acquiring the means to use this right effectively, however, is a matter of justice.

and in what amounts, should legitimately be allocated to whom, but in particular of *how* these goods come into the world in the first place and of *who* decides on their allocation and *how* this allocation is made. Theories of a predominantly allocative-distributive kind are accordingly 'oblivious to power' insofar as they conceive of justice exclusively from the 'recipient side', and if necessary call for 'redistributions', without emphasizing the political question of how the structures of production and allocation of goods are determined in the first place. The claim that the question of power is the first question of justice means that justice has its proper place where the central justifications for a social basic structure must be provided and the institutional ground rules are laid down which determine social life from the bottom up. Everything depends, if you will, on the relations of justification within a society. Power, understood as the effective 'justificatory power' of individuals, is the higher-level good of justice. It is the 'discursive' power to demand and provide justifications and to challenge false legitimations. This amounts to an argument for a 'political turn' in the debate concerning justice and for a *critical theory of justice as a critique of relations of justification.*[56]

The argument outlined makes possible an *autonomous*, reflexively grounded theory of justice that rests on no other values or truths besides the principle of justification itself. The principle in question, however, is not merely a principle of discursive reason but is itself a moral principle.[57] This constitutes the Kantian character of the approach, which means that it emphasizes the autonomy of those for whom certain norms of justice are supposed to be binding – in other words, the autonomy and dignity that consists in being subject to no norms or structures other than those which can be justified towards the individual. This dignity is violated when individuals are regarded merely as recipients of redistributive measures and not as independent agents of justice.

---

[56] See Forst, *Justification and Critique*.
[57] See Forst, *The Right to Justification*, Part I.

10. A comprehensive theory of political and social justice can be constructed on this basis, something at which I can only hint here.[58] First we must make a conceptual distinction between *fundamental* (minimal) and *full* (maximal) *justice*. Whereas the task of fundamental justice is to construct a *basic structure of justification*, the task of full justice is to construct a *justified basic structure*. The former is necessary in order to pursue the latter, that is, a 'putting-into-effect' of justification through constructive, discursive democratic procedures in which the 'justificatory power' is distributed as evenly as possible among the citizens. This calls for certain rights and institutions and a multiplicity of means and specific capabilities[59] and information, including real opportunities to intervene and exercise control within the basic structure – hence, not a 'minimalist' structure, yet one justified in material terms solely on the basis of the principle of justification. The question of what is included in this minimum must be legitimized and assessed in accordance with the criteria of reciprocity and generality. The result is a higher-level, discursive version of the Rawlsian 'difference principle', which, according to Rawls, confers a 'veto' on those who are worst off: 'those who have gained more must do so on terms that are justifiable to those who have gained the least'.[60] This principle does not as a result itself become a particular principle of distribution (as in Rawls), however, but a higher-level principle of justification of possible distributions.[61]

To put it in apparently paradoxical terms, fundamental justice is thus a substantive starting point of procedural justice. Arguments for a basic structure are based on a moral right to justification according

---

[58] For a more detailed discussion, see R. Forst, *Contexts of Justice: Political Philosophy Beyond Liberalism and Communitarianism*, trans. by J. M. M. Farrell. Berkeley: University of California Press, 2002; and *The Right to Justification*.

[59] Here the 'capabilities' approach has a justification, though one associated with the task of constructing fundamental justice.

[60] Rawls, *A Theory of Justice*, p. 131.

[61] Here we must be alert to the fact that the group of the 'worst off' can change according to which good is to be allocated. The unemployed, single parents, the elderly, the sick or ethnic minorities, to mention just a few, could have priority in a given instance and combinations of these characteristics, in particular, aggravate the problem (especially in the light of the history of gender relations).

to which individuals must have real political and social opportunities to determine the institutions of this structure in a reciprocal-general, autonomous manner. Fundamental justice assures all citizens an effective status 'as equals', as citizens with opportunities to participate and wield influence. Fundamental justice is violated when primary justification power is not secured for all equally in the most important institutions.

On this basis it becomes possible to strive for a differentiated, justified basic structure, that is, full justice. Democratic procedures must determine which goods are to be allocated to whom by whom on what scale and for what reasons. Whereas fundamental justice must be laid down in a recursive and discursive manner by reference to the necessary conditions of fair justification opportunities, other substantive considerations and certainly also social-relative considerations (in Michael Walzer's sense), also enter into considerations of full justice.[62] For example, how goods, such as health, work, leisure and so forth, should be distributed must, on this approach, always be determined first in the light of the functional requirements of fundamental justice, and then, in addition, with a view to the corresponding goods and the reasons that favour one or the other distributive scheme (which are also subject to change). As long as fundamental justice pertains, such discourses will not fall prey to illegitimate inequalities of power. Once again it becomes apparent why the first question of justice is the question of power.

11. What, then, is the ultimate difference between the two pictures of justice that I have discussed? Perhaps it resides in two different moral ideas of human beings, as beings who should not lack certain goods that are necessary for a 'good' life or one 'befitting a human being', on the one hand, and as beings whose dignity consists in not being

---

[62] M. Walzer, *Spheres of Justice*. New York: Basic Books, 1983. In later writings, Walzer has modified his approach in such a way that the principle of 'democratic citizenship' plays the leading role in all spheres. See his 'Response', in ibid., and D. Miller (eds), *Pluralism, Justice, and Equality*. Oxford: Oxford University Press, 1995, esp. pp. 286ff.

subject to domination, on the other. Both are important ideas, and any comprehensive moral theory has to include them properly. But on my understanding, only the second idea is central for the grammar of justice.[63]

Translated by Ciaran Cronin

---

[63] An earlier German version of this chapter (which builds in part on the Introduction and Chapter 8 of *The Right to Justification*) was published in R. Forst, M. Hartmann, R. Jaeggi and M. Saar (eds), *Sozialphilosophie und Kritik. Festschrift for Axel Honneth*. Frankfurt am Main: Suhrkamp Verlag, 2009, and reprinted in Forst, *Kritik der Rechtfertigungsverhältnisse*. The revised English version, translated by Ciaran Cronin, is also published in Forst, *Justification and Critique*. Permission to publish this text is kindly acknowledged.

Part Two

Responses

2

Scottish Constructivism and The Right to Justification

Andrea Sangiovanni
Senior Lecturer in Philosophy,
Kings College London, UK

At the centre of *The Right to Justification*[1] is a striking and original claim, namely that the force and content of morality can be grounded in our nature as *justifying beings,* as creatures that cannot but engage in practices of reason-giving and reason-taking. The aim of this paper is twofold. First, I aim to unpack this claim by understanding it as a specific, Kantian form of rationalist constructivism. Second, I will argue that the argument can only take us part of the way: any adequate account of the grounds, force and content of morality must secure a much more central place to the social emotions and their associated capacities and dispositions, the most important of which is empathy. I will end by reflecting on some passages within the book that suggest that Forst is aware of the limits of his own rationalist constructivism, and himself betrays a (hidden?) desire to throw off the Kantian shackles that he otherwise freely accepts. My argument should therefore be read as a kind of immanent critique: I accept most of the premises of Forst's position, but suggest that, when rightly understood, they point us towards Scotland and away from Germany.

---

[1] R. Forst, *The Right to Justification: Elements of a Constructivist Theory,* trans. by J. Flynn. New York: Columbia University Press, 2012. All page references in the text refer to this book.

Constructivisms: Metaethical and normative, restricted and unrestricted

There are mountains, plants, bacteria, tigers, out there, in the world. Their existence does not depend on our attitudes towards them; they exist whether or not we do. Tables, knives and houses are different. Whether something is a house, or a knife or a table, depends on the use we make of it, and hence on the attitudes that we take towards it. A tree stump could be a table, but so could a pile of books, or the hood of a car. There are no natural, causal, attitude-independent properties shared by all these disparate things that explain why they count as tables. It is our (volitional, cognitive, practical) activities that make it true of a tree stump, or the hood of a car or a pile of books, that it is a table.

Are moral claims by which we ascribe moral properties to, for example, actions, or states of affairs, or dispositions, more like the claim that something is a mountain, or more like the claim that something is a table? Do such claims depend for their truth (assuming, for the moment, that moral claims are genuinely truth-evaluable) on our attitudes towards the actions, states of affairs, dispositions which they purport to describe? Or are they true independently? Many have been moved by the thought that moral claims are true, when they are true, not in virtue of their correspondence with a mind-independent reality (like the claim that something is a mountain) but in virtue of bearing the right relations to our practical activities and attitudes (like the claim that something is a table).

Constructivists, among others,[2] are moved in just this way (and, as a constructivist, so is Forst, and so am I). Constructivists believe that moral claims are made true, when they are true, by being the output of a certain (hypothetical or actual) procedure of deliberation. A claim

---

[2]   McDowell and Wiggins, for example, also believe that moral truths are stance dependent, but are not constructivists. See J. McDowell, 'Values and Secondary Qualities', in T. Honderich (ed.), *Morality and Objectivity*. London: Routledge, 1988, pp. 110–29; D. Wiggins, 'A Sensible Subjectivism?', in ibid., *Needs, Values, Truth: Essays in the Philosophy of Value*. Oxford: Oxford University Press, 1987, pp. 185–214.

such as 'happy-slapping is wrong' is true, they say, if and only if it would either be endorsed by an appropriately motivated actual or hypothetical deliberator (or group of deliberators) or entailed by norms that would be selected for mutual governance by appropriately motivated actual or hypothetical deliberators. Constructivists endorse what is sometimes referred to as the *stance-dependence* of moral claims.[3]

Stated in this way, constructivism is ambiguous. This ambiguity is often overlooked, but it is important.[4] Does the right side of the just-stated biconditional give us a test for determining when moral claims are true or does it tell us what moral truth itself consists in? Is it a claim about what it takes to *justify* a moral judgment or a metaphysical claim about the *status* or *nature* of moral truths? Understood in the former sense, constructivists give us a procedure or standpoint for generating (true) moral principles, norms and reasons. Understood in the latter sense, the right side of the biconditional either gives us the moral statement's truth conditions or tells us what it is for an action (like happy-slapping) to be wrong. To prevent confusion, I will call forms of constructivism that affirm only the former, *normative*, and those that affirm only the latter, *metaethical*. Metaethical constructivists aim to provide an account of the logic, semantics and ontology of moral claims. Normative constructivists, on the other hand, remain neutral on such questions. Normative constructivists could hold, for example, that realists or expressivists (rather than metaethical constructivists) provide the best account of the logic, semantics and ontology of moral claims. To illustrate: Imagine that moral properties are best construed as stance-independent, irreducible and non-natural (i.e. a form of realism is true); the normative constructivist could then say that the

---

[3]   See, for example, R. Milo, 'Contractarian Constructivism', *The Journal of Philosophy* 92(1995), 181–204.
[4]   Scanlon, for example, is systematically ambiguous throughout *What We Owe To Each Other*. Cambridge, MA: Harvard University Press, 2008, on whether he should be read as defending primarily a metaethical or a normative constructivism. He concedes unclarity on the issue in T. Scanlon, 'Replies', *Ratio* 16(2003), 424–39, in response to questions by Mark Timmons and Derek Parfit. Mark Timmons is particularly helpful in drawing this distinction. See his M. Timmons, 'The Limits of Moral Constructivism', *Ratio* 16(2003), 391–423.

procedure identified by the right side of the biconditional provides the best way of *discovering* such moral truths rather than *creating* or *legislating* them.[5] I will take Forst to be proposing a form of primarily normative constructivism. While there are points at which Forst seems also to favour a metaethical constructivism, he spends less time defending the position, and the most important and interesting arguments in the book do not contribute to debates on the ontology, logic or semantics of moral claims.

The central obstacle facing any normative constructivism is to specify an account of hypothetical or actual deliberation such that we are warranted in affirming its results as morally correct. Overcoming this obstacle requires the completion of four interconnected tasks. First, the constructivist must show how his proposed procedure of deliberation yields determinate results. The outputs of the procedure must, that is, be at least informative enough to help us in solving the practical problems they are designed to address. In a constructivist theory of *justice*, for example, the procedure ought to identify principles, reasons or norms that tell us more than that we ought to give each person their due, or that we ought to eliminate illegitimate exercises of power. (We still wonder: What counts as a person's due? What forms of power are illegitimate?) The results of construction need not provide solutions to every possible question within the domain of the procedure, of course, but they must at least be capable of meaningfully orienting us with respect to the most important ones. Call this the problem of *determinacy*.

Second, the constructivist must show that his proposed procedure avoids objectionable forms of subjectivism or relativism. If moral truths are discovered or legislated from the point of view of the deliberating agent, then why doesn't each person get to legislate morality for themselves? Why take the point of view of a single *hypothetical or ideal* agent (or agents) as authoritative for every person (and every group of persons) whatever their particular, contingent views on the matter? Or,

---

[5]   Cf. Forst: 'Whether with its help we "make" or just "perceive" a world of norms, like facts that we discover, can be left open' (50).

if we believe that the judgments of some *actual* deliberator or group of deliberators is authoritative, why give *them* rather than some other group such dispositive power? Call this the problem of *objectivity*.

Third, morality is usually taken to generate categorical (or at least very weighty) reasons: moral norms and the reasons they recommend bind us whether or not we desire to be so bound or have an interest in being so bound. But how does merely being the output of a procedure (or selected from a privileged deliberative standpoint) generate such normative force? Why, that is, should we accord the outputs of the deliberative procedure with the importance, priority and authority that we usually accord moral claims? Put another way: Why does the fact that an action is proscribed by norms legislated from the privileged deliberative standpoint provide one with a weighty (or even conclusive) reason not to do it? This is the problem of *normativity*.

Fourth, the heart of any constructivist view will specify relevant constraints on the deliberative procedure (including constraints on admissible motivations for its deliberators). These constraints serve not only to make the procedure determinate but also to motivate it. If one asks–'why this set of constraints rather than that one?'–the constructivist will need to provide an answer that explains why these constraints are required to produce results that have all the hallmarks of genuinely moral claims, including special significance and weight. But there is a problem. What is the moral status of the constraints *themselves*? In justifying the constraints, the constructivist might recommend them on explicitly *moral* grounds. The constraints, the constructivist suggests, are impartial, or fair, or the ideal deliberator benevolent, conscientious or even-handed. In choosing this path, the constructivist finds himself on the first horn of a dilemma. For we then wonder: Are the moral grounds for the constraints themselves constructed from the deliberative point of view? But how could that be, given that they are meant to define and delineate the procedure in the first place? Fearing the first horn of the dilemma, the constructivist might instead try his hand at the second. He might, that is, appeal to *non-moral* grounds for the constraints. The constraints, for example, might be entirely derived from a conception of prudential rationality, or from a purely conceptual analysis of moral terms, or from widely accepted, uncontroversial social conventions governing moral choice. But, here too, the constructivist will find himself impaled, since he now lacks a reason for us to take the outcome of the specified deliberative procedure seriously. Why should we have any moral reason to care what bare prudential rationality requires of us, or what our social conventions happen to be or what is entailed by our moral *concepts* (don't we care about morality *simpliciter* rather than the peculiarities of our moral concepts or their meanings?)? Call this the *Euthyphro* problem.[6]

In the following, I will leave aside the *determinacy* and *objectivity* problems; instead, I will focus on the *normativity* and *Euthyphro* problems. As we will see, there are two common strategies adopted by contemporary constructivists to address both problems. The first is to limit oneself to what Sharon Street has called *restricted* constructivism; the second is to adopt an *unrestricted* constructivism, but argue that the constraints on the procedure are necessary constituents of any practical deliberation or activity.[7] I will discuss both strategies in turn. Forst, as we will see, adopts a version of unrestricted constructivism. Seeing how Forst's view compares to his closest cousins (including Scanlon, Rawls, Habermas and Korsgaard) will be instructive in highlighting the obstacles he faces, and the degree to which he is successful in overcoming them.

Restricted constructivism

According to the restricted constructivist, not *all* moral principles, values or reasons are constructed from the privileged deliberative standpoint;

---

6   Cf. R. Shafer-Landau, *Moral Realism: A Defence*. Oxford: Clarendon, 2003.
7   See, for example, S. Street, 'Constructivism About Reasons', in R. Shafer-Landau (ed.), *Oxford Studies in Metaethics*. Oxford: Oxford University Press, 2008, pp. 207–45; S. Street, 'What Is Constructivism in Ethics and Metaethics?', *Philosophy Compass* 5(2010), 363–84.

only *some* are. Both Rawls and Scanlon are restricted constructivists. For Rawls, for example, only principles of justice are constructed from the original position. The structuring constraints and conceptions that underlie and frame the original position are not. These include the conceptions of the citizen as free and equal, reasonable and rational, and of society as a fair system of cooperation, as well as the argument in favour of the moral arbitrariness of talents. Each of these elements represents a moral commitment flowing from values – toleration, fairness, impartiality, reciprocity – that are not themselves selected from behind the veil of ignorance. For Scanlon, similarly, only those principles that govern 'what we owe to each other' are selected using the contractualist formula. Although often overlooked, the reasons we have for rejecting principles are not themselves constructed (including reasons stemming from our well-being or from considerations of fairness). Neither are the reasons we have for justifying ourselves to others nor, for that matter, the more general 'individualist (or personal reasons) restriction', which limits the kinds of reasons that are admissible in rejecting the principles governing what we owe to each other.[8] Restricted constructivism is best understood, therefore, as a substantive moral view in which a privileged procedure or standpoint is used to connect and organize a set of (often inchoate or incomplete) prior commitments and values, and then to trace their implications for a restricted domain (whether of justice, as in Rawls's case, or what we owe to each other in Scanlon's). Put in Rawlsian terminology, the prior commitments and values are the 'materials' of construction, the privileged standpoint is the 'procedure' of construction, and the restricted domain is the 'target' of construction.[9]

By taking a restricted view, the constructivist adopts a less ambitious position, but also one that allows him to evade, in one stroke, both the normativity and Euthyphro problems. The Euthyphro problem is circumvented by partitioning the grounds for the constraints and

---

[8] On the individualist restriction, and its importance for Scanlon's contractualism, see D. Parfit, 'Justifiability to Each Person', *Ratio* 16(2003), 368–90.

[9] Cf. J. Rawls, *Political Liberalism*. New York: Columbia University Press, 1993, Lecture III.3

the grounds for the target principles. To maintain the partition, the restricted constructivist must ensure that the principles that lie in the domain of the 'target' are not used to motivate the prior commitments and values that serve as 'materials' of construction. As long as this is done successfully, the vicious circularity threatened by the first horn of the Euthyphro dilemma is thereby avoided. The restricted constructivist can then go on to justify all the constraints, inputs and inferences that serve to structure the deliberative standpoint in explicitly moral, non-constructivist terms with a clear conscience. A cursory look at Scanlon's justification of the 'individualist restriction' (most evident in a reply to Parfit) shows exactly an instance of this strategy: nowhere does Scanlon say that the individualist restriction could not reasonably be rejected as a basis for uncoerced, general agreement.[10] This is as it should be: The individualist restriction is meant to tell us which reasons are admissible in rejecting (and hence accepting) the principles that define what we owe to each other. If Scanlon had made the restriction itself a member of the set of principles defining what we owe to each other, he would have squarely begged the question.

The same is true of Rawls. As he writes in Lecture III of *Political Liberalism*,

> What does it mean to say that the conceptions of citizen and of a well-ordered society are embedded in, or modeled by, the constructivist procedure? It means that the form of the procedure, and its more particular features, are drawn from those conceptions taken as its basis. . . . To conclude: not everything, then, is constructed; we must have some material, as it were, from which to begin. In a more literal sense, only the substantive principles specifying the content of political right and justice are constructed. The procedure itself is simply laid out using as starting points the basic conceptions of society and person, the principles of practical reason [viz. the reasonable and the rational], and the public role of a political conception of justice.[11]

---

[10] Scanlon, 'Replies'.
[11] Rawls, *Political Liberalism*, pp. 103–4.

Once again, vicious circularity is avoided by partitioning the justificatory grounds for the 'materials' of construction from the 'targets'
of the procedure itself. On this view, the constructivist procedure (i.e.
the original position) serves to draw out the implications of a set of
(prior) moral commitments to publicity, toleration, reciprocity, fairness, impartiality and so on, in view of (a) a set of specific political
problems (e.g. reasonable pluralism and the 'great political evils')[12] and
(b) a specific understanding of the role principles of justice and legitimacy are meant to play in solving those problems (namely to publicly
order a basic structure via an overlapping consensus).

Once one adopts restricted constructivism, the normativity problem
also becomes easier to solve than for an unrestricted view. An unrestricted
view needs to explain why taking up the privileged deliberative
standpoint or procedure generates results that have the categorical (or
near-categorical) nature expected of moral reasons and principles. The
explanation will need to make exclusive reference to the characteristics
and nature of the deliberative procedure; this is because the procedure
is meant to give birth to (or at least provide a way of revealing) the *entire*
moral order. There is no morality outside of the procedure, and so no
moral normativity; as a result, the deliberative procedure must generate
or reveal not only the governing moral reasons or principles but also
explain their force. The restricted constructivist, on the other hand, is
under less pressure to anchor his account of normativity to the specific
features and character of the privileged deliberative standpoint. He can
either appeal directly to the normativity of the grounding 'materials',
and argue that the target principles simply inherit the normativity of
those starting points, or he can provide an entirely independent, first-
order, non-constructivist account of moral normativity.

Once again, both Rawls and Scanlon provide good illustrations of
the latter two strategies. Let us start with Rawls. In response to the
question, 'Why should principles of justice be given such a categorical,
normally conclusive status in public affairs?', Rawls answers: because

---

[12] John Rawls, *The Law of Peoples*, Cambridge, MA: Harvard University Press, 1999, pp. 6–7.

they provide the most reasonable basis on which to coerce others in conditions of reasonable pluralism. We might then wonder: 'Yes, but why does their being "reasonable" give them (normally) conclusive authority in political conflict? What explains their priority, for example, with respect to people's conception of the good?' Here Rawls points to conception of the free and equal citizen as willing to offer fair terms of cooperation to others similarly motivated. Someone who believes that his own comprehensive conception of the good should govern others' lives, or that denies the authority of principles of justice justified from a freestanding perspective, must therefore deny others' status as free and equal, and hence deny that they are entitled to mutually acceptable terms of justification for the use of coercive power. Notice that, on this picture, the normativity of political principles is explained in terms of a (prior) moral conception of citizens as free and equal, which is itself grounded in a specific (moral) understanding of what is reasonable, and a particular (moral) account of reciprocity and fair-mindedness. None of the latter ideas is constructed; rather, they are merely 'drawn' from the public political culture of a constitutional democracy and justified as fair interpretations of what that culture (already) requires of us. The normativity of principles of justice is, in this way, inherited from the normativity of the (moral) conception of citizens as free and equal.

Scanlon takes a different tack. One of Scanlon's main aims is to explain why the fact that an action is wrong gives us a strong, normally decisive, reason not to do it. It is very important to remember that, on the Scanlonian view, to say that an action is wrong is not just to summarize the balance of reasons against an action. To say that an action is wrong *adds* a further reason not to do it. Say that an action will harm someone but benefit no one. This gives one a conclusive reason not to do it. Compare an action that will cause some discomfort to oneself and benefit no one. This also gives one a conclusive reason not to do it. Stated in this way, both considerations 'weigh' decisively against the action in question. But how much, and in what way, do they count against the action in question? How do we determine the importance and priority of the reasons at stake, including the role they should play in our practical deliberation? The fact that the first action harms someone *else* whereas the second only harms *oneself* makes, let us assume, the first action wrong in a way that the second is not. Someone who performs the first action is subject, as a result, to forms of serious criticism that someone who performs the second is not. But why does the fact that the second action hurts someone else without compensating benefits relevant to the importance and priority of the reasons against it (and the kinds of criticism it merits)? Why, that is, does its wrongness give us not only a decisive reason not to do it, but also a much more weighty one than in the first case?

When we seek to justify ourselves to others, we imply that we are alive to the reasons others might have for stopping us from performing certain actions. By entering into practices of mutual justification, we signal our willingness to desist if it turns out that others cannot reasonably be expected to license our actions. Scanlon argues that the wrongness of an action can be explained as a failure of such mutual justification. If others have decisive reasons to reject any principle allowing us to act, then the action in question, Scanlon argues, is wrong; that fact – the failure of mutual justification – is what makes it wrong. But, assuming that justifying oneself to others implies something like the reasonable rejection test, why 'must' we seek to justify ourselves to others? Why are we subject to criticism if we don't much care what reasons others might have for asking us to stop? Scanlon, at this point, points to the *independent value* of living with others in ways that are mutually justifiable; he points, that is, to the value of a social practice in which people trade in and respect each other's reasons. According to Scanlon,

> When I reflect on the reason that the wrongness of an action seems to supply not to do it, the best description of this reason I can come up with has to do with the relation to others that such acts would put me in.[13]

---

[13] Scanlon, *What We Owe to Each Other*, p. 155.

Here Scanlon points to an analogy with friendship. Loyalty to one's friends is often demanding, requiring us to do things that are costly or otherwise difficult. So why, then, should we be loyal? An answer of the wrong kind would invoke the instrumental benefits of friendship. A person moved only by such instrumental considerations has missed something essential about friendship (just as a person moved only by instrumental considerations has missed something essential about morality). Loyalty itself has to provide one with sufficient reason to do things for one's friends (just as an action's wrongness itself has to provide one with sufficient reason not to act in that way). A loyal friend is moved by the value of the relation itself, by the intimacy and concern and care and love for a specific person that are constitutive of it. Scanlon writes:

> The contractualist ideal of acting in accord with principles that others (similarly motivated) could not reasonably reject is meant to characterize the relation with others the value and appeal of which underlies our reason to do what morality requires. This relation, much less personal than friendship, might be called a relation of mutual recognition. Standing in this relation to others is appealing in itself—worth seeking for its own sake. . . . [Moral] requirements are not just formal imperatives; they are aspects of the positive value of a way of living with others.[14]

While relations of mutual recognition are not founded on the same concern, care, and intimacy, as friendship, they are valuable for their own sake in much the same way as friendship is. This is why Scanlon often says that the importance of justifiability to others reflects our awareness of the value of seeking to live our lives, quoting J. S. Mill, 'in unity with our fellow creatures'. Indeed, Scanlon goes on to claim that the value of mutual justifiability provides the basis of respect, underlying *any* relationship between human beings, whether among family, friends, colleagues or citizens.

---

[14] Ibid., p. 162.

In this way, Scanlon grounds the morality of right and wrong in the value of intrinsically valuable relationships. The right, we might say, is grounded in a further conception of the good.[15] For our purposes, what is important is that nowhere does Scanlon suggest that the ideal of justifiability itself cannot reasonably be rejected. If Scanlon had done that, he would have begged the question. The ideal of justifiability to others undergirds and justifies the contractualist test but is not itself justified by it. It is also important to note that there is no explanation for why we 'must' recognize the value of mutual justifiability. Scanlon does not attempt to show that failing to recognize this value would land one in some sort of practical or rational contradiction or incoherence. The normativity of the ideal itself is assumed; Scanlon believes his readers are already (implicitly) motivated to act in accordance with the ideal, and his aim is merely to show them *that* they are. The normativity of the principles that issue from repeated applications of the contractualist test simply *inherit* the normativity of the ideal that justifies the test itself.

Many have found restricted accounts of this kind not only incomplete but also precariously contingent. Scanlon sets out to explain the special character and role of morality in our lives; he claims to provide a novel and ambitious account of moral normativity that is intended to compete with both consequentialist and Kantian alternatives. Yet, at the crucial point, he seems to simply assume the normativity of the central ideal motivating his entire account. The final appeal to the value of relations of mutual recognition, furthermore, seems – according to this critique – altogether too contingent and underspecified. Is a failure to recognize this value simply a failure to recognize something good (since the failure cannot itself be wrong)? And what, exactly, *is* the value of living in relations of mutual justification? Scanlon seems to assume the value of justifiability (elucidated via a cryptic analogy to friendship) rather than to explain it. After all, relations among strangers *lack* all the crucial features of friendship, including care, love, intimacy, shared

---

[15] Cf. Forst, who writes 'it is necessary for moral action and for being moral at all not to ultimately lead back to an ethical motive' (77).

history and so on. What is the basis for respecting others in relations of mutual recognition, if *not* the special relations and history that are important in relationships like friendship? In what sense are friendship and relations of mutual justification relevantly analogous, if not in those more intimate dimensions? Usually accounts of this kind appeal to something like the value of humanity, dignity or rational agency, or alternatively to the importance of mutual recognition for the formation of a practical identity, yet there is no such appeal here. In the end, the 'positive value of living with others' seems to rest on nothing more than the security we might feel in knowing that others are (or, rather, *should be*) happy for us to carry on. The unconditional, categorical character of morality seems ultimately to rest on quicksand. The same can be said of Rawls, who finally grounds his account of the reasonable in ideas that contingently occur only in liberal democracies. Is there really no further (freestanding) ground for the normativity of his principles of justice?

Unrestricted (Kantian) constructivism

My aim is not to defend this critique of restricted constructivism. Rather, my aim is to give vent to what I believe underlies the ambition to develop a more *unrestricted* constructivism, the most popular versions of which are all, not surprisingly, Kantian. The Kantian ambition is to show that the full set of foundational, ground-level standards of morality can be understood as constitutive of an inescapable practice, such as rational agency, action, communication or deliberation. Korsgaard is representative:

> [T]he only way to establish the authority of any purported normative principles is to establish that it is constitutive of something to which the person whom it governs is committed—something that she either is doing or has to do. And I think that Kant thought this too. The laws of logic govern our thoughts because if we don't follow them we just aren't thinking. . . . [T]he laws of practical reason govern our actions

because if we don't follow them we just aren't acting, and acting is something we must do. A constitutive principle for an inescapable activity is unconditionally binding.[16]

The basic idea, in outline, is quite simple. To act, reason, deliberate or communicate successfully requires guiding one's activity according to the standards constitutive of those domains in the same way as, say, playing chess successfully requires following the constitutive rules and aims of chess. If activities like acting, reasoning or deliberating are inescapable, and if the Kantian can convincingly demonstrate that the moral law (whether understood as the Categorical Imperative, or an ideal discourse procedure or as a procedural ideal of reciprocity and generality) is a constitutive standard for those practices, then morality itself would be inescapable as well. The problem of normativity would be solved. At the same time, the Euthyphro problem would also be solved. Because fundamental moral constraints (on deliberation, or reasoning or communicating) necessarily govern a set of unavoidable practices, there is no 'external' standpoint available from which it can meaningfully be asked whether the constraints themselves are morally desirable. Asking the question – 'Are the basic constraints justifiable?' – would itself require a further stretch of the very deliberation, reasoning or communication that is constituted by the standards in the first place. Notice that if the Kantian project were successful, then it would deliver a comprehensive first-order moral system that also avoided the incompleteness and contingency of more restricted accounts. But is it successful?

In the following, I will argue that specifically Kantian versions of constitutivism (including Forst's) offer at most a set of necessary conditions for solving both the normativity and Euthyphro problems, but they are not sufficient. What is lacking is a place for the social emotions in constituting the moral domain. To prosecute this critique, I will first show that Forst's arguments from Chapters 1 and 2 are best understood

---

[16] C. Korsgaard, *Self-Constitution: Agency, Identity, and Integrity.* Oxford: Oxford University Press, 2009, p. 32.

as a novel form of constitutivism, namely what I will *justificatory constitutivism*. I then seek to reveal the weakest point in Kantian constitutivism (in whatever form) by querying what the constitutivist must say about cases of moral blindness. I will argue that this reflection shows that morality cannot be constitutive of mere deliberation, action, communication or justification; rather, morality is only constitutive of the deliberation, action, justification or communication of *social* beings, of beings, that is, with a distinctive range of social emotions. Perhaps unexpectedly, Forst's own account, I will conclude, already points us towards this (very Scottish) conclusion.

For Korsgaard, morality is a constitutive standard of *action*; for Habermas, it is a constitutive standard of *communication*; and for Forst, it is a constitutive standard of *justification*. Forst writes:

> My own proposal starts from the assumption that the analysis of the moral point of view should begin with a pragmatic reconstruction of moral validity claims and, proceeding recursively, inquire into the conditions of justification of such claims and of the construction of norms. . . . If, starting from [the moral] validity claim, we inquire recursively into the conditions under which it can be redeemed, then the validity criteria of reciprocity and generality take on the role of criteria for discursive justification. It follows that, in justifying or problematizing a moral norm (or mode of action), one cannot raise any specific claims while rejecting like claims of others (reciprocity of contents), and one cannot simply assume that others share one's perspective, evaluations, convictions, interests, or needs (reciprocity of reasons), so that, for example, one claims to speak in the "true" interests of others or in the name of an absolute, unquestionable truth beyond justification. Finally, the objections of any person who is affected, whoever he or she may be, cannot be disregarded, and the reasons adduced in support of the legitimacy of a norm must be capable of being shared by all persons (generality). (48)

The idea, I take it, is this. We find ourselves necessarily implicated in practices of discursive justification, some of which require one to justify oneself in the light of morality. Moral discourses of justification, in turn, have a certain structure, which can be reconstructed by considering what is (necessarily) demanded and expected of others in 'redeeming' a claim to rightness. This requires, in a Habermasian spirit,[17] a reconstruction of the necessary presuppositions of moral argumentation. The argument is therefore classically constitutivist: we cannot but enter into practices of mutual justification; practices of mutual justification, in turn, are necessarily governed by norms of generality and reciprocity, which together make mutual justification what it is (which make it, i.e. a form of *justification* rather than, say, a form of command, advice, warning, exhortation or questioning). If we do not respect the standards, we therefore fail in justifying ourselves to others, and hence fail in something we must do. As Forst writes in the first passages from *The Right to Justification*: 'Human beings' are 'justificatory beings. . . . If we want to understand human practices, we *must* conceive of them as practices bound up with justifications; *no matter what we think or do*, we place upon ourselves (and others) the demand for reasons, whether they are made explicit or remain implicit' (???, emphasis added).

A prominent way of putting pressure on constitutivists is to accept that morality is a constitutive standard of action, or communication, or deliberation or justification, but claim that none of these activities is inescapable. This is often referred to as the 'shmagency' objection (due to David Enoch).[18] If someone says to you, 'If you act, you must obey the categorical imperative, and you must act', then the shmagent objector replies: 'But why must I "act"? If "acting" requires adhering to the CI, then I'd rather "shmact", which is just like "acting" but without the requirement that one must follow the CI.' The objector continues: '"Acting", in the sense required by the constitutivist, is, after all, just like playing chess. Imagine you observe someone playing a game in which he and his opponent follow all the rules for moving pieces typical of

---

[17] For Forst's disagreements with Habermas, see below.
[18] D. Enoch, 'Agency, Shmagency: Why Normativity Won't Come from What Is Constitutive of Action', *The Philosophical Review* 115(2006), pp. 169–98.

chess but where the winner is the one who is checkmated first. You protest: "That's not chess! You're playing it all wrong! One of the constitutive standards of chess is to try to checkmate your opponent rather than yourself!" The players reply: "OK, so this isn't chess, but schmess, so what? Why *must* we play chess?" We can say the same thing with respect to action, deliberation, communication, justification: why must we "act" rather than "shmact" (or "communicate" rather than "shmmunicate", and so on?) If 'acting' or 'deliberating' or 'communicating' or 'justifying' are not things we must do, then the constitutivist argument fails: morality is just as optional as whether to play chess or not.

I don't believe this objection – as popular as it is – is successful. The objection trades on interpreting the constitutivist argument as providing an analysis of the *concept* of action, or deliberation or communication (or, alternatively, of the *social conventions* governing deliberation, communication, action). But then the constitutivist can simply say: 'I'm not interested in the *concept* of action, deliberation, communication, justification or in the *social conventions* governing these activities, I am interested in what action, deliberation, communication, justification actually *are*. I am interested in providing an account of the activities that make up the fabric of our practical lives; those things, in other words, which our concepts are trying to latch onto and our social conventions trying to shape. What I mean by action, deliberation, communication, justification is just what it is that you must do when you reflect on whether you prefer to be a "shmagent" rather than an "agent", or whether you want to play "chess" or "schmess". Morality is a constitutive standard of *that* activity, not simply of the concepts that might be used (some successfully, some unsuccessfully) to refer to the activity, or of the social conventions that may (or may not) contingently govern those activities in particular societies.'[19]

---

[19] A similar response is mooted by L. Ferrero, 'Constitutivism and the Inescapability of Agency', in Shafer-Landau, *Oxford Studies in Metaethics*, pp. 303–33.

Going Scottish

The objection I will pursue in the rest of the chapter takes a very different form. I accept that action, deliberation, communication, justification are inescapable activities. What I will question is whether morality is, in fact, a constitutive standard of those activities *taken on their own*. More precisely, I will claim that, though those activities are necessary conditions for the existence and normativity of morality, they are not sufficient. Morality does not come into being and apply to us simply insofar as we are acting, or communicating, or justifying or deliberating beings. Morality comes into being and applies to us in virtue of the fact that we are also *social* beings whose interaction is shaped by a characteristic range of emotions and dispositions, the most important of which is empathy.

Consider cases of moral blindness. What I have in mind is someone who simply does not *see* others in the way characteristic of someone with a moral sense. The contrast is with someone who is morally bad. The morally bad person acts immorally, but is subsequently moved by guilt or remorse. It is of course possible for someone morally bad to become morally blind (at least in some areas), but to do so would require training or habituation (modern-day soldiers, for example, undergo specific kinds of training whose purpose is to allay or dissolve feelings of moral aversion to killing). Importantly, people trained in this way will often continue to have the characteristic range of moral attitudes in other aspects of their lives.

Moral blindness of the kind that is relevant for our purposes is best exemplified by the psychopath. Psychopaths are identified by the possession of the following characteristics: glibness and/or superficial charm, grandiose sense of self-worth, deceitfulness, manipulativeness, lack of remorse or guilt, shallow affect, callousness, irresponsibility, poor behavioural control, lack of realistic, long-term goals and impulsivity.[20]

---

[20] R. D. Hare, *The Hare Psychopathy Checklist-Revised*. Toronto: Multi-Health Systems, 1991.

Psychophysiological studies of psychopaths show a marked lack of emotional responsiveness to portrayals of others in severe distress and a lack of fear or shock in disturbing situations involving harm to others.[21] This is sometimes explained by lack of what psychologists call a 'Violence Inhibition Mechanism' [VIM], a schema that causes a withdrawal response in the presence of signs of acute distress (e.g. the sights and sounds of someone crying).[22] Lack of this mechanism also seems to contribute to a general difficulty in distinguishing between different types of violations (e.g. between violations of moral and conventional rules) and to judge the seriousness of different violations. Whereas normal people use their own emotional reactions to mediate and judge the seriousness of violations, psychopaths have trouble doing so. Psychopaths, furthermore, often have a working knowledge of common moral expectations and norms, and are able to predict the reactions of others to violations of them; what they lack is the care and concern for others' interests and well-being that underlies normal moral responses. The most important mediating deficit in explaining the psychopath's moral blindness is therefore widely recognized to be a deficit in *empathy*, the capacity to both accurately represent the mental states of others and, more importantly for the psychopath, to respond in an emotionally appropriate way to them.[23]

Other psychological disorders – especially autism – have been associated with lack of empathy, but the way in which such a lack manifests itself is very different from the way it manifests in psychopathy. This difference will become very important in the elaboration of Scottish constructivism below. I will focus on high-functioning autism spectrum

[21] A. S. Aniskiewicz, 'Autonomic Components of Vicarious Conditioning and Psychopathy', *Journal of Clinical Psychology* 35(1979), 60–7; C. J. Patrick, 'Emotion and Psychopathy: Startling New Insights', *Psychophysiology* 31(1994), 319–30; J. Blair et al., 'The Psychopathic Individual: A Lack of Responsiveness to Distress Cues?', *Psychophysiology* 34(1997), 192–8.

[22] R. Blair et al., 'Is the Psychopath "Morally Insane"?', *Personality and Individual Differences* 19(1995), 741–52.

[23] R. Blair, 'Responding to the Emotions of Others: Dissociating Forms of Empathy through the Study of Typical and Psychiatric Populations', *Consciousness and Cognition* 14(2005), 698–718.

disorders, in which there is little or no impairment in linguistic ability (though there may have been language delay) or IQ. Those suffering from high-functioning autistic spectrum disorders – to which I'll refer using the general term 'autistics' in what follows – are characterized by severe social impairment, limited capacity to engage in role-playing, narrow interests and repetitiveness of behaviour. Autistics are often confused by others' reactions, and find social situations very difficult to negotiate. A growing consensus traces the autistic's difficulties in social adjustment and response to a failure to 'mind-read', that is, to predict or attribute mental states (such as desires and beliefs) to self and others.[24] Autistics can learn to predict and attribute mental states to others, often on the basis of mere correlation between cues and outcomes, but such learning is difficult and often inaccurate. However, autistics typically report feeling bad if someone indicates that their behaviour was hurtful, and feel that hurt should be avoided where possible.[25] They are also able to distinguish moral from conventional violations in the same way as normal individuals, and have normal physiological arousal responses to perceived distress.[26] Importantly for our purposes, autistics are much less prone to the range of anti-social and criminal behaviour characteristic of psychopaths. The problem is that they are typically unable to determine both when someone is in distress and what they should do as a response to the distress. This is why the failure to mind-read is often invoked to explain the absence of 'pro-social' responses (i.e. empathy) in the presence of others' suffering. Oliver Sacks reports the response to distress of one of his patients, Jim Sinclair, who says:

> I have to develop a separate translation code for every person I meet. . . . Does it indicate an unco-operative attitude if someone doesn't

[24] See, for example, S. Baron-Cohen et al., 'Does the Autistic Child Have a "Theory of Mind"?', *Cognition* 21(1985), 37–46; S. Baron-Cohen, *Mindblindness: As Essay on Autism and Theory of Mind*. Cambridge, MA: MIT Press, 1995.

[25] S. Baron-Cohen and S. Wheelwright, 'The Empathy Quotient: An Investigation of Adults with Asperger Syndrome or High Functioning Autism, and Normal Sex Differences', *Journal of Autism and Developmental Disorders* 34(2004), 163–75, at p. 169.

[26] R. James and R. Blair, 'Brief Report: Morality in the Autistic Child', *Journal of Autism and Developmental Disorders* 26(1996), 571–9, at p. 577.

understand information conveyed in a foreign language? Even if I can tell what the cues mean, I may not know what to do about them. The first time I ever realized someone needed to be touched was during an encounter with a grief-stricken, hysterically sobbing person who was in no condition to respond to my questions about what I should do to help. I could certainly tell he was upset. I could even figure out that there was *something* I could do that would be better than nothing. But I didn't know what that something was.[27]

The morally inappropriate behaviour of autistics is therefore more often seen as a failure to coordinate an appropriate behavioural response to distress or the prospect of distress (both their own and others') or explained as a failure to understand the moral valences of more complex social situations.[28] It is not triggered by a lack of general concern for others.

We can now compare the lack of empathy characteristic of autism and psychopathy. Recall the definition of empathy I gave above, which emphasized *both* the ability to accurately represent the mental states of others *and* the ability to respond in an emotionally appropriate way to them. As we have seen, both psychopaths and autistics do not respond in an emotionally appropriate way to signs of distress in others. The key difference is that this failure in autistics can be traced to a failure to mind-read – namely to accurately simulate the mental states of others – and then to coordinate socially appropriate responses to them. Psychopaths, on the other hand, have no impairment in their ability to mind-read; indeed, this is what makes them particularly good at deceit, charm and manipulation. The lack of empathy for psychopaths is entirely traceable to their 'cold' emotional responses to violence, harm and fear. Psychopaths understand what other people are doing, what they are thinking and what reactions they are likely to have, but they just do not care (except in instances where it might further some end). It is

---

[27] Quoted in J. Kennett, 'Autism, Empathy and Moral Agency', *The Philosophical Quarterly* 52(2002), 340–57.

[28] See James and Blair, 'Brief Report: Morality in the Autistic Child' at p. 577ff.

no surprise that psychopaths are typically not very good at carrying out systematic plans that extend beyond the very near future: such an ability requires a kind of empathy for one's own future selves. Once again, the way in which the lack of empathy manifests itself in autism couldn't be more different: there is no sense in which autistics are left entirely 'cold' to the responses of others. Quite on the contrary, they often care very much what others think, and why they are thinking it; what makes them anxious and clumsy in their responses is, first, others' perceived opacity and unpredictability and, second, the perceived indeterminacy and malleability of social rules and conventions, whose application, of course, varies quite significantly (and to autistics, often unintelligibly) according to context and circumstance. We might say that where psychopaths are morally blind, autistics are merely short-sighted. This difference will become quite important in our development of Scottish constructivism.

Of what relevance are such cases of restriction in moral vision? Psychopathy (and amoralism generally) is usually invoked either in discussions of moral motivation and its connection to moral judgment, or in an attempt to answer the amoralist in terms he might accept, or as a step in an argument for skepticism. Those are not the questions I am interested in here. I am also only indirectly interested in whether and to what extent psychopaths and autistics should be held morally responsible. The question I want to pose is another one: How do we understand the moral failures, insofar as they do fail, of psychopaths and autistics? What capacity or faculty or disposition do each of them lack that diminishes or extinguishes their moral sight, which we can gloss here (for the sake of argument) as a failure to see or respond to moral reasons?

If the Kantian constitutivists are right, then moral failures of these kinds must ultimately lie in an incapacity to reason, or to communicate, or to act, or to justify oneself to others. When the Korsgaardian, for example, observes someone who does not respond to or see the moral reasons that apply, she will (ultimately) say: 'You are failing to see and act according to the standards that make what you are attempting to do an *action*! (And you must perform actions.).' The Habermasian will say: 'You are failing to see and act according to the standards that make what you are attempting to say a form of *communication*! (And you must communicate.).' The Forstian will say: 'You are failing to see and act according to the standards that make what you are attempting to vindicate (e.g., a claim, an action, an attitude) a *justification*! (And you must justify.).' The Kantian will say: 'You are failing to see and act according to the standards that make what you are doing a conclusion of practical *reasoning*! (And you must reason.).'

Let's take each one in turn. In what sense are the moral failures of psychopaths and autistics due to a failure to *reason*? Psychopaths and (high-functioning) autistics have normal inferential capacities, normal IQ and normal (or superior) mathematical abilities. Deficits in none of these areas seem at all relevant to explaining the particular ways in which each of them fails to see or respond to the moral reasons that apply (when they do fail). Similarly, in what sense do psychopaths or autistics lack the ability to *act* in the relevant Korsgaardian sense? Both, after all, can act for reasons; both of them are capable of 'intentional movement . . . that is guided by a representation or conception . . . of [the] environment'.[29] Both have the ability to 'constitute themselves' through their choices; both, that is, can give themselves a practical identity by choosing what to do. There is no sense in which either of them is acting from merely 'external' causes (as long as one does not beg the question by saying that all moral failures are by definition caused 'externally'). What about *communication*? While it is true that, sometimes, autistics will not be very effective communicators, this failure is due to an inability to express or recognize their own or others' mental states; it is not an inability to understand the presuppositions of argumentation or their implications (unless one builds in the capacity to express or recognize mental states as part of the necessary presuppositions of communication). And, whatever we say about autistics, there is surely no similar impairment in the case of

---

[29] Korsgaard, *Self-Constitution*, p. 97.

psychopaths, who are as able to communicate as normal individuals. And, finally, much the same thing can be said of the capacity to justify oneself to others. Both psychopaths and autistics understand what is needed to enter into practices of justification (indeed, one might say that psychopaths are particularly good at it, given their ability to deceive and manipulate others).

As should be clear by now, the incapacity that best characterizes the moral failures of both psychopaths and autistics is not an incapacity to reason, communicate, act or justify but an incapacity to *empathize*. Continuing with the analogy to sight, the 'organ' that is responsible for the inability to see or respond to moral reasons is empathy, the capacity to represent others' mental states and to coordinate appropriate behavioural responses to them. It may seem that so far the constitutivist need not deny anything I've said so far. Why can't constitutivists simply reply: 'You may be right that empathy is required to see or respond to moral reasons, but the moral reasons there are and that apply to us are either discovered or created by reflecting on the conditions necessary for action, justification, communication, and so on; empathy has nothing to do with that (more fundamental) task. It is one thing to *justify* or *create* moral reasons, another to explain what might aid us in recognizing them'? This response only raises a further question: If empathy has nothing to do with the creation or justification of moral reasons, then why does its *lack* cause such a profound impairment of our moral sense? Why is the capacity for empathy so fundamental in 'seeing' the reasons there are?

This is a relevant question *especially* for a constructivist view. The constructivist position, as we have seen, is motivated by one of two metaethical starting points. It is either motivated by the view that there are no stance-independent moral facts that make moral claims true (when they are true). On this view, the truth of a moral claim simply *consists in* being the outcome of a certain (stance-dependent) deliberative procedure. For constitutivist versions of such a metaethical constructivism, the truth of higher-order moral claims consists in being the necessary constituents of a necessary activity, and the truth of any lower-order moral claims consists in being entailed by the higher-order claims. Alternatively, constructivism is motivated by the view that, whatever the nature of moral truth, there is no *access* to such truths except insofar as we see them as the output of a certain (stance-dependent) deliberative procedure. On this more agnostic view, the constitutivist would say that reflection on the necessary constituents of deliberation, justification, action and so on is necessary to know the true moral claims that apply to us. With this reminder of the motivation for constructivism, our question to the objector can be put more pointedly: 'If stance-dependence is so important (on either metaethical version of constructivism), and if empathy is a necessary capacity required to see the moral reasons there are, then why *shouldn't* empathy be part of the characterization of the appropriate morality-generating (or morality-discovering) procedure?' The pointedness of the question is reinforced when we reflect (as we have above) that there is a plausible sense in which the psychopath and autistic have unimpaired capacities to act, reason, communicate and so on. The argument can be recast in terms of our visual analogy. The constitutivist answer to our question has the same structure as someone who, when presented with multiple cases of colour blindness, replies that, though he agrees that the eye is essential for explaining most patients' colour blindness,[30] denies that the eye is essential in either discovering (or constituting) the colours there are, which are discovered (or constituted) by (say) the brain alone. If that were true, then how is most patients' colour blindness caused by a defect in the eye rather than the brain?

---

[30] That is, it's not a case of cerebral achromatopsia, where colour blindness is caused by a lesion to the brain, but rather a deformation of colour receptor cells in the retina. The analogy to cerebral achromatopsia would be to someone who behaves in ways that would otherwise be considered immoral, but for the fact that the person has Tourette's syndrome. In that latter case, there is no sense in which the person is an agent during an episode; he is not acting for a reason, or in the light of a conception of the world. His capacity to act, reason, communicate and so on really is impaired, and it is that impairment which causes his apparently immoral behaviour (once again, recall that we are leaving aside whether autistics and psychopaths should be held morally responsible for their actions). As I have already said, I do not deny that action, communication and so on are necessary conditions for the knowledge or generation of moral reasons, I am only denying they are also sufficient.

Perhaps, at this point, the Kantian constitutivist might try to change tack, and deny that empathy ultimately explains the moral failures of our two psychological disorders (analogous to the way in which someone might deny that no colour blindness is caused by the eye). Instead, they might try to argue in the following way: 'I reject the view that the psychopath and autistic have unimpaired capacities to act, reason, and so on. Indeed, their lack of empathy is only important *insofar as* it impairs their capacity to act, reason, communicate and so on. The lack of empathy triggers the impairments in action, communication and so on, but it is ultimately those further impairments that explain the relevant moral failures.' Once again, the constitutivist's response raises the following question: 'Yes, but *how* does a lack of empathy trigger a failure of action, communication, and so on?' Imagine our objector answers in this way: 'Lack of empathy impairs our ability to act, communicate, and so on, precisely because lack of empathy leads people to fail in successfully taking the moral point of view. And because morality is a constitutive standard of action, communication, and so on, failing to act morally necessarily counts as a failure to act, communicate, and so on.' This answer begs the question. What we are putting in question is whether action, communication and so on can be sufficient conditions for the existence and/or knowledge and application of moral reasons; the response just assumes that at least one of them is. A more plausible response would go like this: 'Empathy is *itself* constitutive feature of successful communication, action, and so on; therefore, a failure of empathy is necessarily also a failure of communication, action, justification, and deliberation in the relevant sense.' The response is a good one, but it concedes exactly the point I am trying to make, namely that empathy is a crucial (constitutive) component of the activities that create or justify the moral reasons that apply to us. Action, communication, justification and deliberation are only jointly sufficient conditions for the existence/justification of moral reasons *in conjunction with* the operation of empathy.

What is the upshot of the discussion thus far? If what I have said is correct, then whatever one's metaethical point of view, and whatever one's preferred specification of normative constructivism, the deliberative standpoint from which we either create or discover moral reasons must also model the particular character of our shared human empathy. The substantive claims that morality makes on us cannot be understood without such a model. This is also true of constitutivist views like Forst's: whatever one thinks about the constitutive relation between action, reason, communication, justification and fundamental moral norms, the operation of our shared human empathy must also be considered as one of the 'activities' that creates (or gives us access to) moral reasons. The important role given to empathy ('sympathy') makes the view under consideration best understood as a form of *Scottish* constructivism:

> When a man denominates another his enemy, his rival, his antagonist, his adversary, he is understood to speak the language of self-love, and to express sentiments, peculiar to himself, and arising from his particular circumstances and situation. But when he bestows on any man the epithets of vicious or odious or depraved, he then speaks another language, and expresses sentiments in which, he expects, all his audience are to concur with him. He must here, therefore, depart from his private and particular situation, and must chuse a point of view, common to him with others: He must move some universal principle of the human frame, and touch a string, to which all mankind have an accord and symphony. If he mean, therefore, to express, that this man possesses qualities, whose tendency is pernicious to society, he has chosen this common point of view, and has touched the principle of humanity, in which every man, in some degree, concurs.[31]

The mechanism that takes us from the personal point of view to the 'common point of view' is, of course, empathy ('sympathy' in Hume's vocabulary), which connects, transmits and harmonizes our emotional responses with those of others. 'As in strings equally wound up, the motion of one communicates itself to the rest; so all the affections

---

[31] D. Hume, *An Enquiry Concerning the Principles of Morals*, ed. T. L. Beauchamp. Oxford: Oxford University Press, 1998, IX.1.

readily pass from one person to another, and beget correspondent movements in every human creature.'[32]

Before concluding with the promised demonstration that Forst's own arguments point in this direction, I want to suggest one important advantage of the Scottish constructivism when compared to his Kantian cousin, and mention some of the obstacles standing in the way of a full elaboration of such a view. The advantage is this. One of the difficulties Kantian constitutivists face is that they seem to mischaracterize the special force of moral requirements. According to Scanlon, for example, constitutivists do

> not give a very satisfactory description of what is wrong with a person who fails [to care about morality]. The special force of moral requirements seems quite different from that of, say, principles of logic, even if both are, in some sense, "inescapable." And the fault involved in failing to be moved by moral requirements does not seem to be a form of incoherence.[33]

This seems right. The wrong involved in someone's failing to take up the moral point of view – to see its special importance – is not simply a type of first-personal rational inconsistency.[34] About someone unmoved by others' moral claims, we ought to be able to say more than: 'They're failing to act according to very norms which constitute them as agents! (And they must act.)' or 'They're engaged in a pragmatic contradiction, violating the very norms of argumentation they invoke in communicating!'. The wrong involved should at the very least take into account the importance of others' independent interests or perspectives. As we have seen, Scanlon tries to account for this special importance via an invocation of the independent value of relations of mutual recognition. But, as we have also noted, this seems to leave important questions open including: 'What, exactly, *is* the special value

[32] D. Hume, *A Treatise of Human Nature*, ed. L. A. Selby-Bigge. Oxford: Oxford University Press, 1978, 3.3.1.

[33] Scanlon, *What We Owe to Each Other*, p. 151.

[34] For a similar critique see R. Forst, *The Right to Justification*, pp. 101m, 4m.

of mutual recognition (and how does an explanation of that value not appeal to the very moral notions it was meant to explain)? And, whatever value explains the importance of mutual recognition, what explains the special importance of that further value?'

Scottish constructivism, on the contrary, maintains the structure of the constitutivist's solution to the normativity and Euthyphro problems (empathy-informed communication, deliberation, action, justification are activities that beings like us cannot avoid), but provides a much more plausible description of the failure of those who do not see the special force of moral reasons (when compared both with Kantians and with Scanlon). I have argued that those left cold by morality lack the capacity not merely to reason or communicate consistently but to 'vibrate in sympathy' with others' 'feelings and operations'. In Humean terms, what such individuals lack is the ability to see others' *humanity*, the ways in which others are moved and hurt in ways just like we are. So when we fail to take the moral point of view, we fail to see others as bearing the same range of sensibilities, concerns, emotions as we do, and that are typical of all human beings. Moral failures are failures to see, to *feel*, the humanity in others. Insofar as we fail in this way, we fail to 'touch a string to which all mankind have an accord and symphony'. On this view, the seat of normativity lies in the range of contingent human sensibilities, concerns and emotions evoked by the operation of empathy in contexts of action, communication, justification. Notice that this account also allows us to distinguish the moral failures of psychopaths from those of autistics. Recall that autistics *are* concerned and preoccupied with other people's concerns, emotions and interests; they are just not very good at determining what those are, or how to coordinate their behaviour in reaction to them. This makes their moral failure (in those cases in which there is such short-sightedness) much less vicious and thorough-going than the psychopath's, whose mind-reading and role-taking capacities are fully intact, but who simply does not care why others' perspectives should matter.

I have only given a very cursory sketch of Scottish constructivism. Much more would be needed to fill it out. I cannot do that here. But it may be useful at least to outline what some of the obstacles in the elaboration of such a view might be. I will mention three. First, the Scottish constructivist must provide a more specific characterization of the deliberative standpoint from which moral claims are justified or created – a characterization that models the operation of empathy and that explains why the characterization helps us to account for the moral reasons there are. Second, he must provide an account of moral responsibility that coheres with the empathy-based characterization of the deliberative standpoint. For example, does a failure of empathy, or a general lack of empathy, provide 'excusing' conditions? Third, and closely related, he must explain how the Scottish constructivist can secure the right kind of objectivity for moral claims, especially in view of the wide differences in both our capacities to empathize and their structure. I do not think these are insuperable difficulties; indeed, many of them are just as difficult to overcome for Kantian constitutivists.

Forst's humanity

At a critical point in the book, Forst bemoans Habermas's attempt to overcome the gap between 'a "must" in the sense of weak transcendental necessitation by "unavoidable" presuppositions of argumentation, and the "prescriptive 'must' of a rule of action"' by pointing to our 'existential' interest as a species in maintaining a 'communicative way of life' (102). Forst worries that this makes morality optional: '[such an existential] interest cannot provide the basis of morality, for morality must possess a normativity of its own that makes the maintenance of such a form of life a duty that one simply has toward others' (103). In response to Habermas's 'retreat' to an ethical ground, Forst resists the temptation to reassert a more uncompromising, Kantian interpretation of discourse ethics. He explicitly recognizes the central difficulty facing any such purely 'transcendental-pragmatic' justification of morality, namely that it seems to make failures to take the moral point of view into failures of *self-relation* – failures, for discourse ethicists like Karl-Otto Apel, merely to abide by the pragmatic presuppositions of one's own communicative acts. Just as we have above, Forst wonders about the place of *others* in this interpretation of Kantian constitutivism.

Forst's alternative is complex and nuanced, but I believe it points him well beyond his Kantian starting point. It is worth quoting him in full:

> This reflection on the capacity for being a "rational animal" is bound up with the reflection on being a "social" and also a "natural" animal: not only a justifying being but also a being who *needs* reasons. This completes the second-order practical insight as a "human insight," which is at the same time an insight into the kind of being human that is relevant for morality. For one owes other humans reciprocal and general reasons not only as autonomous beings but also as finite beings with whom one shares contexts of action in which conflicts are unavoidable.
>
> [The insight into finitude] is an insight into the various risks of human vulnerability and human suffering, bodily and psychological. Without the consciousness of this vulnerability and the corresponding sensibility, without the consciousness that one's own actions must account for the "wills of suffering subjects," as Kant puts it, moral insight that is an insight into human responsibility remains blind. A morality of justification also rests therefore on the insight that human beings as vulnerable and finite beings require moral respect and thus justifying reasons; and in this sense this is not a morality for mere "rational beings" but for those who have a sense of the evils that follow from denying someone's right to justification and not being respected as an author and addressee of validity claims. Here we see . . . that the moral point of view must combine cognitive (the capacity for justification), volitional (willingness to give justification and act justifiably), and affective (the sensorium for moral violations) components. . . . Precisely because, with the moral insight, the awareness of the *conditionality* of human beings as finite beings becomes part of a person's identity—and thereby also his or her emotional life—it represents an insight into the

unconditionality of the demand for moral respect and the criteria of reciprocity and generality, which cannot be replaced by other criteria (52-3m).

The way I read this passage is that the moral point of view is presupposed by any recognition of another as a vulnerable, suffering, finite being. The moral point of view is always already included in any such recognition of another as a human being. On this view, when you fail to take the moral point of view, you fail to recognize the (vulnerable, finite, suffering) humanity of another person (rather than merely failing to recognize their capacity to set and pursue ends as on traditional Kantian accounts). But why, we might wonder, is the moral point of view always already included in any such recognition? Here Forst makes, I believe, a false move. He writes, referring to Levinas:

> it is the "face" of the other that makes clear to me where the ground of being moral lies, namely, in a certain fundamental understanding of what "being human" means. It makes sense to describe this phenomenon as one of both cognition and recognition. For morality is concerned with the cognition of a human being *qua* human being (105m).

What force does 'being human' have? Forst here seems to be appealing to something like the concept of 'being human', as if reflection on what we mean when we refer to human beings as human beings requires us to recognize them as finite, suffering and vulnerable. This is certainly true, but how does that recognition require us to treat them a certain way? Why does recognizing someone as a human being entail that I shouldn't take advantage, say, of his finitude, vulnerability and suffering? Sometimes Forst refers to Wittgenstein and the idea that when we recognize another as person, we must recognize that the other is not merely an 'automaton' but a being with a 'soul'. Yes, but why should the fact that he is a soul entail that we should treat him one way rather than another?

The Scottish constructivist can provide the missing piece in Forst's puzzle. When we reflect on the finitude, suffering and vulnerability of others, the capacity that moves us to be concerned for them, to take their perspective into account, to justify ourselves to them, is empathy. Human beings who have a normally functioning capacity for empathy *cannot but* feel others' finitude, suffering and vulnerability as if it were their own; they *cannot but* respond to their reasons (even if they end up disregarding them). For the Scottish constructivist, the reason that morality is inescapable is that we cannot avoid recognizing and then feeling others' perspectives on the world. It is in virtue of that recognition that we then owe them a justification, a reason, for our actions that they can accept from their standpoint. This is why the Scottish constructivist says that the existence and operation of this capacity, in conjunction with the capacity for deliberative reflection and action, is what grounds morality. And it is only by recognizing the central place of this social emotion that Forst's justificatory constitutivism can work. Or at least that is what I have tried to argue. Through a reconstruction of Forst's grounding of the right to justification, which I have tried to do by placing him in dialogue with his constructivist cousins, we have seen that Forst himself points the way from Germany to Scotland. Will he join us on the journey there?

Texts cited

Aniskiewicz, A. S. (1979), 'Autonomic Components of Vicarious Conditioning and Psychopathy', *Journal of Clinical Psychology* 35: 60–7.

Baron-Cohen, S. (1995), *Mindblindness: As Essay on Autism and Theory of Mind.* Cambridge, MA: MIT Press.

Baron-Cohen, S. and S. Wheelwright (2004), 'The Empathy Quotient: An Investigation of Adults with Asperger Syndrome or High Functioning Autism, and Normal Sex Differences', *Journal of autism and developmental disorders* 34: 163–75.

Baron-Cohen, S., A. M. Leslie, and U. Frith (1985), 'Does the Autistic Child Have a "Theory of Mind"?', *Cognition* 21: 37–46.

Blair, J., L. Jones, F. Clark, and M. Smith (1997), 'The Psychopathic Individual: A Lack of Responsiveness to Distress Cues?', *Psychophysiology* 34: 192–8.

Blair, R. (2005), 'Responding to the Emotions of Others: Dissociating Forms of Empathy through the Study of Typical and Psychiatric Populations', *Consciousness and Cognition* 14: 698–718.

Blair, R., L. Jones, F. Clark, and M. Smith (1995), 'Is the Psychopath "Morally Insane"?', *Personality and Individual Differences* 19: 741–52.

Enoch, David (2006), 'Agency, Shmagency: Why Normativity Won't Come from What Is Constitutive of Action', *The Philosophical Review* 115: 169–98.

Ferrero, Luca (2009), 'Constitutivism and the Inescapability of Agency', in Russ Shafer-Landau (ed.), *Oxford Studies in Metaethics*. Oxford: Oxford University Press.

Forst, Rainer (2012), *The Right to Justification: Elements of a Constructivist Theory of Justice*. New York: Columbia University Press.

Hare, R. D. (1991), *The Hare Psychopathy Checklist-Revised*. Toronto: Multi-Health Systems.

Hume, David (1978), *A Treatise of Human Nature*, ed. L. A. Selby-Bigge. Oxford: Oxford University Press.

—(1998), *An Enquiry Concerning the Principles of Morals*, ed. Tom L. Beauchamp. Oxford: Oxford University Press.

James, R. and R. Blair (1996), 'Brief Report: Morality in the Autistic Child', *Journal of autism and developmental disorders* 26: 571–9.

Kennett, J. (2002), 'Autism, Empathy and Moral Agency', *The Philosophical Quarterly* 52: 340–57.

Korsgaard, Christine (2009), *Self-Constitution: Agency, Identity, and Integrity*. Oxford: Oxford University Press.

McDowell, John (1988), 'Values and Secondary Qualities', in Ted Honderich (ed.), *Morality and Objectivity*. London: Routledge.

Milo, Ronald (1995), 'Contractarian Constructivism', *The Journal of Philosophy* 92: 181–204.

Parfit, Derek (2003), 'Justifiability to Each Person', *Ratio* 16: 368–90.

Patrick, C. J. (1994), 'Emotion and Psychopathy: Startling New Insights', *Psychophysiology* 31: 319–30.

Rawls, John (1993), *Political Liberalism*. New York: Columbia University Press.

Scanlon, Thomas (1998), *What We Owe to Each Other*. Cambridge: Harvard University Press.

Scanlon, Tim (2003), 'Replies', *Ratio* 16: 424–39.

Shafer-Landau, Russ (2003), *Moral Realism: A Defence*. Oxford; New York: Clarendon.

Street, Sharon (2010), 'What Is Constructivism in Ethics and Metaethics?', *Philosophy Compass* 5: 363–84.

Street, Susan (2008), 'Constructivism About Reasons', in Russ Shafer-Landau (ed.), *Oxford Studies in Metaethics*. Oxford: Oxford University Press.

Timmons, Mark (2003), 'The Limits of Moral Constructivism', *Ratio* 16: 391–423.

Wiggins, David (1987), 'A Sensible Subjectivism?', in *Needs, Values, Truth: Essays in the Philosophy of Value*. Oxford: Oxford University Press.

3

The Power of Justification

Amy Allen

Professor of Philosophy, Dartmouth College, USA

The first question of justice, according to Rainer Forst, is the question of 'the justifiability of social relations and the distribution of the "power of justification" within a political context'.[1] This insight is central to a critical theory of justice, which insofar as it is critical must also be radical, that is, it must uncover the roots of social injustice. The first good of a critical theory of justice is therefore 'the socially effective power to demand, question, and provide justifications, or to turn them into the foundations of political action and institutional arrangements' (RJ, p. 5). Similarly, the core idea of a just order is the idea that 'its rules and institutions of social life be *free of all forms of arbitrary rule or domination*'; guaranteeing this freedom from arbitrary rule or domination is the first 'task' of justice (RJ, p. 189). Justice is 'first and foremost about ending domination and unjustifiable, arbitrary rule, whether political or social in a broader sense; it is about citizens' status as equals in political and social life; i.e., as persons with what I call a basic right to justification'.[2]

Hence a critical theory of justice that puts the issue of justification at its centre is one that, as Forst puts it elsewhere, puts 'first things first', where this means that it puts the issue of 'justificatory power' first.[3]

---

[1] R. Forst, *The Right to Justification: Elements of a Constructivist Theory of Justice*, trans. by J. Flynn. New York: Columbia University Press, 2012, p. 4. Henceforth cited in text as RJ.
[2] R. Forst, 'First Things First: Redistribution, Recognition and Justification', *European Journal of Political Theory* 6(3), (2007b), 291–304, p. 295.
[3] Ibid., p. 299.

Justice, Forst rightly insists, is a matter not of the distribution of goods but of the subjection of some individuals to the domination and/or arbitrary rule of others. This is why the first question of justice is the question of power.

The essential conceptual or philosophical elements of Forst's critical theory of (in)justice as it is articulated in the *Right to Justification* are the following: (1) a constructivist account of the source of moral (and, derivatively, political) normativity; and (2) an ultimate grounding of constructivism in a conception of practical reason and of what it means to be a human being that cannot itself be constructed (only reconstructed). Using this constructivist strategy together with his account of practical reason and the irreducibly moral dimensions of personhood, Forst develops the notion of a fundamental human/moral right to justification and a principle of justification centred on two basic criteria: reciprocity and generality. Throughout the *Right to Justification*, Forst puts this idea of the basic right to justification to work in a number of insightful and productive ways: in a masterful reconsideration of Rawls/Habermas and liberalism/communitarianism debates, and in original and well-developed accounts of deliberative democracy, social justice, human rights and transnational justice.

My main interest, however, in what follows is not so much on the ways in which the theory can be put to work, but rather on the key conceptual elements of Forst's theory, and of how well they serve his aim of putting first things first, that is, of making the question of power central to his account of justice. I share Forst's sense that the first question of justice is the question of power, so my overarching aim in what follows is to offer a kind of internal critique of his theory, focusing on the question of whether Forst's framework does in fact succeed in putting first things first, in the sense of doing justice to the question of power. My argument is that, as that framework is developed in the *Right to Justification*, it does not, and the reason for this is that Forst tends to envision the power of justification in positive terms – as an empowering force to be wielded against domination, as a weapon of the weak, as it were – and does not pay sufficient attention to the ways in which practical reason itself can and often does serve not only to legitimate existing relations of domination but also to enact them. Notably, the claim that our notion of practical reason is premised on and serves to reinforce relations of domination and subordination figures prominently in the critiques of reason offered by many feminist, queer, critical race and postcolonial theorists. While this doesn't mean that the claim should be accepted uncritically, it does mean, I think, that a theory that aims to be truly critical should take such claims seriously. The more interesting question, I think, however, is not whether Forst's framework *does* accommodate the idea that practical reason and justification, as these have been understood in the Enlightenment philosophical tradition that we have inherited from Kant, are mechanisms of both empowerment and domination at the same time. The more interesting question is whether or not Forst's framework *could* accommodate such an idea. That's a more difficult question for me to answer, but one that I hope my remarks will at least invite Forst to reflect upon further.

Constructivism, reconstructivism and the problem of ideology

There is a sense in which Forst's project is a foundationalist one, insofar as he seeks to ground his account of political justice – and his related accounts of deliberative democracy, human rights, social and transnational justice – in a fundamental moral right, which is also a human right. This is the right to justification. In this sense, there is an avowedly Platonic aspect to Forst's project, insofar as it seeks to ground all normative phenomenon in a '*single* root' which forms the 'normative core' of talk of justice in all social and political contexts, 'the one basic human *right to justification*' (RJ, p. vii). Indeed, talk of foundations is prominent in this book: the introduction is called 'The Foundation of Justice' and the first section of the book bears the title 'Foundations' while the subtitle of the first chapter is 'the foundation of morality'. As we will see below, however, Forst stops short of claiming that there is an 'ultimate' foundation or ground for normativity[4]; so all talk of foundations aside, his theory of normativity is non-foundationalist.

If there is no ultimate foundation or ground for normativity, then what accounts for the validity of our moral and political norms, in particular, the fundamental principle of justification? In response to this metaethical question, Forst initially offers a constructivist answer.[5] Morality rests upon its own validity, it does not draw its normativity or validity from God or any other source. In this sense, morality is autonomous. And yet moral norms are capable of being genuinely valid.[6] Their validity is a function of their having survived an idealized procedure of practical deliberation, what Forst calls a justification procedure. Forst formulates the core insight of constructivism as follows: 'there is no objective, or in any other sense valid, order of values that takes priority over the justification procedure. Only those norms that can successfully withstand this procedure count as valid' (RJ, p. 48).

On Forst's particular version of constructivism, the justification procedure centres on two criteria: reciprocity and generality. The reciprocity criterion holds that: 'one cannot raise any specific claims while rejecting like claims of others (reciprocity of contents), and one cannot simply assume that others share one's perspective, evaluations, convictions, interests, or needs (reciprocity of reasons), so that, for

---

[4] Hence, Forst claims that his theory of justification 'starts from the unavailability of "ultimate" grounds for principles of justice' (*Right to Justification*, p. 81).

[5] Note that since Forst grounds political norms in a constructivist account of the validity of moral norms, his version of constructivism is more Kantian than Rawlsian. Compare Rawls's classic statement of constructivism, which is limited to a political conception of justice: J. Rawls, 'Kantian Constructivism in Moral Theory', *Journal of Philosophy* 77(1980), 515–72. For Forst's account of the differences between his constructivism and Rawls's, see *Right to Justification*, pp. 111ff.

[6] In line with Habermas's discourse ethics, Forst focuses on the validity of moral norms rather than their truth. For Habermas's argument that normative validity is analogous to but not a species of truth, see J. Habermas, 'Discourse Ethics: Notes on a Program of Philosophical Justification', in ibid., *Moral Consciousness and Communicative Action*, trans. by C. Lenhardt and S. Weber Nicholsen. Cambridge, MA: MIT Press, 1990, pp. 43–115.

example, one claims to speak in the "true" interests of others or in the name of an absolute, unquestionable truth beyond justification' (RJ, p. 49). The generality criterion holds that: 'the objections of any person who is affected, whoever he or she may be, cannot be disregarded, and the reasons adduced in support of the legitimacy of a norm must be capable of being shared by all persons' (RJ, p. 49). Hence, for Forst, the world of moral normativity is constructed by means of a principle of reciprocal and general justification; the binding force of norms rests on the fact that no good reasons can be offered against them (RJ, p. 50). The relevant sense of 'no good reasons' is a way of cashing out the Scanlonian idea of 'reasonable rejection'. Hence, Forst writes, 'Normativity is generated by a discursive justification procedure that equips norms with reasons that cannot be [reasonably] rejected. These reasons are the ground on which the normativity of autonomous morality rests' (RJ, p. 51). But what it means to say that a norm can't be reasonably rejected is just that it meets the criteria of reciprocity and generality.

And yet, as Forst realizes, there is a limit to the work that constructivism can do. This limit is expressed in the following question: what is the source of the normativity of the justification procedure – the principle of justification – itself, on the basis of which moral and political norms are to be constructed?

Forst's answer to this question is to assert that the ought 'brings its own reasons with it so that there can be no question of other reasons' and that recognizing this just is what it means to be a moral subject (RJ, p. 53). Hence, he claims, 'the moral law does not need any further justifying reasons over and above the practical knowledge that one is a "justifying being" with a fundamental duty to provide justifications and ... [that] "being human", insofar as it necessarily implies being a "fellow human", already has a normative character that entails the duty to provide justifications in moral contexts' (RJ, p. 54). So the 'ultimate' foundation – keeping in mind that Forst denies that the foundation is truly ultimate – of Forst's moral and political constructivism is a certain conception of what it means to be human, a conception that is essentially equated with an account of practical reason.[7] Forst is quite explicit that this account cannot itself be constructed, though it can be reconstructed.[8] This is fair enough – it is a common criticism of constructivism that it must either bottom out in some foundation that is not itself constructed but instead forms a realist ground – or end up being circular.[9] Forst explicitly denies that his constructivism ultimately rests on a moral realist ground[10]; this is the basis for his repeated insistence that there is no 'ultimate' foundation for morality. Rather, he adopts the strategy of admitting to a kind of circularity to the way in which the construction procedure itself is grounded – he uses the term 'recursive' – though he insists that this circularity is virtuous and reflexive rather than vicious and question-begging. This is where the notion of reconstruction comes in.[11]

But what precisely does it mean to say that the account of practical reasons that underlies Forst's constructivist procedure can be reconstructed? What does 'reconstruction' mean here? Forst doesn't say explicitly here what he means by this, but his usage of the term seems close, at least in this text,[12] to Habermas's. As Thomas McCarthy explains, rational reconstruction for Habermas is the reflective articulation, refinement and elaboration of 'the intuitive grasp of the normative presuppositions of social interaction that belongs to the repertoire

---

[7]   Note that Forst distinguishes his account of practical reason from Kant's because he takes Kant to fail to appreciate the intersubjective nature of morality's demands; see *Right to Justification*, ch. 2, sec. 13. Being human has its normative character for Forst only 'insofar as it necessarily implies being a "fellow human"' (*Right to Justification*, p. 54).

[8]   For example, in the Introduction, Forst writes, 'the "ultimate" foundation of constructivism cannot itself be constructed, but must prove itself as being appropriately reconstructed in an analysis of our normative world' (*Right to Justification*, p. 5).

[9]   C. Bagnoli, 'Constructivism in Metaethics', *Stanford Encyclopedia of Philosophy*, published 27 September 2011 at http://plato.stanford.edu/entries/constructivism-metaethics/, accessed 19 January 2012.

[10] See, for example, *Right to Justification* ch. 2, especially sec. 19, where Forst responds to the work of Charles Larmore.

[11] Hence, Forst claims that 'the principle of justification is thus a principle that must be "recursively" reconstructed' (*Right to Justification*, p. 81).

[12] Note that, as Forst himself notes, it is also possible to approach the right to justification from the point of view of a historical reconstruction of the ways in which discourses of justification have emerged in various social and political conflicts. Forst pursues this kind of reconstructive strategy in his book, *Toleration in Conflict*, trans. by C. Cronin. Cambridge: Cambridge University Press, 2013a. See Forst, *Right to Justification*, p. 3.

of competent social actors in any society'.[13] For Habermas, rational reconstruction draws on work in the empirical sciences to generate a quasi-transcendental account of the rational-normative potentials built into linguistic communication[14]; this quasi-transcendental account plays an important justificatory role in his discourse-ethical constructivism.[15] Although Forst indicates that he does not wish to take on board the whole of Habermas's 'comprehensive theory of truth and argumentation', (RJ, p. 271, n. 29), his use of the term reconstruction in this text nonetheless has affinities with Habermas's. Hence, Forst's reconstructive approach to the moral point of view starts with a pragmatic analysis of moral validity claims and inquires 'into the conditions of justification of such claims' (RJ, pp. 48–9). This recursive, reconstructive analysis generates the criteria of generality and reciprocity, in the sense that by means of a reflexive articulation of what we are implicitly committed to as moral agents it uncovers that what it means for a competent moral actor to redeem a moral validity claim is just for him or her to be able to defend that claim in a reciprocal and general way, in a way that no one can reasonably reject.

So it turns out that all of the talk of foundations of morality notwithstanding, Forst's approach 'ultimately' rests on a non-foundationalist ground, namely, the reconstructive analysis of what we are implicitly committed to as practically reasoning moral agents. This sort of strategy is open to some standard worries that are raised in debates about constructivism: If constructivism ultimately rests

---

[13] T. McCarthy, 'Kantian Constructivism and Reconstructivism: Rawls and Habermas in Dialogue', *Ethics* 105(1), (1994), 44–63, at p. 47. Habermasian rational reconstruction plays a similar role in his theory to the role played by the reflective articulation of our considered convictions about justice in Rawlsian political liberalism. For Forst's discussion of the different ways in which Habermas and Rawls combine reconstructivist and constructivist strategies, see *Right to Justification*, pp. 82–92.

[14] J. Habermas, 'What is Universal Pragmatics', in *Communication and the Evolution of Society*, trans. T. McCarthy. Boston: Beacon Press, 1979; and J. Habermas, *The Theory of Communicative Action, volume 1: Reason and the Rationalization of Society*, trans. by T. McCarthy. Boston: Beacon Press, 1984, especially ch. 3.

[15] But note that for Habermas this account doesn't bear all of the justificatory weight, for related to this quasi-transcendental account of the pragmatics of language use is Habermas's historical account of the normative content of modernity as having emerged out of a cultural and social learning process.

on some view about practical reason, then isn't the problem to which constructivism is supposed to offer such an elegant solution – namely, how to ground the validity of our moral judgments in a way that avoids relativism but without recourse to moral realism – just shifted back a level, to the level of the account of practical reason? What grounds the appeal to the normative content of the account of practical reason itself? If, in an effort to avoid moral realism, one answers this question, as Forst does, by saying, in effect, 'this is just what it means to be a practical reasoner', then the norms that are taken to be constitutive of practical reason threaten to become arbitrary.[16]

A nearby worry, not typically raised in discussions of constructivism in metaethics, is the problem of ideology. If the 'ultimate' grounds of the normative values that are modelled in our constructivist procedure are just our own practices and conception of practical reasoning, then what are we to do if, built into those practices and that conception, are certain ideological distortions? Suppose that the conception of practical reason on the basis of which we construct our normative world is itself, in some sense that remains to be fully spelt out, normatively suspect or problematic? What resources, then, would a normative theory such as Forst's give us for criticizing that world? (How) can an account of moral and political justice that grounds its understanding of normativity in this way help us to diagnose such distortions?

Nor should this be seen as an empty worry, since there has been lots of criticism over the last 30 years or more, from feminist, queer, postcolonial and critical race theorists, of just the sort of account of practical reason on which Forst's moral constructivism rests.[17] Such critiques claim that the Kantian Enlightenment conception

---

[16] On this point, see Bagnoli, 'Constructivism in Metaethics'.

[17] In feminist theory, the locus classicus of such discussion is G. Lloyd, *The Man of Reason: 'Male' and 'Female' in Western Philosophy*, 2nd edition. Chicago: University of Chicago Press, 1993; in critical race and postcolonial theory, the central text is F. Fanon, *Black Skin, White Masks*, trans. by R. Philcox. New York: Grove Press, 2008; for a recent articulation of this critique from the point of view of queer theory, see L. Huffer, *Mad for Foucault: Rethinking the Foundations of Queer Theory*. New York: Columbia University Press, 2010.

of practical reason explicitly or implicitly excludes, represses or dominates all that is associated with the so-called Other of reason, whether that be understood in terms of madness, irrationality, the emotions, the affects, embodiment or the imagination, all of which are symbolically associated with black, queer, female and colonized subjects. These symbolic associations serve both to rationalize and justify existing relations of racial, heterosexist and ethnic oppression and domination – by defining women, blacks, queers and colonized peoples as not rational and therefore as not fully human – at the same time that they reinforce certain stereotypical understandings of black, queer, feminine and subaltern identity as closer to nature, more tied to the body, more emotional, more prone to madness, irrationality or violence and so on.

Indeed, taking seriously the ways in which 'our' conception of practical reason is connected not just to empowerment – understood here as the ability to demand justification for the norms by which one is ruled, as what Forst calls 'justificatory power' – but also to the domination and exclusion of all those who have been affiliated with reason's others – the body, affects, unreason or madness, primitive nature, etc. – seems especially important for Forst, who, contra Rawls, understands the construction procedure itself not as a thought experiment but rather as a social practice. But, if the construction procedure is itself a social practice, then shouldn't we be worried about the extent to which our procedures of justification and the account of practical reason on which they are based may themselves be inflected with existing relations of social subordination, domination and oppression? Shouldn't we be worried about the ways in which the power of justification is both a weapon of the weak – a means by which subordinated individuals demand justification for their subordination – and tool of the powerful – a means by which powerful individuals rationalize their own dominance? And isn't raising such questions necessary if we are really to put first things first, to make the first question of justice the question of power?

Practical reason and subjection

But these sorts of questions can only be fully addressed through a more detailed consideration of Forst's account of practical reason, which is defined as the ability and disposition to 'enter into the normative space of intersubjectively supportable reasons' (RJ, p. 17) which means 'the basic capacity to respond to practical questions in appropriate ways with justifying reasons within each of the practical contexts in which they arise and must be situated' (RJ, p. 18). The fundamental principle of practical reason is the already mentioned principle of justification. What precisely this principle demands, for Forst, will vary by context of justification. So, for example, in moral contexts, the bar for justification is higher than it is in ethical or political contexts, and higher in these, in turn, than in pragmatic contexts. In moral contexts (where the bar is highest), the 'defining feature of reasons that can justify moral claims is . . . that they must be *reasons that cannot be reasonably – that is, not reciprocally and generally – rejected*' (RJ, p. 21).

So we get an image here of the space of justification as a space populated with 'reasonable, autonomous, and moral beings who must be able to account for their actions to one another' (RJ, p. 22). But how does one enter this space? What motivates one to take up the moral point of view? In contrast to neo-Humeans such as Bernard Williams, Forst insists that the reasons for taking up the moral point of view cannot be external, in the sense of fear of external sanctions or guilt or considerations of self-interest. And this is so because 'a categorical and unconditionally valid morality cannot stand on an instrumentally or ethically hypothetical foundation. It requires an *unconditioned ground*' (RJ, p. 34). So, the motivation for taking up the moral point of view has to be 'respect for the fundamental right to justification of every autonomous moral person' (RJ, p. 37), which Forst characterizes as a 'second-order practical insight' that is 'fundamental for morality' (RJ, p. 37). Through this insight, 'humans recognize themselves and each other reciprocally as members of the moral community of justification that includes all human beings, as autonomous and responsible beings, endowed with reason, who are members of a shared (and commonly constructed) space of justifying reasons' (RJ, pp. 37–8).

On Forst's view, one cannot arrive at this insight into what it means to be moral by being convinced that doing so is in your interest, for the phenomenon of being moral 'consists in the fact that anyone who realizes that he is morally obligated toward others also knows that he cannot have reasons for this obligation rooted in primarily self-regarding empirical interests, such as the avoidance of sanctions' (RJ, p. 58). In support of this point, Forst paraphrases Heidegger's attempt to dissolve (rather than solve) the problem of epistemological skepticism about the external world. As Heidegger famously argues in *Being and Time*,[18] the problem of skepticism arises only if one accepts an artificial and problematic view of the relationship between subject and object, whereby the subject is understood as a unique kind of being, set over against a world of objects. Once one sets things up in that way, the subject is separated from objects by a chasm that it can never quite manage to get back across; it is forever after plagued by sceptical worries about whether its experience of the world in fact matches up with the way the world really is. Heidegger's (dis) solution of this problem rests on showing it to be a false problem, based on an abstraction from our primordial way of existing, which is to be immersed in the world, to experience our being-in-the-world as a unified phenomenon. Forst runs an intriguing parallel argument with respect to moral skepticism. As Forst puts it, 'from the perspective of someone who understands himself as a moral being, from the perspective of moral "being-in-the-world", so to speak, this question [i.e., why be moral?] does not even arise; and someone who does not understand himself morally can never be brought to see the point of morality in this way [i.e., by means of external sanctions]' (RJ, p. 58).

But note that there's an important disanalogy between epistemological and moral skepticism that Forst does not acknowledge, and it is a

---

[18] M. Heidegger, *Being and Time*, trans. J. Stambaugh, ed. and rev. by D. Schmidt. Albany, NY: SUNY Press, 2010.

difference that casts doubt on Forst's strategy here. The difference is this: no one starts out in life a skeptic about the reality of the world. Quite the contrary, we all start out naïve realists, who understand ourselves as immersed in the world in just the way that Heidegger's phenomenology attempts to recover. Typically, one needs a fair amount of philosophical argumentation to motivate sceptical doubts about our knowledge, and they tend to dissipate as soon as, as Hume says, we leave the room, when we quite naturally leave by the door rather than the window. But in the case of moral skepticism, the situation is much less clear. There's some reason for thinking that we *do* all start out life as moral skeptics, or at least as creatures who do not inhabit the moral point of view. Anyone who has spent a significant amount of time with toddlers has some experience with this phenomenon. Children have to be *socialized into* morality and the central mechanism for this socialization is precisely the threat of sanctions (whether positive or negative), which (hopefully, if all goes well) through the mechanism of guilt leads to the internalization of structures of parental authority. This basic insight is found not only in the work of Nietzsche and Freud but also in the work of less pessimistic or ambivalent theorists of moral development such as Lawrence Kohlberg and Habermas.

Forst acknowledges that there's a degree of socialization required here but insists that this socialization is benign: 'To become part of such contexts means to learn to recognize what justifications are, when one owes them, and to whom. Such processes of formation do not "ram" an "absolute must" into us in an inexplicable manner, as Tugendhat puts it. Rather, they constitute the way in which we are as fellow human beings and through which we become individual persons' (RJ, p. 61). But he gives no discussion of how one is socialized into the space of moral reasons, nor does he acknowledge the role that accepting and internalizing the superior power of the parent (or other normative authority) inevitably plays in this process. Nor does he appreciate the fact that *from the point of view of the child,* these formation processes *necessarily* have an element of inexplicability and arbitrariness to them; the child can only appreciate the reasons that justify such socialization processes *after the fact*, after she has taken up a position within the space of reasons. Until that point is reached, parental reasons, from the point of view of the child, all seem to rest on one ultimate ground: because I said so. In other words, the space of reasons is also a space of power in the sense that it is constituted through a certain kind of power relation that can only be justified to the participants after they have entered it and accepted its demands and constitutive norms.

This line of thought can also be connected to a kind of communitarian critique of Forst's Kantian account. What, after all, are we being socialized into when we are being socialized into the space of reasons? Are we being socialized into a reasoning practice that allows us to arrive at or at least approximate a truly universal, context-transcending perspective, one that affords us a genuinely critical perspective on any form of life whatsoever, including our own? Or are we being socialized into a particular form of life, one that is rooted in and carries with it both the ethical values and, perhaps, the ideological biases of that form of life? Forst considers such worries in his discussion of Charles Taylor's work, since Taylor argues that belief in the power of reason and the autonomous subject are not, in fact universal moral values, but rather part of the uniquely modern spirit or identity (RJ, pp. 73–4).[19] Hence, on Taylor's view, the normative concepts such as practical reason and autonomy that undergird universalistic Kantian moral theories are themselves rooted in thick ethical values or constitutive goods of a particular form of life, namely, the modern (European) form of life.

To this sort of worry, Forst responds that the validity of morality cannot be grounded in this way, since 'morality is about a sphere of categorically binding norms whose observance is not required for the sake of *one's own* good, but is *unconditionally* required for the sake of the good of *others* according to the criteria of reciprocity and generality' (RJ, p. 74). Morality and its central principle, the principle

---

[19] See C. Taylor, *Sources of the Self.* Cambridge, MA: Harvard University Press, 1989.

of justification, must be grounded instead in 'practical reason itself' (RJ, p. 74). However, to the non-Kantian, this response sounds a bit like emphatically stamping one's foot, inasmuch as it presupposes precisely what is supposed to be at issue here, which is whether or not the validity of the moral can have an unconditioned ground, whether or not it can be defended independently of any and all thick, culturally specific, conceptions of the good. The most that Forst seems entitled to say at this point is that in order to count as a genuine morality, a system of normative principles would have to have an unconditioned ground; but claiming that this is a necessary feature of morality as such is not, by itself, sufficient to show that this unconditioned ground actually exists. It is worth nothing that part of Taylor's historical story is about the 'belief in the power of reason of the autonomous subject' as one of the goods particular to modernity (RJ, p. 74). If Taylor's historical genealogy is plausible, then even Forst's account of practical reason comes from somewhere, is rooted a particular point of view, something like the point of view of European Enlightenment modernity.[20] And in that case, the communitarian challenge is a serious one – and it isn't just about how to draw the distinction between ethics and morality. Rather, it is about whether all attempts, such as Forsts's, to articulate morality in the strong universalist and categorical sense are not, in fact, thick, particular, ethical values and substantive conceptions of the good in disguise.

To be sure, Forst is right that 'excluding a Hegelian recourse to the absolute, [Taylor's] narrative reconstruction of the goods underlying modern identity is confronted with the problem of justifying the validity of this kind of ethics' (RJ, p. 74). But notice that this is only true to the extent that one understands validity in the fairly demanding sense

[20]   In connection with this it is worth noting that Forst's central concept, that of justification, is also central to the Christian tradition, as can be seen in the theological writings of the apostle Paul, St Augustine and Martin Luther. On the centrality of justification to the Christian tradition, see 'Justification', in L. Jones (ed.), *Encyclopedia of Religion*, 2nd edition. Detroit, MI: Macmillan Reference, 2005, pp. 5039–42. It would be interesting to trace the genealogy of the concept of justification from its theological beginnings to the role it comes to play in Kantian and post-Kantian moral philosophy.

that Forst himself does. If, by contrast, one is comfortable with a less demanding, more contextualist conception of normative validity, then one wouldn't have to have recourse either to a theory of the absolute or to the notion of an unconditioned ground.

Now, I suspect that Forst would say that even granting the concerns I have raised thus far – concerns about possible ideological distortions in our understanding of practical reason and about the relationship between socialization into the space of reasons and power relations – still we have no other resource on which to rely in analysing and critiquing such relationships but reason itself. As he puts it, 'a morality of justification is a morality that can be criticized and revised in its details: a human morality "without a banister" that cannot in principle exclude the possibility of failures and errors. There is, however, only one "authority" for revising any reasons that no longer seem defensible: reason itself' (RJ, p. 39). And this shows why he regards the normative concepts of autonomy and practical reason as genuinely universal, not just the expression of a particular form of life. These concepts form the core of a notion of responsibility for which there is no conceivable alternative, and on the basis of which the legitimacy of all forms of the good life are debated. As Forst sees it, this notion of moral responsibility is 'not the result of shared conceptions of the good life, but rather of a realistic consideration of the results of conflicts and learning processes that have made it clear what people owe one another. This is more than agreement concerning a few "procedural" rules, but less than the sharing of a form of life that constitutes the ethical identity of citizens' (RJ, p. 121).[21]

I can't really settle this point about whether the Kantian conception of practical reason and autonomy that Forst defends is genuinely universal or ethically particular here, though I admit I'm doubtful

---

[21] The reference to learning processes is interesting here, since it suggests that Forst's view is tied to some sort of story about historical development; but this, as Thomas McCarthy has argued recently, only heightens the worries I have raised about the entanglement of the normative values of modernity with relations of (neo)colonial, (neo)imperial, racist domination. See T. McCarthy, *Race, Empire, and the Idea of Human Development.* Cambridge: Cambridge University Press, 2009.

about Forst's claim, particularly to the extent that it relies on the reconstruction of certain historical developments as learning processes. The central point I want to make is this: It may be true that reason is all 'we' have, that reason is the best weapon we have as we try to adjudicate the kinds of questions I have raised about ideological distortions and power relations, and that, in that sense, reason is self-correcting. In other words, it may be true that, as Forst says, 'there is . . . only one "authority" for revising any reasons that no longer seem defensible: reason itself' (RJ, p. 39).[22]

But, even if we grant Forst this point, this is all the more reason to be attentive to what Albena Azmanova calls, following Kant and Hannah Arendt, the scandal of reason. The scandal of reason consists in its capacity *both* to stabilize and legitimate *and* to destabilize and delegitimate relations of domination and subordination.[23] A greater focus on this scandal, and on the relationship between 'our' ideals and practices of reasoning and the power relations with which they are intertwined, would not lead us to abandon the ideal of practical reason, though it might lead us to conceptualize it differently.[24]

Putting first things first (and the methodology of critical theory)

The two conceptual issues I've been laying out can both be understood as raising questions about how Forst's theory makes sense of the relationship between practical reason and the practice of justification, on the one hand, and relations of power over others – domination and

---

[22] See also his related claim, in the context of his discussion of his justificatory account of deliberative democracy, that 'there may always be better answers than the ones arrived at in democratic procedures; but the meaning of "better" is: more justifiable in a process of deliberation and argumentation' (*Right to Justification*, p. 186).

[23] A. Azmanova, *The Scandal of Reason: Toward a Critical Theory of Political Judgment*. New York: Columbia University Press, 2012.

[24] For a compelling attempt to conceptualize reasoning in a way that is attentive to its actual and potential entanglements with relations of domination, see A. S. Laden, this volume; and A. S. Laden, *Reasoning: A Social Picture*. New York: Oxford University Press, 2012.

authority – on the other. The question of the problem of ideology in relation to constructivism as a metaethical position can be construed in more neutral ways – as a question about whether our construction procedure might lead us systematically astray about some moral facts of the matter – but it can also be construed, as I argued above, as a question about whether 'our' conceptions of practical reason and practices of justification might be entangled with relationships of exclusion and domination. Hence, the worry is about whether the foundation for our normative construction, which is a reconstruction of 'our' point of view as practically reasoning moral agents, is itself inflected with relations of domination and subordination. In order to theorize this possibility, we would have to understand terms such as the 'power of justification' and 'justificatory power' as having two distinct meanings. These terms can refer, as they do in Forst's work, to the empowering power of justification, that is, to the ability on the part of subjects of domination and/or arbitrary rule to demand justification for their situation.[25] But they can also refer to the subordinating power of justification, that is, to the ways in which certain conceptions of practical reason and practices of justification can and do serve to entrench, rationalize and legitimate relations of domination[26]. Although Forst offers us a compelling account of the former aspect of the power of justification, he does not provide an account of the latter, which means that he also does not offer an account of how these dimensions of the relationship between power and justification are often entangled with one another. Since power and domination are pervasive features of our social world, it seems especially incumbent upon a theory that understands practical reason as a social and discursive practice of giving and asking for reasons to attempt to theorize both aspects of the power of justification.

[25] Hence, Forst claims that justificatory power is 'the highest good of justice (though one that cannot be distributed like a material good)' and he defines it as 'the "discursive" power to provide and to demand justifications, and to challenge false legitimations' (*Right to Justification*, p. 196).

[26] For insightful discussion of this issue, see Kevin Olson, "Complexities of Political Discourse," this volume.

The question about the conception of moral personhood that underlies the account of practical reason can also be understood as a question of justificatory power, though in a somewhat different way. The process of socialization into the moral point of view inevitably and necessarily involves the internalization of a certain relationship of power, as a result of the child's radical dependence on her parents.[27] As I mentioned above, this is a central insight in the work of Nietzsche and Freud, and it is a point that was not lost on the First Generation of the Frankfurt School. As Horkheimer and Adorno put it, 'humanity had to inflict terrible injuries on itself before the self . . . was created, and something of this process is repeated in every childhood'.[28] To be sure, this power relation can be construed as an authority relation, but, significantly, whether that authority is dictatorial or legitimate can be determined only after the fact, after the child has taken up the moral point of view. The threat of parental or social sanctions – whether positive or negative – and the mechanisms of guilt and shame play a crucial role in this process. The conclusion we should draw from this is not that all authority is illegitimate, that we shouldn't discipline children, or that freedom means a wild, schizophrenic, anarchic transgression of the boundaries of moral personhood. Rather, the conclusion is a more complicated and ambivalent one: that power relations are constitutive of subjectivity and moral personhood, that power relations provide the condition of possibility for entering the space of reasons in the first place, which means that the space of reasons is also always already a space of power. And this suggests that our confidence in the ability that reason itself gives us to distinguish between legitimate and illegitimate forms of power and dependency shouldn't be overly strong.

---

[27] I discuss this issue in more detail, in relation to Judith Butler's theory of subjection, in chapter four of A. Allen, *The Politics of Our Selves: Power, Autonomy, and Gender in Contemporary Critical Theory*. New York: Columbia University Press, 2008.

[28] M. Horkheimer and T. Adorno, *Dialectic of Enlightenment: Philosophical Fragments*, trans. E. Jephcott. Stanford: Stanford University Press, 2002, p. 26.

I suspect that this conclusion would be quite worrisome to Forst, whose division of labour between the constructive and critical tasks of a theory of justice seems designed to avoid precisely the sorts of considerations that I've been raising. The constructive part of the theory of justice 'lies in identifying the premises, principles, and procedures of the project of establishing a (more) just society' (RJ, p. 117); the critical part 'lies in uncovering false or absent justifications for existing social relations and the corresponding relocation of the *power of justification* to the subjects themselves' (RJ, p. 117). The centrepiece of the constructive part of the theory is the justification of a just basic structure, which rests on the constructivist and reconstructivist account of the principle of justification itself. The centrepiece, the critical part of the theory of justice is the 'analysis and critique of legal, political, and social relations that are not reciprocally and generally justifiable. It requires a *critique of relations of justification* in a double sense, namely, both with respect to the real, particularly institutional possibility of discursive justification and (in terms of discourse theory) with regard to allegedly "generally" accepted and acceptable results, that in truth are missing a sufficient grounding' (RJ, p. 121).

The advantage of distinguishing between the constructive and critical tasks of a theory of justice in this way is relatively clear: it allows Forst to confine questions of the relations of domination in existing social relations to the critical part of the theory, allowing him to focus in the constructive part on the normative defence and elaboration of the principle of justification. This allows Forst to develop a strong normative principle on the basis of which power relations can be critically assessed. But the shortcomings of such an approach are, in my view, equally clear. This sort of approach seems to be an instance of what has recently been called political philosophy as applied ethics.[29] The strategy seems to be to develop and defend

---

[29] R. Geuss, *Philosophy and Real Politics*. Princeton: Princeton University Press, 2008.

the normative philosophical framework on independent grounds and then, in a second step, to apply this theory to the task of criticizing existing social relations.

The merits of such an approach as a general approach to political philosophy are debatable.[30] The more specific question that I would prefer to focus on here has to do with the merits of adopting this sort of approach when what one endeavours to do is to offer a critical theory of justice that puts the question of power at its centre. Can an approach such as this do justice to the depth and complexity of power relations, especially as these pertain to the conditions and practice of justification and practical reasoning? As I've already suggested, it seems to me that an approach that puts first things first would be one that focuses not only on the emancipatory role that the demand for justification can and does play but also on the role that practices of justification and conceptions of practical reasoning also play in legitimating and undergirding existing relations of domination and subordination, particularly along lines of race, ethnicity and gender/ sexuality. Moreover, such an approach would also highlight the ways in which these two aspects of the power of justification are often entangled with one another.

This way of understanding the inherent duality of the power of justification would be in line with an alternative conception of the methodology of critical theory: an approach that envisions critical theory not as a kind of applied ethics but, rather, takes the distinctiveness of critical theory to lie in its understanding of practical reason as impure, by which I mean embodied and embedded in history, culture, society, language and so on, which is to say, entangled with power relations. On this view, the methodological distinctiveness of critical theory lies precisely in its attempt to grapple with the essential tension between reason and power relations, an essential tension that needs to be

---

[30] For compelling critical discussions of Rawls that foreground this issue, see Geuss, *Philosophy and Real Politics*, and F. Freyenhagen and J. Schaub, 'Hat hier jemand gesagt, der Kaiser sei nackt? Eine Verteidigung der Geussschen Kritik an Rawls' idealtheoretischem Ansatz', *Deutsche Zeitschrift für Philosophie* 58(3), (2010), 457–77.

confronted not just at the empirical level but also at the conceptual level.[31] In other words, the methodological distinctiveness of critical theory rests in its acknowledgement that, as Foucault once put it, we are 'fortunately committed to practicing a rationality that is unfortunately crisscrossed by intrinsic dangers' and the task of critical theory is both to accept and to think through this spiral.[32] Such an approach to critical theory is actually more fully reflexive than the political philosophy as applied ethics approach, insofar as it has built into itself a genealogical reflection on the contingent and possibly ideological grounds of its own theoretical formation.[33]

To all of this, I imagine that Forst might reply by complaining that the approach that I advocate makes it difficult, if not impossible, to distinguish between legitimate and illegitimate relations of power. And indeed, it is true that I have not, in the course of this discussion, distinguished clearly between power relations as such and relations of domination and subordination.[34] I think that an approach to critical theory that foregrounds a genealogical analysis of power relations still can – indeed: must! – make such distinctions, though it will need to understand the normative validity of such distinctions as based on a more contextualist metaethical position than the one defended by Forst.[35] Still, I admit that the methodological approach to critical theory that I have (only rather sketchily, to be sure) proposed here as an alternative to Forst's will have a more difficult time making such distinctions in a

---

[31] I argue for this way of understanding the project of critical theory in A. Allen, 'The Unforced Force of the Better Argument: Reason and Power in Habermas's Political Theory', *Constellations* 19(3), (September, 2012), 1–16. Interestingly enough, Habermas himself comes closer to the view I am advocating – though not, in my view, close enough – in his discussion of law in *Between Facts and Norms: Contributions to a Discourse Theory of Law and Democracy*, trans. by W. Rehg. Cambridge, MA: MIT Press, 1996a. Forst explicitly distances himself from this aspect of Habermas's thought in ch. 4 of *Right to Justification*; see especially, pp. 113–16.

[32] M. Foucault, 'Space, Knowledge, and Power', in J. Faubion (ed.), *Essential Works of Michel Foucault, volume 3: Power*. New York: The New Press, 2000, p. 358.

[33] Freyenhagen and Schaub, 'Hat hier jemand gesagt', p. 464.

[34] This is a task that I attempt to carry out in A. Allen, *The Power of Feminist Theory: Domination, Resistance, Solidarity*. Boulder, CO: Westview Press, 1999.

[35] I attempt to work out such a position via a critical engagement with Habermas in chapters 5 and 6 of Allen, *The Politics of Our Selves*.

firm and fast way, with a great degree of confidence. But I see this as an *advantage* of the view that I'm proposing, because it seems to me that the great difficulty we have in distinguishing legitimate from illegitimate relations of power is a feature of the cultural, social and political world we inhabit, something that critical theorists should place at the very centre of our theorizing. It does no good to pretend that this is not a deep and pervasive feature of our social world, nor to assume that this practical issue doesn't affect our own theorizing. To do so, it seems to me, would be to engage in a kind of wishful thinking that we would do well to avoid.[36]

---

[36] On the concept of wishful thinking, see David Owen's insightful critique of Geuss, D. Owen, 'Die verlorene und die wiedergefundene Wirklichkeit. Ethik, Politik und Imagination bei Raymond Geuss', *Deutsche Zeitschrift für Philosophie* 58(3), (2010), 431–43.

4

Complexities of Political Discourse

Class, Power and the Linguistic Turn[1]

Kevin Olson
Associate Professor of Political Science,
University of California, USA

The linguistic turn began as an epistemological revolution against metaphysics. During the initial onslaught of this rebellion, political thought was a victim of collateral damage – a subject about which philosophy could not speak, so it must remain silent.[2] After the dust settled, however, the linguistic turn proved surprisingly useful for politics. It has furnished core insights for a wide array of perspectives in political theory, revealing exciting vistas that would have been unimaginable 50 years ago.

With these advances also come problems, however. As language has become more and more the lens through which politics is viewed, we are forced to deal much more incisively with the complex social and political character of linguistic practices. The proliferation of political theories based on language requires a critical counterpart of equal weight, especially when normative – which is to say, prescriptive – conclusions hang in the balance. If we are to organize

[1] I'm grateful to Rainer Forst for several rounds of stimulating dialogue, including his insightful comments on an earlier draft of this essay. I've also benefitted greatly from conversations with Amy Allen, Maeve Cooke and Keith Topper on these themes. This research was supported by the Critical Theory Institute at the University of California, Irvine.
[2] L. Wittgenstein, 'Whereof one cannot speak, thereof one must be silent'. *Tractatus Logico-Philosophicus*, trans. by C. K. Ogden. London: Routledge, 1922, §7. Cf. A. J. Ayers, *Language, Truth, and Logic*, 2nd edition. New York: Dover, 1952, ch. 6.

our society around something like the public use of language, we must have a finely honed analysis of the dangers and pitfalls that we might encounter along the way.

As a contribution to this critique, I will enter into conversation here with Rainer Forst's innovative version of the linguistic turn. Forst bases his political theory on the idea of a right to justification. It establishes a view of politics centred on the reciprocal trading of reasons for proposed norms and laws. This view inscribes a linguistic turn in politics by connecting justification with ideas of recognition, generality and reciprocity. Because justification is so basic to politics, especially when we think of it as discursive in character, this provides a normative fulcrum for critical perspectives on a wide array of issues, from multiculturalism to toleration, deliberative democracy, social justice and transnational justice.

In this essay I will focus on an issue lying at the heart of Forst's work: the argument he makes for the right to justification itself. I am particularly interested in his account of the claims we can make for such a right. I believe that Forst's answer to that question has a great deal to say about the normative bases of a discursive politics, while also exemplifying the linguistic turn's entwinement with some of the very social issues it aims to criticize. Chief among these, I will claim, are issues of power and class in political discourse. When taken together, these concerns call into question the universality of something like a right to justification. Rather than forming the core of any discursive politics, reason-giving may well be a class-specific political practice that favours elite groups over others. The connection of such practices with class power and domination gives us cause to rethink the way we inscribe a linguistic turn in political theory.

These are not claims that I take lightly, nor do I mean to impugn Rainer Forst's admirable insights and conceptual subtlety. I single out his work here because it theorizes political discourse in a robust, clear and compelling manner, making it possible to see the underlying problems in a uniquely perspicuous way as well. My claims apply equally to many other political theories based on discourse and language.

Jürgen Habermas's work springs to mind, as do other attempts to make a linguistic turn in political theory, including, I hasten to add, some of my own. In a spirit of friendly engagement and self-criticism, then, I join with Rainer Forst to see what can be made of a linguistic turn in politics when we take issues of class and power into account.

Rights to justification

Forst's political theory is based on moral premises, particularly on a conception of the autonomy of morality. He understands morality 'as a system of categorically obligating norms – and corresponding duties and rights – that count as reciprocal and general for humans *as humans* in their character as moral persons, and do not presuppose any thicker context of interpersonal relations like particular communities (family, friends, political community, etc.)' (75–6).[3] The bases of morality are independent of cultural or ethical contexts, then, such as particular notions of the good, or culturally embedded ideas of right and wrong. Instead, morality rests on the character of human beings as moral agents.

The humanity from which morality arises is not our own, however. We do not act morally out of respect for ourselves, but out of respect for others (89–90, 94). As a moral insight, this has a double character, with both cognitive and recognitive components (89). We understand others as human, in the sense of free, rational beings subject to suffering. Similarly, we recognize others as human, seeing them as vulnerable to suffering and thus deserving of respect. This, Forst claims, is tantamount to recognizing them as moral beings to whom we have particular obligations (67). Invoking Levinas, he writes: 'It is the face of

---

[3] Emphasis in the original. Parenthetical references in the text refer to R. Forst, *Das Recht auf Rechtfertigung: Elemente einer konstruktivistischen Theorie der Gerechtigkeit.* Frankfurt am Main: Suhrkamp, 2007a. I have translated all quotations of this work from the original German.

the other that makes it clear to me where the ground of being moral lies: in the fact that we are humans' (95). People are given to us – recognized by us – as moral others. Understanding and recognition come to the same conclusion, then: we see others as moral agents to whom we have categorical moral obligations.

Because moral norms are based on the cognition of shared humanity and the recognition of others as moral agents, they have an inherently intersubjective character. They raise validity claims that must be discursively negotiated within a 'shared space of justifying reasons' (65, 106). The discursive character of moral norms implies the second-order practical insight that we have of duties of justification towards those others (66–9, 124). Insofar as people are affected by a given norm or action, we have a duty to justify it to them, to provide reasons that show our respect for them as persons affected. Symmetrically, this duty implies that each person has a right to justification. The right to justification provides each person with what Forst calls a 'moral veto', being able to object when particular norms or actions seem not to be justifiable (173, 198).

In Forst's view, the right to justification can be fulfilled only by discourses of a particular form. Those discourses are characterized above all by reciprocity and generality. Reciprocity ensures symmetry between the interests and points of view considered in discourse. No one can determine unilaterally what counts as a good reason, and any reason I apply to my own case must apply equally well to others. Generality guarantees that no affected person's participation can be excluded from the discourses that create an agreement. Agreement is general only when the discourses forming it are open to all those who may be affected by the issue under consideration (34–6, 81–2, 106–7).

Although Forst's conception of a right to justification is philosophically elaborated, he does not intend it as an abstract view from nowhere. Rather, he says that the right to justification is 'disclosed from a first-person perspective' (126). It is 'the unconditional claim of the other' (124). This right is based on an 'evaluative perception' of others: we recognize them as human beings and moral agents (96). As such, the right to justification is immanent in concrete contexts and actual practices. It is something we understand and perceive for ourselves, based on the attitudes we take towards others as human.

These insights about morality, intersubjectivity, discourse and justification have far-reaching political significance. The moral insights we derive from our experience of others imply particular forms of politics. Norms, laws and actions must be justifiable in a reciprocal and general sense. The duty to justify in turn requires political procedures and institutions that can facilitate justification. At the same time, it puts limits on the kinds of interests and perspectives that count in public discourse. The right to justification has broad implications for politics, then, from face-to-face discursive interactions in the political arena, to justice and toleration, to human rights and international politics.

Complexities of the normative world

Forst's view makes an elegant linguistic turn in politics. It starts from a particular notion of humanity, describes it as a characteristic of our experience of others, shows that this experience has a distinctively moral character, and finally, elucidates a duty of justification towards others on that basis. The view moves from basic ideas about human existence to a form of discursive proceduralism. Here Forst's view acquires its greatest normative weight as a critical theory of contemporary society. The duty of justification is not simply a moral prescription, but a way to evaluate actually existing systems of law and politics. It provides a basis for criticizing institutions and human relations in which justification is insincere, incomplete, impeded or non-existent.

I take this kind of argument very seriously. It describes a carefully specified mode of politics without making any pre-determinations about the issues that actual participants would discuss. Its conclusions are drawn from concrete forms of experience and public practices of reasoning, rather than moral absolutes or metaphysical notions of a person. Yet I wonder to what extent it depends upon assumptions about practice and culture that we may have a hard time redeeming. In particular, I wonder whether the theory can do justice to what Forst himself refers to as 'the complexity of the normative world' (111).

As I have accounted for it, Forst's view rests on particular assumptions about our cognition and recognition of others as human beings. It is based on a specific and morally charged conception of what it means to be human. This view gives humans a dignity by virtue of their humanity, and describes moral orientations we should take towards them in recognition of this humanity. In Forst's case, the moral and political results of the theory rest on our experience: they are 'disclosed from a first-person perspective'; they are impressed upon us by the recognition of human finitude and by our confrontation with 'the face of the other'. Here Forst evokes the spirit of Kant's investigation of the conditions of experience. Like Kant, he draws broader conclusions from the fact of our experiences. Kant details the preconditions necessary for us to have coherent experience as such. Forst, following a slightly different path, traces the consequences of experiencing others as humans and moral agents. Forst's view starts from a more particular point than does Kant's: not experience as such, but the experience of others as particular kinds of human beings. The view rests on an empirical claim about the way we actually experience others, rather than an analysis of the necessary presuppositions of experience in general. The normative force that we can draw from seeing others as humans depends on the *de facto* practice of those forms of cognition and recognition. We must actually experience others as humans to whom we owe reciprocal and general justification for the theory to have normative traction.

This kind of humanism is part of a distinguished intellectual tradition that reaches back at least to Suarez and Bellarmine in the sixteenth century and the English Levellers in the seventeenth. It has a long history of levelling hierarchies and providing the bases for egalitarianism and (quasi-)universal suffrage. Variants of this view are still highly favoured by philosophers and other thinkers today. Given Forst's emphasis on the actual experiences of people in general, however, we must ask how well this outlook characterizes the practices of contemporary societies. Do all – or at least a significant number – of our fellow citizens really recognize one another as human beings with moral standing in a way that implies a right to justification? Do all individuals, or all individuals in modernized, rationalized societies – or at least a significant number of them – share the kind of humanist outlook described here? Does this form of recognition actually characterize the norms and attitudes of the real people around us?

I believe that this conception of recognition is only partly on target. There are many different ways of recognizing others, and not all of them take the form Forst describes. Indeed, the social sciences provide persuasive evidence that our practices of recognition are much more varied. Those practices oscillate between broad-ish (sometimes close to universal) recognition of others as something like human, and differentiated forms focusing on distinctions in group difference.

At times, people recognize others as sharing certain common traits. If comprehensive and robust enough, this kind of recognition can be interpreted as an experience of basic human commonality. It is, however, a rather thin and abstract form of recognition. This experience is typical of contexts in which we know very little about the other person or her culture: in the cases of 'first contact' that we find described in early anthropology or science fiction, for instance, in which the language and culture of the others is so foreign that we are reduced to the most abstract commonalities in trying to understand them. It can also be characteristic of situations of duress: emergencies in which the blood and pain of another forcibly negates any more subtle, socially differentiated conclusions one might draw about them. Here the impulse to focus on differences is set aside in favour of a more general, less differentiated response.

More often, however, things run in the opposite direction. We see others in identitarian ways rather than egalitarian, universalist, humanist ones. These socially differentiated identities are generated through categories of social perception and classification. Pierre Bourdieu has catalogued these mechanisms in careful detail, showing how individuals are classed into groups by various markers of group identity. Subtle cues of speech, dress, taste and bodily posture are taken as signs of group belonging. They provide criteria for determining who functions as a 'natural' (i.e. thoroughly enculturated) member of a given group. The ubiquitous use of these criteria in turn forms a system of social distinction. There is nothing necessary about this logic of group formation, but it seems to be a durable pattern of human behaviour that has been observed in a wide variety of societies across several continents.[4]

The process of group distinction is largely unconscious and intuitive. We classify people without thinking about it, and attach various valuations, orientations, biases and stereotypes accordingly. We do this in many ways, but language is one important mechanism. Differences in the way people use language, their skill at using it and their fluency in the idioms of argumentation and speech are an important mechanism for determining a person's group identity.[5] Differences in accent, grammar, vocabulary, word choice, rhetorical ability, style and self-confidence within a given language constitute an important way to tell 'who a person really is'.[6] In this sense, language use operates in the same way as many other markers of distinction that we draw on constantly to assess and value other people.

It is important to realize that these habits of social differentiation are not simply perceptual or phenomenal. They are not simply a matter of recognition, but equally a matter of cognition. They are part of the sense, as Bourdieu characterizes it, in which 'ordinary experience of the social world is a cognition, . . . [and] primary cognition is misrecognition,

---

[4]   For example, concerning France, North Africa, Japan and East Germany, respectively: P. Bourdieu, *Distinction: A Social Critique of the Judgement of Taste*, trans. by R. Nice. Cambridge: MA, Harvard University Press, 1984; P. Bourdieu, *Outline of a Theory of Practice*. Cambridge: Cambridge University Press, 1977; P. Bourdieu, 'Social Space and Symbolic Space: Introduction to a Japanese Reading of Distinction', *Poetics Today* 12(4), (1991a), 627–38; P. Bourdieu, 'Distinction Revisited: Introduction to an East German Reading', *Poetics Today* 12(4), (1991b), 639–41.

[5]   P. Bourdieu, *Language and Symbolic Power*. Cambridge, MA: Harvard University Press, 1991c.

[6]   C. R. Hayward, 'Doxa and Deliberation', *Critical Review of International Social and Political Philosophy* 7(1), (2004), 1–24.

recognition of an order which is also established in the mind'.[7] Our practices of social differentiation are both cognitive and recognitive, then. We recognize others as different, and we understand the social world to be structured through such differences in a way that seems both natural and intuitive to us, because it is part of the very fabric of our experience of society.

The empirical realities of social differentiation seem to undermine the humanist orientation described by Forst. In his terms, our cognition of the shared humanity of others must live in tension with our cognition of them as different. Similarly, our recognition of others as moral agents competes with our recognition of them as falling into certain types based on (quasi-)intuitive categories of classification. In this case, universalism has no distinctive normative privilege over distinction. Rather, the principle we seem to endorse in our actions is one of polyvalence: universalism sometimes, distinction other times. At times we treat others as equals, like us, deserving of respect because of their similarity to us. At other times, however, we treat them as members of different and perhaps competing social groups, different from us, and valued (positively or negatively) for their embodied characteristics as members of those groups.

Consider, for example, the biblical story of the Good Samaritan. We are told that Samaritans and Jews were largely hostile to one another in this era. Each group recognized the other as different and disliked it. Against this background, the 'Good' Samaritan strikingly rejects such differentiating tendencies and recognizes the basic humanity of an injured Jewish traveller. This recognition causes him to care for the traveller, even at some expense to himself. Tensions between universalism and difference give this parable its heuristic force. The parable is able to valorize the Good Samaritan's behaviour precisely because we see it as such an atypical response. His recognition of a more-universal humanity stands as a reproach to our own differentiating tendencies to see others as alien, of less value and not worthy of our aid.

[7]   Bourdieu, *Distinction*, p. 172.

This example, one among a great many, shows that we do not simply recognize others as universally human, nor do we recognize them as thoroughly different. Rather, there are many different ways to recognize others, and within that, there are many different ways to recognize them 'as human'. As a result, principles like reciprocity and generality sometimes characterize our practices and sometimes do not. This examination tells us that we cannot derive any determinate conclusions about the moral status of others from practices of recognition as such. Those practices are polyvalent and often contradict one another. By extension, it is not clear that others have a right to justification based on our recognition of them. The multiplicity of practices through which we assign value to others throw this conclusion into doubt.

The ruling ideas of the ruling class

Now that we have examined some of the complexities of the normative world, it is important to clarify that I am not referring to what is often called 'the fact of pluralism'. That expression refers more narrowly to discussions about whether 'the right' can accommodate different conceptions of 'the good' (cf. 101–2). Here I am identifying something much less connected with abstractions of moral theory and much more connected to the complex texture of our practices themselves: the fact that we recognize others in a great variety of ways; that we combine practices that have distinctively moral or ethical content with those that have an altogether different character; that our practices are so complex that it is difficult to say how one can gain normative leverage on them.

Unfortunately, failing this normative challenge may cause us to remain blind to some of the power and class dynamics that can occur within democratic politics. In particular, it is important to be aware of the implicit class character that ideas of discourse and justification can have. The primary constituency of such views is the class-fraction that Pierre Bourdieu refers to as high in cultural capital and occupying professions that emphasize words and speech.[8] That is to say, it is the domain of knowledge experts: writers, consultants, politicians and, of course, academics. The members of these professions specialize in the self-confident articulation of opinions through language, complex, persuasive forms of discourse, thematization of problems, criticism of opposing positions, taking of stances, peer review of written results, building a career based on the uptake received by one's opinions, controversy as a source of interest, intellectual life as a privileged mode of practice. Giving reasons is one of their primary aptitudes and most sharply honed skills. Correspondingly, the public use of reasons is most closely associated with the shared orientations and habits of these knowledge experts.

We must acknowledge, then, that the value intellectuals place on discourse is to some extent subcultural and group specific. Giving reasons seems natural to this group because of the deep centrality of language to its own practices. It is not surprising that such people would see others as deserving of justification. Nor is it surprising that they would see practices of justification and public reasoning as an essential aspect of being human. The naturalness of these ideals is very much an aspect of their group identity, one not necessarily shared by other groups. In fact, some groups specialize in skills that have very little to do with the public use of reasons. For them the public use of reasons is a much less intuitive practice, and perhaps worse, one at which they perceive themselves as less competent.[9] From this perspective, justification is not a basic human right, but a mode of practice that is the expert domain of others. It does not recognize one's basic humanity, but implicitly universalizes a vision of humanity whose signature characteristics are most comfortably practiced by the members of elite groups.

This line of criticism suggests that a conception of recognition based on humanist criteria, implying moral obligations to justification, may

---

[8] P. Bourdieu, *Homo Academicus*. Stanford: Stanford University Press, 1988; Bourdieu, *Distinction*, ch. 1, esp. tables 2 and 3.

[9] Bourdieu, *Distinction*, ch. 8.

not be as universally practiced or as naturally human as the members of that group suppose. The subject-position of intellectuals as a group, with our specific identities, orientations and taken-for-granted knowledges and practices, may lead us to suppose that certain things about ourselves are also true of people as a whole. And this mistaken assumption may lead us falsely to universalize those skills and activities.[10] This would be a kind of social myopia, taking all of society in one's own image. It would be a product of what Bourdieu calls the 'unconscious universalization of the particular case'.[11] And this universalization has an implicit class character. As Marx and Engels noted, each dominant class tends to 'represent its interest as the common interest of all the members of society, that is, expressed in ideal form: it has to give its ideas the form of universality, and present them as the only rational, universally valid ones'.[12] In this manner, we academics might see reason-giving as a fundamental aspect of being human, when it is actually a group-specific behaviour that defines the borders and criteria of entry to certain privileged groups.

If we fail to see the group-specific character of this set of linguistic practices, we risk misrecognizing the exclusions and biases they covertly bring along with them. At core, these are problems of class position and power, and the joint effects of the two when they coincide. They raise the prospect of a cultural imperialism *within* developed societies: not the imposition of Western ideals on the rest of the world, but the imposition of the ideals of the thinking and talking classes on the rest of society. Here seemingly open and fair conceptions of political practice can have a dark side as well. Rather than bracketing or challenging power relations, such theories risk reproducing them.[13]

[10] K. Olson, 'Legitimate Speech and Hegemonic Idiom: The Limits of Deliberative Democracy in the Diversity of its Voices', *Political Studies* 59(3), (2011), 527–46.

[11] P. Bourdieu, *Practical Reason: On the Theory of Action*. Oxford: Polity, 1998, p. 136; P. Bourdieu, *Pascalian Meditations*. Stanford: Stanford University Press, 2000, p. 65.

[12] K. Marx and F. Engels, *The German Ideology*. New York: International Publishers, 1970, pp. 65–6.

[13] K. Topper, 'Not So Trifling Nuances: Pierre Bourdieu, Symbolic Violence, and the Perversions of Democracy', *Constellations* 8(1), (2001), 30–56; K. Topper, 'Arendt and Bourdieu between Word and Deed', *Political Theory* 39(2011), 358–61; Hayward, 'Doxa and Deliberation'.

They universalize as 'human' activities those that are practiced at differential levels of expertise throughout the population and are differentially valued by members of different groups. Thus well-intentioned ideas such as recognizing the humanity of others through the public use of language can rationalize a political system that privileges some while framing others as less competent. Rather than recognizing the universal humanity of others, such a conception might establish a seemingly neutral domain of politics that is differentiated along pre-existing lines of group privilege.[14] Wittingly or not, such a political theory could become another case in which 'the ruling ideas are nothing more than the ideal expression of the dominant material relationships; the dominant material relationships grasped as ideas'.[15] That is to say, it could become a mechanism for reproducing relations of class and power, rather than challenging them.

Critique, idealization, practice

One might call the line of criticism I have been outlining a 'critique of socially differentiated epistemology' or a 'critique of socially differentiated practice'. It ultimately raises two questions. First, it forces us to ask how we can justify political theories based on a linguistic turn – like a right to justification – without appealing to universalist notions of humanity. Second, it poses the problem of how we can combine those theories with a critical understanding of power, class and social differentiation. In sum, we must determine under what circumstances language can serve as a medium for justifying norms and actions, and under what circumstances it is co-opted by pre-existing relations of class and power.

These questions have a special urgency for neo-Kantians. Their approach has great normative power, but often has difficulty bridging the

---

[14] I have developed this line of thought more fully in Olson, 'Legitimate Speech and Hegemonic Idiom'.

[15] Marx and Engels, *The German Ideology*, p. 64.

gap between theoretical idealizations and actual people and practices. One's response to these challenges depends on how exactly one wants to tap Kantian insights. Rainer Forst draws on many varieties of neo-Kantian political thought in rich and subtle ways. Overall, though, I take his view to fall closer to the constructivist side of contemporary neo-Kantianism than the reconstructivist side. The difference is something like this: A constructivist theory builds an idealized model of political or moral practice, then brings it into reflective equilibrium with current cultural norms. The model has internal consistency because of the care with which it is constructed, then it tries to acquire binding force by being adapted to actual contexts. A reconstructive view, in contrast, is interpretative from the start, working within actual practices to discern their implicit norms and presuppositions. It must interpretatively characterize people's practices in a rich enough way to show those people the implicit, hidden logic of their own action. This logic typically takes the form of unrecognized presuppositions that provide the interpreter with leverage to criticize the practices in question.

Each paradigm has advantages and disadvantages. Constructive views develop a strong idealized consistency from the start, but then must bridge the gap to the messy world. They are more theoretically pure, but correspondingly more distant from the normative complexities of real life. Reconstructive views acquire a strong normativity from their starting point within the lived world, but then have corresponding difficulties developing critical distance and philosophical consistency from that basis.

Forst advertises his view as a constructivist one, and I think he does fall closest to that side of contemporary neo-Kantianism. For instance, he characterizes his insights about the reciprocal and general character of norms as 'a practical, not metaphysical constructivism', emphasizing that 'for us' there is no other path to moral norms than this kind of practical constructivist insight (83–4). He unequivocally rejects metaphysical notions of moral personhood, putting in their place a non-metaphysical though still idealized view of a moral human being. When the idealized humans in question are thought in relation to one another, we arrive at the idea of an idealized moral community. It would be a community of people who recognize one another as moral persons and feel a responsibility to justify actions and norms to one another as a result. The idea of a right to justification, then, is implied by the postulated features of this construct, particularly its conception of moral personhood.

This argumentative strategy has the hallmark advantages of a constructivist theory. It draws clear lines from moral personhood to rights to justification, framing a robust notion of discursive politics on that basis. The concerns I have outlined do not challenge the internal consistency of that vision so much as its relation to our actual practices of recognizing and thinking about one another. They are concerns, in other words, about a gap between the theory's idealized claims and their basis in lived experience. To fully elaborate the potential of this vision, we would need to think carefully about bringing its idealized claims together with lived experience to ensure that the theory retains its critical force.

My own suggestion would be to embrace a more thoroughly reconstructive approach. This would require us to interpret and reconstruct practices that people actually engage in, as opposed to practices they ideally would or hypothetically should engage in. By reconstructing the ways that people actually recognize one another, we may be able to identify practices that would serve as a basis for reciprocal, general commitments towards one another. In this revised view, it is possible that reason-giving would not emerge as a privileged mode of human action. Justification may not be something we owe to one another *as humans*. Indeed, there may be no 'humanity as such' in such an account. It may wind up relying on multiple modes of politics to avoid the potential problems that could be associated with a view based solely on a linguistic turn. However, such a strategy would come closer to fulfilling the desiderata I laid out above. It would stay closer to actual social and political contexts, giving it stronger critical purchase against problems of class and power. It would also make possible a more differentiated view of subtle group differences in knowledge and practice.

Conclusion

The problems I have outlined are troubling ones. They threaten what has seemed for a long time like a robust source of normativity for political theory. The linguistic turn promised that political theorists could get out of the business of substantive critique and focus on procedure. We would tame language as a neutralized medium of communication, allowing normative content to rise out of the fissures of daily life and harden into already-binding, already-contextualized norms and obligations.

Whatever variety of the linguistic turn one subscribes to, that strategy is now thrown into doubt. Before such a project can succeed, we must find critical strategies that take the social differentiation of discursive practices into account. What I have called a 'critique of socially differentiated epistemology' must be a necessary component of such an understanding. It requires us to take account of the social and political complexities of language, particularly their tendency to reproduce class and power relations. Such a theory must conduct a finely textured critique of the faultlines of real life, even if they complicate philosophical conclusions or render theorists unable to make normative pronouncements on their own. Answering these questions will help us to make a linguistic turn that can comment incisively on the actual politics of our time, without becoming entangled in the very issues it aims to criticize.

5

The Practice of Equality

Anthony Simon Laden
*Professor of Philosophy, University of Illinois
at Chicago, USA*

Rainer Forst presents his approach to justice as a kind of dialectic advance on earlier Kantian and Hegelian conceptions. But as we all know, dialectical advances always prepare the way for their own overcoming. This chapter unpacks some of the potential latent in Forst's work for a further dialectical advance in our thinking about justice and invites him (and others) to embrace it. But it makes this invitation somewhat hesitantly, keeping in mind Ralph Ellison's warning about dialecticians in the 'Prologue' to *Invisible Man:* 'Beware of those who speak of the *spiral* of history; they are preparing a boomerang. Keep a steel helmet ready.'[1]

In the introduction to *The Right to Justification*, Forst situates his own work on justice alongside those who, like Iris Marion Young, picture justice as a matter of relationships rather than distribution.[2] Because advocates of relational approaches to justice have been primarily focused on contrasting their work with those within a distributivist paradigm, they have been less attentive to a division within the relational approach itself. In particular, the focus on relationships as the subject matter of justice can be understood impersonally or intersubjectively. One of the most exciting features about Forst's work on the right to justification is that it provides the materials to make this distinction plain. By speaking of justice in terms of justification, he offers a handy way of thinking

---

[1]   R. Ellison, *Invisible Man*. New York: Vintage, 1995 (orig. pub. 1947), p. 6.
[2]   R. Forst, *The Right to Justification*, trans. by J. Flynn. New York: Columbia University Press, 2012. Young's initial criticism can be found in I. M. Young, *Justice and the Politics of Difference*. Princeton: Princeton University Press, 1990.

of justice as an activity rather than a state of affairs, something we do rather than something to bring about. He thus opens the door for the fully practical conception of justice that this chapter explores. I situate such an approach, point to some of its features and implications, and then consider why, despite its many attractions, Forst might be hesitant to accept my invitation.

Two pictures of justice[3]

Both distributive and relational pictures of justice conceive of injustice in terms a form of arbitrariness. They disagree, however, about the domains in which arbitrariness is a threat to justice. The distributive picture takes justice to require the non-arbitrary distribution of goods, so that each subject of justice has what is rightly hers. So understood, the distributive picture of justice is consistent with any number of theories of justice, depending on how we specify the set of relevant goods to be distributed, the criteria for determining rightful versus arbitrary claims, and the proper recipients of the goods, as well as what, if any, concerns of justice extend beyond questions of distribution. As this list of issues suggests, the distributivist picture of justice has been the dominant picture in recent political philosophy, shared by so-called luck egalitarians, many people who take themselves to be working downstream of John Rawls and those working out a capability approach to justice.[4] In contrast, what I call the 'relational picture of justice' conceives of injustice in terms of arbitrary rule, of relations of domination and subordination.[5] On this picture, as Forst puts it, 'the

---

[3] I take the title from Forst's lead essay for this volume.

[4] Luck egalitarians include Richard Arneson, Brian Barry, Jeremy Waldron, Ronald Dworkin and G. A. Cohen. Those advocating a capabilities approach include Amartya Sen and Martha Nussbaum. Forst discusses some of the shortcomings with these views in *The Right to Justification,* chs 8 and 11 as well as in the lead essay of this volume.

[5] Prominent advocates of the relational approach to justice among contemporary political philosophers include Catherine MacKinnon, Iris Marion Young, James Tully and Elizabeth Anderson, as well as Forst. On some readings, Jürgen Habermas, Axel Honneth and John Rawls are also relational justice theorists, though Rawls is most often placed in the distributivist camp (though not by Anderson, Forst or myself).

first question of justice is the question of power,[6] and so the primary questions a theory of justice concerns itself with is not directly who gets how much, but who decides and how?

Forst follows other advocates of relational justice in motivating his relational picture via a criticism of the distributivist picture, thereby developing that picture around a set of contrasts.[7] Let me note three of them. First, the distributivist approach makes the subjects of justice basically passive recipients rather than active agents. It pictures the just distribution of goods as what John Rawls calls a matter of 'allocative justice': handing out a fixed quantity of goods to a fixed set of recipients, with no attention paid to the role of the recipients in the production of the goods to be distributed.[8] Distributive justice, so conceived, is not a matter of regulating cooperative schemes, but of handing out products. In contrast, a relational approach to justice treats the subjects of justice as active agents, who stand in various relations to one another, whether as participants in a cooperative scheme, fellow co-authors of democratic law, or enmeshed in social structures of domination and subordination.

Second, justice as conceived by the distributivist picture has no tight connection to democracy. That is, unless we add political participation or certain political rights to the list of goods to be distributed, and specify that the proper distribution of these goods is universal and equal, democracy is not conceptually necessary for distributive justice. If we could figure out the right formula for a just distribution and the

---

6   Forst, *The Right to Justification*, p. 195.
7   See, for instance, the lead essay in this volume, as well as C. MacKinnon, 'Difference and Dominance: On Sex Discrimination', in ibid., *Feminism Unmodified*. Cambridge, MA: Harvard University Press, 1987, pp. 32–44. Young, *Justice and the Politics of Difference*; I. M. Young, 'Structural Injustice and the Politics of Difference', in A. S. Laden and D. Owen (eds), *Multiculturalism and Political Theory*. Cambridge: Cambridge University Press, 2007, pp. 60–88; R. Forst, 'First things First: Redistribution, Recognition and Justification', *European Journal of Political Philosophy* 6(2007b), 291–304; and E. Anderson, 'What's the Point of Equality?', *Ethics* 109(1999): 287–337.
8   J. Rawls, *A Theory of Justice*, rev. edn. Cambridge, MA: Harvard University Press, 1999a, pp. 76–7. This is admittedly an overly crude characterization. Theorists working within this picture will often attend to questions of production and political voice by classifying these as further goods to be distributed: the good of meaningful work or leisure, the good of political influence or the powers and prerogatives of various offices.

appropriate social levers to pull to bring it about, then we could achieve justice by leaving that distribution in the hands of a machine or a dictator. And even if we add equal rights to political participation to the list of goods to be properly distributed, we end up with a conception of democracy as primarily a voting scheme, rather than a more full-blown form of collective self-government. In contrast, the relational approach to justice draws a strong connection between justice and democracy. If injustice is primarily a matter of some arbitrarily ruling over others, then it looks like full justice requires that people share collectively in governing their society, so that no individual or group rules over any others.

Third, in order to make something into a proper object of justice within the distributivist picture, it must be conceived of as a distributable good. So if political power or a set of rights or social positions are to be treated as objects of distributive justice, we must imagine them as goods, so that we can talk about bundles of rights, equal access to or voice in political decisions, or the various ingredients necessary to shape a good life. What gets lost in such descriptions is the value that comes from, as Rawls puts the point, being able 'to face one another openly', of standing in reciprocal, recognitive and respectful relations to one another.[9]

We can sum up these contrasts by saying that whereas the distributivist picture of justice treats justice as a matter of relative or absolute standing, the relational picture treats justice in terms of the relationships we stand in to others. Note that treating justice as a matter of standing rather than relationships does not preclude analysing some among the goods that are to be distributed as positional goods, goods whose value is dependent on who else has them and how much they have. The difference, then, is not whether or not you pay attention to relationships, but what kind of relationships you pay attention to. The distributive picture attends to relationships like 'having more than' or 'being further up the queue than'. In contrast, the relational approach

---

[9] J. Rawls, 'Justice as Fairness', in *Collected Papers*. Cambridge, MA: Harvard University Press, 1999b, pp. 47–72 at p. 59.

focuses on relationships like 'being a friend to' or 'being under the dominion of.'[10]

The debate between these two pictures of justice is by no means over and done with, and there is a fairly important question as to how or whether these two pictures can be fruitfully combined. But as it is not here that I wish to enter the discussion, I take it as given that there are sufficiently good reasons to abandon a distributive picture for a relational one.

Two pictures of justification

In an effort to show why both pictures are pictures of *justice*, Forst claims that each involves overcoming a form of arbitrariness: the arbitrary distribution of goods versus arbitrary rule. In so framing the matter, he occludes the fact that 'arbitrary' is not a univocal concept, and that how one understands arbitrariness colours one's picture of justice. It is not that Forst is insensitive to the need to analyse the idea of arbitrariness. In fact, much of what I want to highlight in Forst's work involves his particular analysis of what arbitrariness involves. But he is not as clear or explicit as he might be that he is taking a particular view of arbitrariness, one that is not merely a result of adopting a relational picture of justice. To bring out the possibilities within the relational picture we can contrast two senses of arbitrariness. Being arbitrary involves being without reason, without justification. So the two senses of arbitrariness turn on a distinction between two pictures of justification.

Consider a teacher who justifies a course of study to her students by explaining that this is what the state mandates or what she, qua expert, has decided is the best way to learn. She justifies her action by grounding it in a system of thought, rules, or authority that she takes to hold, regardless of whether the person to whom she is justifying her actions also accepts these premises. I am going to call this kind of justification 'impersonal' to

---

[10] On the importance of recognizing that some goods are positional, even within a distributivist picture, see H. Brighouse and A. Swift, 'Equality, Priority, and Positional Goods', *Ethics* 116(2006), 471–97.

have a name for it, but I'm also going to ask you not to read too much into the name. The key for me is that this sort of justification involves securing a kind of warrant from the universe or the existing social structure that what one is doing is rational. A picture of justification as impersonal can be appropriately humble and fallibilist, and so can leave room for criticism of a particular line of justification. It need not (and rarely does) define justification as what those in power say. Nevertheless, one important feature of impersonal justification is that it does not make the validity of justification in any way dependent on uptake from the one to whom the justification is offered. So, our teacher may have misunderstood the statutes or be relying on outdated and disproven pedagogical theories, and if so, her justification of her decision will fail even if no one recognizes this fact. But barring these kinds of mistakes, she can, secure in her justification, fail to take seriously her students' criticisms of her decisions without rendering those decisions arbitrary. In such a case, she is likely to point out that their failure to follow her directives is a sign of their immaturity, and the strength of their resistance an indication of their lack of self-control and full rationality. If her justification is valid, then their failure to accept it is a sign of their failings, not her injustice.

But there is another way we might understand justification: as essentially intersubjective. Intersubjective justification is justification *to* those ruled, rather than in virtue of its grounding in some theoretical apparatus that others may not accept or understand. It is this conception of justification that Forst adopts. It is one that John Rawls also clearly articulates: 'justification is argument addressed to those who disagree with us, or to ourselves when we are of two minds. It seeks to convince others, or ourselves, of the reasonableness of the principles upon which our claims and judgments are founded'.[11] Justification of this sort aims at uptake from the one to whom it is offered, and modulo several qualifications that we can ignore for the moment, only succeeds when it is accepted as adequate.[12] It is this dependence on acceptance that makes

---

[11] Rawls, *A Theory of Justice*, p. 508.
[12] Attentive readers will note a slippage in modality here, from what is acceptable to what is accepted. I will come back to this below.

justification a practice of equality and reciprocity as well as a means of overcoming arbitrariness. To treat you as an equal, one whose words and concerns matter as much as my own, I must be able and willing to justify what I do to you in this second sense. If, relying on an impersonal picture of justification, I try to dismiss your rejection as a sign of your irrationality, as the teacher above does, then I fail at this intersubjective activity of justification. That doesn't mean that my justification can't advert to inequalities in knowledge or expertise or the need for some to make decisions for others. But it does mean that these considerations have to be ones that those to whom I offer my justifications accept as grounds for allotting decision-making power unequally. Put another way, a necessary feature of engaging in this practice of intersubjective justification is being responsive to those to whom you are offering justification.

Our teacher might shift to this second kind of justification by elaborating her original justifications: by explaining why her greater knowledge of the subject allows her to see why this approach will make it easier to learn, although her students' lack of knowledge at the moment makes it impossible for her to explain what she knows to them. Note that in offering a justification of this sort, the teacher is asking her students to trust her and perhaps reminding them of why she is trustworthy rather than baldly asserting her authority to make these decisions without challenge. Her justification will thus succeed only to the extent that her students find her trustworthy. Whether they find her trustworthy may depend on their previous interactions with her, and her responsiveness to them, considering the fact that they are particular individuals and not merely abstract placeholders or possible test scores or disciplinary problems to be managed.[13] Note also that in this kind of example, it is really the intersubjective activity of justification and not the prior fact that the reasons the teacher adverts to are good ones, or that the students see them, on their own, as good.

---

[13] The generation of trust in hierarchical authority relationships deserves at least a whole other paper. Although I think engaging in the practices of justification that the paper discusses is one way to generate trust, I am not claiming it is the only or even the most important way to do so.

Philosophers have not always fully appreciated the importance of the difference between impersonal and intersubjective pictures of justification for thinking about justice. One reason for this is that to see clearly the deep differences between them requires situating intersubjective justification within a picture of the very activity of reasoning that is different from the one we are used to working with. If, as we are used to, we think of reasoning as an end-driven activity of basically problem-solving, then it will be tempting to think that what ultimately makes even intersubjective justification successful is that it adverts to a set of reasons that are, independently, there, and not dependent on the response of those to whom the justification is offered. In order, then, to picture intersubjective justification as truly intersubjective, we need to situate the practice of offering justifications that are answerable to others within a larger practice of offering and evaluating and responding to reasons, of reasoning, seen not as an activity of problem-solving, but as an activity of interacting with and being responsive to, others. On such a social picture of reasoning, what is essential to an activity being reasoning is not that it follows rules of calculation or the manipulation of formal rules and symbols, but that it is a form of interaction with others that is reciprocal and respectful. In other words, we have to think about the activity of reasoning as a way of neither commanding nor blindly deferring to others, but of treating them as equals, as people whose words and ideas and points of view matter and to which our own actions are answerable. Although there is much to be said about how to understand reasoning on this picture, for our purposes it is enough to note that excellence at reasoning in this sense

---

[14] For a much fuller discussion of this picture of reasoning, see A. S. Laden, *Reasoning: A Social Picture*. Oxford: Oxford University Press, 2012. The picture of reasoning developed there makes reasoning a much more capacious category than standard pictures do. In particular, it does not exclude certain forms of interaction that depend on affect or emotion, and so by focusing on the place of reasoning in being and becoming equal I do not mean to exclude such activities. That said, however, I also don't mean to say that the only form of interaction that makes us equal is reasoning, even broadly construed, nor to deny that the capacity to reason in my sense may require other forms of capacity that are best not thought of in terms of reasoning, such as an ability to be emotionally open, and not gripped by various fears. I am grateful to Maggie Schein for discussion on this point.

is manifested in someone being reasonable.[14] That is to say that a skilled reasoner on this alternative picture of reasoning is someone who is fully responsive to the people with whom she talks and relates, rather than someone who is particularly skilled at maneuvering within formal and symbolic systems. This kind of reasoning requires a set of skills that are not always associated with reasoning. The skills include listening to and understanding others, allowing their words to matter, as well as, when appropriate, being able to trust others, which may require being open to being vulnerable to them.[15] They also include being trustworthy and manifesting that trust-worthiness, which may include being open about our own limitations and partialities and forms of blindness.[16] Reasoning with others is thus a way of showing them respect, of recognizing them, and thus taking seriously their differences from us in a positive way and not as grounds for their exclusion or dismissal. In other words, reasoning with people in the sense gestured above is one, perhaps the central, practice of the kind of justice that Forst's work pictures.

Justice as a practice of equality

This distinction between pictures of justification provides a different way to distinguish pictures of justice. If justice requires that our relationships to one another include a right to justification, then our picture of justice will depend on whether we have impersonal or intersubjective justification in mind. And what I now want to ask is: What does an account of justice that is both relational and intersubjective look like? How does it differ from a conception that rests on relations that are impersonally justifiable? One set of answers to that question is to be found in the essays of *The Right to Justification*, but I want to bring out some further implications of this view that Forst does not, although I believe he would be willing to accept at

---

[15] For further discussion of the place of trust and vulnerability in reasoning with others, see A. S. Laden, 'Negotiation, Deliberation and the Claims of Politics', in Laden and Owen (eds), *Multiculturalism and Political Theory*, pp. 198–217.

[16] J. Tully, 'Diversity's Gambit Declined', in C. Cook (ed.), *Constitutional Predicament*. Montréal: McGill-Queen's University Press, 1994.

least those worked out in this section. In particular, I want to make clear how, on a picture like Forst's, justice itself becomes a practice, something we do rather than something we aim for or try to bring about.[17] And I want to say a bit about what that practice might look like.

First, notice how an intersubjective relational picture of justice shifts our view of equality. Although each picture of justice we've been discussing is championed in the name of egalitarianism, each conceives of equality differently. The debates I have in mind here are not about equality of what, but over the more fundamental question that Catherine MacKinnon asks: 'What is an equality question a question of?'[18] And once again, the debates on this point between the distributivist and relational pictures of justice are somewhat familiar, but occlude a third possibility. We can see the salient differences by thinking about how each yields different lessons about what we need to teach and learn in order to realize a more equal society. On the distributional picture of justice, equality is a matter of mirroring. That is, one of the criteria for a distribution being non-arbitrary is that it mirrors some more or less natural feature of the population among whom it is distributed. Most often, this mirroring move involves citing something that all targets of distributions have in common (we are all human) or disputing that some difference (race, gender, class, etc.) is morally relevant, by showing that it is, in Rawls's words, 'arbitrary from a moral point of view'.

What is significant in this approach to equality is that it starts from a premise about the world or about people that is taken as a given.[19] The kind of underlying equality that the distributive picture of justice begins

---

[17] In this, it returns in a sense to Rawls. See C. Korsgaard, 'The Reasons We Can Share', in ibid., *Constructing the Kingdom of Ends*. Cambridge: Cambridge University Press, 1996, pp. 275–310; T. M. Scanlon, 'Contractualism and Utilitarianism', in B. Williams and A. Sen (eds), *Utlitarianism and beyond*. Cambridge: Cambridge University Press, 1982.

[18] Most recently in, C. MacKinnon, 'Making Sex Equality Real', in ibid., *Are Women Human?*. Cambridge, MA: Harvard University Press, 2006, pp. 71–6 at p. 74; but see also C. MacKinnon, 'Difference and Dominance: On Sex Discrimination', in ibid., *Feminism Unmodified*. Cambridge, MA: Harvard University Press, 1987, pp. 32–44.

[19] At least, in the short term. We can accept that some or all of these factors are affected or even constructed by social institutions and practices in the long run and yet still adopt this mirroring conception, as long as we don't conceive of being equal as itself a way of acting with others, and thus something constituted by what we do here and now.

with is a prior fact, not one that comes about as a direct result of the social processes in question. The question that remains for policy and the design of social institutions is whether or not our society adequately responds to this pre-social fact. On such a view, we may need to learn and to teach others that and how we are already equal, and how that fact is or is not properly treated by our social institutions, but there is nothing for us to do that might be described as making each other equal.

On relational pictures of justice, equality is understood as a result of standing in certain kinds of relationships (reciprocal, non-dominated). Whether we stand in one kind of relationship or another is not a natural or pre-social fact about us, but is a result of how our society is organized and how we act within that organization. While a large part of what determines our possibilities in the short run is a result of social factors that may well be beyond our individual control, there are also plenty of ways that we shape our relationships through how we and others act within them. So, what we need to learn on this picture is that we should be equals and what sorts of changes in our society might bring that equality about. In other words, the pursuit of justice on this second picture involves, in the words of the Canadian Constitutional Court approvingly cited by MacKinnon, 'promoting equality'.[20]

If we shift all the way to a relational picture of justice with an intersubjective picture of justification at its core, our conception of equality shifts again. Although we still think of equality in terms of relationships not marked by arbitrary rule, our attention is brought to how those involved in these relationships act towards one another: Are they prepared to offer justifications to one another and do they take themselves to be bound by the uptake or rejection that their justifications meet? Our focus here is not so much on which kinds of

---

[20] For further discussions of the importance and robustness of this form of relational equality, also called democratic equality, see Anderson, 'What is the point of equality?' and J. Cohen, 'Democratic Equality', *Ethics* 99(4), (1989), 727–51. Both argue that a focus on democratic equality has robust implications for distributional schemes in part because of the expressive value of those schemes, and thus what justifying them to our fellow citizens might entail. In so doing, they also rely on an intersubjective picture of relational justice.

relationships to bring about, but how we relate to one another within those relationships. How we relate to one another will, of course, be conditioned and shaped by the institutional structures within which we live. No amount of good will and equal regard will make it possible for the slaveowner to treat his slave as an equal. But equality is not here exhausted by our place within various social structures. Part of what determines whether I am equal to others is my interactions with them. I can act in ways that are servile towards or contemptuous of some or all of my peers, students and fellow citizens, or I can learn to treat them with respect as equals. Which of these I do shapes to what extent a basic right of intersubjective justification is realized in our society? And so these facts, just as much as my social position, will constitute or undermine our equality. Since equality here is something we actively do, it is something that we can and must learn.[21] In other words, equality is neither a natural fact nor a social goal but a kind of practice. Learning the practices of equality involves not only developing the ability to offer and demand justifications, but also to do so in a way that is accountable to others.[22] And that may very well require learning to recognize others as appropriate subjects of our love or respect or moral regard.[23] Justification meets recognition.

Before moving forward, it helps to sum up these differences: On a distributivist picture the equality that justice requires involves everyone

[21] It should not be surprising, then, that one of the earliest political philosophers to develop this picture of justice, Jean-Jacques Rousseau, was also so concerned not only with education in general but also with the particular problem of how to educate people into being and acting as equals. For a somewhat different path to a similar set of conclusions about equality being a matter of our civic practices and habits, see D. S. Allen, *Talking to Strangers*. Chicago: University of Chicago Press, 2004. I discuss the implications of this view of equality for education in A. S. Laden, 'Learning to be Equal: Just Schools and Schools of Justice', in D. S. Allen and R. Reich (eds), *Education, Justice and Democracy*. Chicago: University of Chicago Press, 2013, pp. 62–79, from which much of the foregoing analysis is taken.

[22] Accountability is one of the requirements of valid justifications on Forst's view. See Forst, *The Right to Justification*, p. 129. For further elaboration of accountability as a requirement in order for deliberation to be reasonable, see my 'Outline of a Theory of Reasonable Deliberation', *Canadian Journal of Philosophy* 30(2000), 551–80; and more generally, A. S. Laden, *Reasoning: A Social Picture*.

[23] On the importance of this initial capacity for seeing others as objects of our moral regard, see R. Gaita, *A Common Humanity*. New York: Routledge, 2000.

having the same slice of the pie because of some inherent feature that gives them an equal claim. On the impersonal relational picture, justice requires the kind of equality that is achieved when no one is standing on another's neck. Finally, on the intersubjective relational view, justice requires the kind of equality that is achieved when no one sees another as beneath her notice or concern, as invisible or undeserving of reciprocal justification.

At this point, partisans of the impersonal relational approach will worry that I have turned justice into an activity that takes place in everyday and face-to-face personal encounters. The problem is that a theory of justice that keeps its gaze firmly focused on such encounters appears to lose sight of the importance of *social* justice, returning in some sense to an ancient conception of justice as a personal virtue. Although this *is* a danger in thinking of justice as a practice, it is one that we can easily avoid. We need only note that institutions play a mediating role, shaping what we can say to one another by way of justification in at least two ways. First, among the things for which we can demand justifications are the particular shape that certain institutions take in our society. Second, we advert to certain institutional structures in the course of justifying our relative positions to others. Part of the justification you might offer me for your greater wealth is that you are entitled to it as a result of the basic structure of economic and social institutions we live under, one that I also consider fair. And, one way your justification can fail to satisfy my demand is if it relies on the functioning of institutions that are not fair or have been imposed on me. Since how we relate to one another is a function of what we can say to one another, the institutions that mediate our relationships continue to play an important role in our conversations about justice.

Consider now, a second feature of an intersubjective conception of justice. As my remarks about learning the practices of equality above suggest, this approach to justice brings squarely into view both the general educative role of institutions and the important institutional role of education in realizing justice. In establishing particular rules and forums for demanding and offering justifications, institutions serve to teach those interacting with them and with others through them a set of techniques of reasoning and justification. Furthermore, an institution that establishes practices of accountability and justification within its structures teaches lessons about who is worthy of and owed such justifications. They thus initiate us into the practices of justification that serve to realize justice in our world. Institutions can be schools of democracy and justice or schools of despotism, and these features as well as their efficiency and productivity and contribution to fair schemes of distribution are ones we need to take heed of as we evaluate them in terms of justice. Think, for instance, about the institutions of the modern welfare state, which may more justly distribute income and relieve certain dependency relations, but which nevertheless too often treat their clients with a kind of arrogance and officiousness that violates the practices of equality I have been describing. In the process, they teach us unjust lessons about the kind of regard we owe one another.

Of course, there is one set of institutions in any society whose primary function is educative: schools and universities. And so if we begin to think of justice as a practice we can and should learn, then we need to think more carefully than many political philosophers have about whether and how schools serve these functions. Schools, rather than financial institutions or taxation schemes, may be, to use a phrase of G. A. Cohen's, 'where the action is'.[24]

Finally, notice that by picturing equality in terms of the practices that constitute our relationships to one another as reciprocally accountable, we make room for certain forms of hierarchy within a just society. Since one of the insights that supports the move from the distributivist to the relational picture of justice is that hierarchies are precisely the form of inequality our theories of justice should address, this looks, at first sight, like a step backwards. Nevertheless, it is also

---

[24] G. A. Cohen, 'Where the Action Is: On the Site of Distributive Justice', *Philosophy and Public Affairs* 26(1), (1997), 3–30.

the case that no modern society can exist without some forms of hierarchical authority relationships. Even the staunchest advocate of radical democracy accepts that teachers should have some sort of non-reciprocal authority over their students, that managers should have the authority to manage workers, judges to pass down rulings, and so forth. If all forms of such social organization are forms of injustice, then complete justice is not only far-off but also not to be desired. So what we need is a way to distinguish between legitimate and illegitimate hierarchies, and picturing justice as a practice of equality provides one.

Here, it helps to distinguish hierarchy from arbitrariness of rule. Hierarchy involves some having authority over others, and thus having the status to make decisions or take actions that others do not. Teachers who determine lesson plans and assessment mechanisms and assign grades and enforce classroom rules without consulting with or receiving the approval of their students stand above them in a hierarchy. But an institution can have within it, hierarchical relations of this sort without granting those in higher positions the further privilege of non-accountability, of arbitrary rule. A teacher has this further privilege when demands that he justify his decisions can be peremptorily refused on the ground of his position in the hierarchy, with a 'because I know better' or 'because I am the teacher' or 'because that's what the rules say' where these are offered as final answers. But it is possible to stand in a hierarchical relation with others while nevertheless being accountable to them. In such cases, deference to one's authority must rest on earned trust and the ability to justify one's decisions, neither of which requires handing over authority to one's subordinates. It requires only that those in authority are accountable to those over whom they have authority, just as those under their jurisdiction are accountable to them. So an institution within a just society, whether a school or a workplace, can enact an intersubjective form of relational justice by making sure people within the institution are accountable to one another (and to those outside) without having to do away with all hierarchies of authority.

Moving beyond Forst

Although it isn't an explicit part of Forst's view, I think he would be perfectly happy with the idea of equality as a practice. But this is where his dialectical advance starts to overcome itself, because once we start picturing justice as involving practices of justification, it begs the question as to how we should understand the very justification of this picture. In other words, might the justification of our picture of justice as intersubjective justification be intersubjective as well? What would that mean? Let's try to get there through a somewhat different route:

Consider the role experts on justice play within the various pictures. On the distributivist picture, justice involves the correct allocation of the appropriate goods. Since distributive pictures of justice treat their subjects as passive recipients, it makes no difference to the justice of a distribution that some people neither accept nor understand it. Justice is a kind of social engineering problem, and like other engineering problems, is best left to be worked out and implemented by an expert, call him Jeremy (Bentham, not Waldron): justice demands government by lawyers and trained civil servants.

If we shift to a relational picture of justice, but hold on to an impersonal conception of justification, then we need to shift to a genuine democracy, where policies are decided upon and authorized by the people themselves, not handed down by experts. Nevertheless, on this view, there still remains a role for a certain kind of, as it were, philosophical expert, call him Ronnie (after Dworkin): someone who can determine which relations are just and which are not, who can give us a theory of justice.

Next, move to an intersubjective conception of justification within our politics. Here there is no possibility of a prior theory of justice: justice has to be worked out by the citizens of a society themselves as they work out what they can justify to one another, what justifications they can accept. But if we nevertheless hold that philosophical justification of our picture of justice must be impersonal, there may still be a role for a different kind of philosophical expert here, call him Jürgen. Such an expert cannot directly lay out the most just institutions or distributions or give us a substantive theory that authorizes particular justifications, but he can lay out the boundaries of public reason or the structure of genuine moral discourse. He can tell us why the right to justification is fundamental to justice, and thus when we are engaged in genuine practices of justice-realizing justification.

If this is right, then moving from a distributivist to a relational picture of justice is a dialectical step forward insofar as it lessens the role of experts in the realization of justice. And this makes the move from an impersonal to an intersubjective picture of justification within a relational picture of justice similarly a step forward. But note that seen this way, there is another natural step to take. Jürgen retains the role of an expert because even though this third picture treats justifications within a political society as intersubjective, it treats the philosophical justification of the basic right to justification itself as impersonal. And that raises the question of whether we can also treat this stage of philosophical justification as intersubjective as well.

Because such a view would be intersubjective all the way down, it would make us active not only with respect to working out the details of our relations to one another in ways that make them non-arbitrary, but also with respect to the terms in which the justification of those relationships plays out. Justice, on this fourth model, is no longer a matter for experts and theorists to figure out or implement at all. It comes about only through our shared implementation of our shared ideas about how to live together, a process that is ongoing and goes all the way up and down.

We can understand this fourth picture as applying the intersubjective picture of justification to philosophy itself, and it is this picture of justice and of political philosophy that I want to invite you to consider. I don't think it is necessary in order to treat equality as a practice, but it does seem to be where doing so takes us. It is also, I think, where Forst and I part ways, so those who reject this invitation will be in good company.

Space constraints prevent a full description of what an intersubjective conception of philosophical justification would look like. But I want to try to sketch some of the underlying issues at stake in the choice between these pictures of political philosophy.

First, note two roles a so-called ideal theory of justice can play. On a traditional picture, justice is generally seen as a goal and philosophers doing ideal theory as laying out a kind of blueprint about where to aim our policies. Philosophy sets out a theoretical goal, and then we apply our philosophical conclusions to particular policy questions in part by trimming our ideals by considerations about what is feasible. This model fits nicely with the idea that ideal theory is theoretically justified. If, however, justice is first and foremost a practice of justification, then ideals serve as constraints on our present action, rather than as a goal to aim for.[25] I realize justice by, here and now, holding myself and others accountable and only acting in ways for which I can offer reciprocally accepted justifications. In abiding by this constraint, I realize an ideal. Because the ideals pictured in intersubjective accounts of relational justice serve as constraints not goals, we are not to figure out what relational justice demands and then work out which policies will bring it about. Rather, we must ask of various policies, regardless of the ends they seek to promote, are these consistent with relational justice? Ideal theory so understood does not then require trimming by concerns of feasibility. Rather, it tells us which among the feasible alternatives should be off the table because it is inconsistent with the demands of justice. But this, in turn, offers a rather different view of political philosophy's role.[26] Political philosophy, so understood, is not the most abstract branch of political science, but rather a way to make our practice, here and now, more reflective, more reasonable, and thus, more just.[27] In doing this, it

---

[25] I discuss this contrast at greater length in reference to Amartya Sen's criticisms of Rawls in A. S. Laden, 'Ideals: Goals vs. Constraints', *Critical Review of International Social and Political Philosophy*, 16(2), (2013), 205–19.

[26] For the most part, this is not how contemporary analytic political philosophers think of the role of political philosophy. For a clear articulation of that more common view, see A. Swift, 'The Value of Philosophy in Non-Ideal Circumstances', *Social Theory and Practice* 34(3), (2008), 363–88. I don't think the possibility of one rules out the possibility or value of the other. But it is important to understand which one is undertaking and why.

[27] J. Tully, 'Political Philosophy as a Critical Activity', in ibid., *Public Philosophy in a New Key*, vol. 1. Cambridge: Cambridge University Press, 2008, pp. 15–38.

does not give recipes and policy proposals to bureaucrats and princes, but helps ordinary citizens enact the justice we seek by helping us to see the meaning and power our actions can have when they are animated by a picture of justice.

Second, note the modality in which the various pictures of justice are expressed. A picture that treats philosophical justification as impersonal will talk, as Forst does, about whether everyone *could or would* accept a political justification.[28] An intersubjective picture, however, will ask us to ask whether our justifications *do* meet with uptake, *are* accepted. Is this shift from acceptability to acceptance a dangerous one? There are two reasons to think so, and both of them appear to concern Forst. The first involves the actual acceptance of faulty justifications, possibly as a result of manipulation or pressure. The traditional housewife who accepts her subordinate role within the household and the wider society and thus accepts justifications for various practices that subordinate her on the basis of this role is not, despite this, being justly treated. She has accepted justifications that are reasonably rejectable. The second kind of case involves stubborn rejection of good justifications. Here, just because someone obstinately rejects a perfectly good justification, we don't want to say that this rejection makes the justification insufficient. Hypothetical acceptability allows us to liberate the housewife while not being held hostage to the forces of unreason.

But not without costs. In particular, if all that matters is the acceptability of justifications, then it does not look as if the actual offering of justifications is essential at least at some level. We can work out what actions and laws and rights regimes are acceptable in the comfort of our studies, shifting to the hypothetical mode of thinking so beloved of philosophers; we are back relying on Jürgen and Ronnie, and perhaps even Jeremy. So taking this route tends to push us back towards an impersonal conception of justification. We can try to hold our ground by distinguishing between the intersubjective form of political justification and the impersonal form of philosophical justification

[28] Forst, *The Right to Justification*, p. 15.

(this is what Habermas tries to do). Forst takes another tack, by trying to assure us that our impersonal philosophical justification just *has* to be intersubjectively accepted. That, as I understand it, is what his recursive justification of the right to justification amounts to. But this position strikes me as unstable. What happens when a justification that has to be accepted just isn't? Luckily, there is another way forward.

We can also avoid the worrisome cases without shifting into a hypothetical register. A model for how to do this is Rawls's idea of pure procedural justice. Pure procedural justice obtains in cases where there is no way of determining the just result without actually going through a procedure. Rawls's example is gambling. The only way to know that a particular outcome is the result of a fair gamble is to play out the game. No amount of hypothetical reasoning will help here. But reliance on an actual procedure being carried out does not mean there are no justice-inspired constraints on the procedure. For the outcome of the game to be fair, the play of the game must be fair, and this will involve it following various rules. Similarly, we might say that for the acceptance or refusal of a justification to be determinative of the justice of the relationship in which it is offered, certain basic rules and norms of justification must be observed. These can look a whole lot like Forst's criteria of accountability, reciprocity and generality.[29] Someone whose rejection of a proffered justification violates these norms will not thus render the justification offered insufficient, so stubbornness is no bar to justice. And accepting a justification that violates these norms will not make the justification a good one, so the accepting housewife is not being treated justly. But the mere fact that an acceptable justification is available will not render a relationship just if there is no means for it to be demanded or willingness for it to be given. We realize justice in how we talk to one another, not in the space of abstract possibilities. And to avoid a different criticism, we can hold that these norms must gain

---

[29] Forst, *The Right to Justification*, p. 20, where they are presented more or less as I have presented them here, as constraining criteria.

their authority in the very same way that the justifications they make possible do: through being accepted.

But even if you accept that not laying out ideal goals and not offering theories that speak in hypotheticals are attractive possibilities, you may still find the idea that philosophical justification could be intersubjective all the way down unattractive, even downright unphilosophical. Many, probably most, philosophers do. So I want to end by trying to locate that resistance, and maybe suggest some of the attractions of the position I have been laying out.

What, ultimately, seems to lie at the bottom of the difference between an approach that distinguishes philosophical and political justification or in other ways tries to impersonally ground our conception of justice and one which aims to be intersubjective all the way down is something like what William James called philosophical temperament. The point here is subtle and tricky and I am not sure I am yet articulating it well, but the basic thought has to do with our tolerance for uncertainty in the struggle for justice.

Let me try to get at it in a roundabout sort of way. Kant taught us to think about morality (and much else besides) in terms of necessity and unconditional grounding. And to think in terms of necessity is to adopt the language of duty and inevitability.[30] It is to search for unavoidable, if not metaphysical or foundational, grounds of those duties in our condition or nature. It is to focus on what we must, inevitably, do or be.[31] By resting our conception of justice on such unconditional and firm grounds, we secure our footing, as it were, and can rest assured that we will be able to counter injustice where we find it. For those as concerned to respond to injustice as Forst is, that is not something to give up lightly.

---

[30] Forst, *The Right to Justification*, pp. 33–4.

[31] Forst's own Kantianism is constructivist and post-metaphysical, to be sure (see e.g. Forst, *The Right to Justification*, p. 36). But it is still suffused with the search for the unconditional ground of duty, of the necessity of acting in a certain way. Forst claims that this ground, though not constructed, must be re-constructed, and must thus be answerable to the very criteria it supports (ibid., pp. 22, 272n.46, ch. 2). And so neither Forst's Kant nor Forst's own view rests on a form of substantive realism. But in adverting to this re-construction, he is constantly brought back to something like its necessity or the necessity of the practical insight on which it rests (ibid., p. 60).

The problem is that once we have found an inevitable source of obligation in our condition, then it looks as if any failure to uphold and acknowledge that obligation is a kind of existential confusion, a failure to be human. But this is overly dramatic: it leaves no room for all the more or less ordinary ways we fail to live up to our ideals of justice without thereby failing to be human.

In contrast, the kind of view I have offered here can be thought of as holding out an ideal set of practices for others to join us in realizing. Rather than insisting on these practices as obligatory or inevitable or grounded in who we are, it holds them out as ideals, as something towards which we might aspire. It thus speaks in the language of exemplars, not principles. Since we can accept an ideal that we do not yet live up to, we can also at the same time accept all the myriad ways we currently fail to be just without failing thereby to be who we are.

Now, from the point of view of the impersonal view of philosophical justification we find in Kant and Forst and most other political philosophers, holding out ideals will appear to be insufficiently critical and grounded. It will seem too weak a position with which to confront the world's many injustices. For one, it looks as if letting go of the impersonal philosophical grounding of the basic right to justification leaves us with nothing to say to those who do not recognize it.

But I would suggest that giving up the project of finding unconditional grounds does not need to render us mute in the face of injustice. There is another way philosophical argument might proceed: rather than search for grounds for our principles, we might attempt to describe our ideals in ways that make them attractive, and invite others to see them as we do and to join us in the shared project of working out ideals we can share. This is inevitably a more collaborative enterprise. It requires that we also be open to being changed by what others say to us. In that sense, it does leave more up for grabs. But in doing so, it recognizes and respects those with whom we talk and argue in a way that arguing from already established philosophical foundations does not. It thus realizes justice by failing to guarantee it. (This is where the choice turns on your tolerance for uncertainty in the struggle for justice).

We might understand this as a project of coming to be creatures for whom justice is inevitable, or simply a project of taking responsibility for taking on the obligations of justice. Note that this is a project we undertake first and foremost not by theoretical study or the implementation of particular social policies, but by, to quote Gandhi, being the change we want to see in the world, by enacting in our relationships with one another these very practices of justification and thus equality. And we do this not only as fellow citizens, but also as philosophers, for on this conception of philosophy's role, there is no difference.

As I said above, adopting this intersubjective picture of political philosophy can be seen as applying an intersubjective picture of justification to philosophy itself. Not, as Forst tries to do, by making the grounding of the principle of justification recursive and thus unavoidable, but by giving philosophy a different role to play: helping us to see more clearly the costs of adopting or abandoning certain ideals or ways of acting in the world and thus giving us a language in which to offer justifications to each other for thinking one way rather than another. If this strikes you as insufficiently philosophical, note that it may be where Kant's recognition of the autonomy of reason eventually takes us. It is arguably where it took Hegel and Nietzsche and, I would argue, Rawls.[32] For if the justification of justice is as intersubjective an exercise as the justification of particular actions or principles or cooperative schemes, then we must construct our philosophical ground as we construct our political and social grounds, by reasoning together, by talking to one another. We cannot hope to discover or re-construct it by careful philosophical study alone. Similarly, if justice is our aspiration, not our condition, then we have to take it upon ourselves to be the change by engaging in practices of equality with one another,

---

[32] For the further development of this argument with respect to Rawls, see A. S. Laden, 'The Justice of Justification', in F. Frayenhagen and J. G. Finlayson (eds), *Debating the Political: Rawls and Habermas in Dialogue*. New York: Routledge, 2010, pp. 135–52.

rather than to look for authorization or permission or necessitation in a grounding argument. This is the picture of the practice of equality that I invite you to consider. I find it attractive, but I realize that many readers, like Forst, will see such a leap into thin air as jumping off a cliff rather than taking flight. And they may well be right about that. It is certainly not an issue that I can settle now. It will, no doubt, require the coming of the dusk, when owls and boomerangs fly free.

6

The Boundary Problem and the Right to Justification

Eva Erman

Department of Government, Uppsala University, Sweden

Introduction

Democracy presumes a collective, a group of individuals, who are in a specific sense self-governing or self-determining. The problem of who should be included in this collective and thus take part in collective democratic decision-making, what is sometimes called the boundary problem in democratic theory, is an increasingly pressing political problem in the light of growing asymmetries between rule-makers and rule-takers in a globalized world. While the boundary problem can and has been approached in a variety of ways pleading to moral theory, through which democracy is justified instrumentally for realizing some other normative ideal, such as justice, the present chapter is a contribution to this debate with the intent to hold on to the ideal of democracy – that is, where democracy as collective self-determination (the 'rule by the people') is intrinsically justified[1] as the foundation of legitimate authority.[2]

---

[1] For sure, the question what is intrinsic value and what sort of things can have intrinsic value is contested among philosophers. The argument here remains neutral towards the much more complex questions concerning whether intrinsic value is non-derivative and whether it supervenes on intrinsic properties alone (see M. Zimmerman, *The Nature of Intrinsic Value*. Lanham: Rowman and Littlefield, 2001). Instead, it is the broader distinction between *valuable for its own sake* and *valuable for the sake of something else* that is of interest here, which perhaps makes it more appropriate to follow Christine Korsgaard and speak of 'final value' (C. Korsgaard, 'Two Distinctions in Goodness', Philosophical Review 92(1983), 169–95). On a normative pragmatic view, which I find convincing, something that has intrinsic (or final) value in one context might have instrumental value in another.

[2] Of course, such an intrinsic justification of democracy could – and in my view must – also draw on moral values or principles (or both).

A basic presumption of this chapter is that to the extent that we wish to hold on to democracy as a normative ideal when approaching the boundary question about justified inclusion (henceforth the 'B question' for simplicity), whatever solution we come up with, it must be *compatible* with the basic conditions of democracy, answering what is henceforth called the 'C question', that is, what conditions must an arrangement fulfil in order to be minimally democratic? The overall aim is to show that a particular discourse-theoretical approach has resources to achieve this. This will be done at the level of 'ideal theory'[3] in the sense that the chapter will bracket questions of feasibility and the realization of democracy under non-ideal circumstances, for example, dealing with problems of immigration and border control.[4] The thesis defended is that the so-called 'equal influence principle' is preferable to solutions to the boundary problem drawing on what is commonly called 'the all affected interests principle' as well as on the alternative discourse-theoretical views of Jürgen Habermas and Rainer Forst, since it can offer a criterion of justified inclusion compatible with a criterion of democratic legitimacy (thus answering the B and C questions in a compatible way).

The argument is pursued in four steps. In the first step, I call attention to the relationship between the B and C questions as well as

---

[3]   See, for example, J. Simmons, 'Ideal and Nonideal Theory', *Philosophy & Public Affairs* 38(2010), 5–36; L. Ypi, 'On the Confusion between Ideal and Non-ideal in Recent Debates on Global Justice', *Political Studies* 58(2010), 536–55; E. Erman, and N. Möller, 'Three Failed Charges Against Ideal Theory, *Social Theory & Practice* 39(1), (2013), 19–44; L. Valentini, 'On the Apparent Paradox of Ideal Theory', *Journal of Political Philosophy* 17(2009), 332–5.

[4]   Cf. A. Abizadeh, 'Democratic Theory and Border Coercion: No Right to Unilaterally Control your Own Borders', *Political Theory* 36(1), (2008), 37–65; A. Abizadeh, 'Democratic Legitimacy and State Coercion: A Reply to David Miller', *Political Theory* 38(1), (2010), 121–30; J. Carens, 'Fear vs. Fairness: Migration, Citizenship and the Transformation of Political Community', in K. Lippert-Rasmussen, N. Holtug, and S. Laegaard (eds), *Nationalism and Multiculturalism in a World of Immigration*. Houndmills: Palgrave Macmillan, 2009; J. Carens, 'Aliens and Citizens: The Case for Open Borders', in R. Bellamy and A. Palumbo (eds), *Citizenship*. Aldershot: Ashgate Publishing, 2010; D. Miller, 'Why Immigration Controls Are Not Coercive: A Reply to Arash Abizadeh', *Political Theory* 38(1), (2010), 111–20.

address the common claim that the B question is 'prior'. I also propose an answer to the C question by presenting two basic conditions that I suggest are reasonable to require of an arrangement for it to qualify as minimally democratic, namely, *political equality* and *political bindingness* (I). In the second section, I take a look at 'all affected solutions' to the boundary problem in the light of these two conditions in an attempt to show why the all affected principle is not appropriate for solving the boundary problem (II). In the third section, the so-called equal influence principle is defended as the proper criterion of justified inclusion, which is a version of what is sometimes labelled 'the all subjected principle'. Attention is drawn to the strengths of the equal influence principle for answering the B question in comparison with the discourse-theoretical alternatives of Habermas and Forst (III). In a final step, I specify in what contexts democracy is an applicable ideal, arguing that the equal influence principle is only applicable under circumstances of interdependent interests. Further, drawing on Forst's distinction between different contexts of justification, I position the proposed equal influence principle in the larger context of justificatory practices among discursive agents in the space of reasons and suggest how we may approach contexts where democracy is not an applicable normative ideal but we still reasonably require of authorities to be politically legitimate (IV).

The boundary question versus the basic conditions question

In stark contrast to what has traditionally been the case among political theorists, those who today approach the boundary problem consider the question of *who* should be included in the 'demos' of a democracy to be the basic and first question of democracy, in particular in a transnational context. In fact, it is almost a truism among democratic theorists that the B question is *prior* to the C question in democratic theory. The controversies have instead tended to revolve around the conceptual and normative implications of this claim.[5]

However, a crucial aspect that is overlooked is what exactly 'prior' alludes to in this context. Most importantly, from the fact that the B question is causally and empirically prior, it does not follow that it is also normatively prior. In fact, it would be peculiar to argue that it is normatively prior, since there are a lot of boundary problems 'out there' in normative space, concerned with the 'who question' from various normative ideals, such as who should be included and excluded from having group rights or certain primary goods. The particular boundary question of relevance here concerns the ideal of democracy. In other words, when approaching the B question, we need a pair of 'democratic glasses', specifying at least the basic requirements for an arrangement to qualify as minimally democratic (answering the C question), in order to know where to look.[6]

So let us take a closer look at the C question. What conditions are required for an arrangement to qualify as minimally democratic? Indeed, similar to most (if not all) normative concepts, democracy is highly contested. At the same time, we seem to need at least some shared idea of what the ideal of the rule by the people means in order to make comparisons and critical judgments about different conceptions of democracy.[7] In broad strokes, what seems indisputable is that democracy,

---

[5] For example, compare R. Goodin, 'Enfranchising All Affected Interests and Its Alternatives', *Philosophy and Public Affairs* 35(1), (2007), 40–68, at pp. 40–1; with R. Dahl, *Democracy and its Critics*. New Haven: Yale University Press, 1989, pp. 119–31; and J. Habermas, *Between Facts and Norms: Contributions to a Discourse Theory of Law and Democracy*, trans. by W. Rehg. Cambridge, MA: MIT Press, 1996a.

[6] Naturally, there is a considerable amount of conceptual and normative work left for a full-fledged democratic theory when we have answered the B and C questions in a compatible way, not least pertaining to the institutional and practical dimensions of democracy, such as the contextual specification of these requirements and further conditions following from them. However, for the present purposes, the chapter is confined to an analysis of the boundary problem from a normative and conceptual point of view in ideal-theoretical terms.

[7] Indeed, even to the extent that we would agree on the basic conditions of democracy, democratic theorists would certainly disagree on what needs to be done in order to fulfil them. However, we should distinguish the question of what democracy is from what it requires. The latter question is not of immediate interest in this section.

'the rule by the people', is a form of political arrangement in which people collectively rule themselves as political equals. Democracy expresses the idea of 'equal political power' or 'equal decision-making power', as it were. If we unpack this idea, *two* conditions come to the fore as fundamentally important and seem to me hard to dismiss for any modern account of democracy. The first condition is *political equality*. What distinguishes democracy from other forms of government, such as dictatorship, monarchy or aristocracy, is that it has components that express and secure some form of political equality, according to which anyone who is relevantly affected by a political decision (or law) has an equal opportunity, secured through an equal right, to participate (directly or indirectly) in the decision-making about it.[8]

Apart from this 'deontological' dimension of being given an equal *opportunity* to participate in the decision procedure through equal rights, the rule by the people also involves what we might call a 'teleological' dimension, in that people rule over themselves and shape their institutions only if they, at least a sufficient number of them, act politically by 'exercising' their political equality.[9] In other words, democracy requires some sort of *democratic practice* (through informal and/or formal processes, depending on which conception of democracy is favoured). I call this condition *political bindingness*. More specifically, in order for people to rule over themselves through a political authority (i.e. a decision-making body), thereby making themselves authors of the laws, they have to *bind* themselves as equals to this authority, which requires certain forms of political action.[10] Under modern conditions this *authorization* is usually made by taking part (directly or indirectly) in the decision-making or at a minimum

[8] T. Christiano, 'A Democratic Theory of Territory and Some Puzzles about Global Democracy', *Journal of Political Philosophy* 17(2), (2006), 228–40.

[9] On this point, compare Rawls' theory of justice as fairness, which insists on the 'equal *worth* of political rights' (*Justice as Fairness. A Restatement*. Cambridge, MA: Harvard University Press, 2001). Of course, what is considered a 'sufficient number' will vary between different conceptions or models of democracy.

[10] E. Erman, 'In Search of Democratic Agency in Deliberative Governance', *European Journal of International Relations*, (2013), pp. 847–68.

accepting the constitutionalized procedures as valid, without which the right to participate would not have any binding force.[11] We will have reason to return to this below.

The ideal of democracy and the all-affected principle

A common solution to the boundary problem is often referred to as the 'all affected interests principle (or the all affected principle for short)', which roughly states that all whose relevant (or significant) interests are affected by a decision should have influence over it.[12] There are of course as many versions of this principle as there are contestations about how to best interpret 'decision-making' or 'relevantly affected'. There is also disagreement as to whether the principle should refer to those 'possibly affected' or those 'actually affected'.[13] But these internal disputes are bracketed here since of primary concern is how the general normative

---

[11] Again, what is of interest in this section is specifying the conditions for answering the C question, not what needs to be done in order to properly fulfil them. The answer to the latter question will vary among democratic theories.

[12] See, e.g. D. Archibugi, 'Principles of Cosmopolitan Democracy', in ibid., D. Held, and M. Kohler (eds), *Re-Imagining Political Community: Studies in Cosmopolitan Democracy.* London: Polity, 1998; G. Arrhenius, 'The Boundary Problem in Democratic Theory', in F. Tersman (ed.), *Democracy Unbound.* Stockholm: Stockholm University Press, 2005; S. Benhabib, *The Rights of Others: Aliens, Residents and Citizens.* Cambridge: Cambridge University Press, 2004; Goodin, 'Enfranchising All Affected Interests and its Alternatives'; C. Gould, *Globalizing Democracy and Human Rights.* Cambridge: Cambridge University Press, 2004; D. Held, *Democracy and the Global Order.* Cambridge: Cambridge University Press, 1995; I. Shapiro, *Democratic Justice.* New Haven: Yale University Press, 1999; F. G. Whelan, 'Democratic Theory and the Boundary Problem', in J. R. Pennock and J. W. Chapman (eds), *Liberal Democracy.* New York: New York University Press, 1983. For a discussion of the different roles of the all affected principle for dealing with the problem of democratic boundary-making, see S. Näsström, 'The Challenge of the All affected Principle', *Political Studies* 59(1), (2011), 116–34. For a sceptical view of the principle, see J. Karlsson Schaffer, 'The boundaries of transnational democracy: alternatives to the all-affected principle', *Review of International Studies*, available on CJO 2011 doi: 10.1017/S0260210510001749.

[13] Goodin, 'Enfranchising All Affected Interests and its Alternatives'; D. Owen, 'Constituting the Polity, Constituting the Demos: On the place of the all affected interests principle in democratic theory and in resolving the democratic boundary problem', *Ethics and Global Politics* 5(3), (2012), 129–52.

structure of the principle feeds into the ideal of democracy. Despite the attractiveness of the all affected principle as a normative principle underpinning democracy, it is argued that it seems unable in its *general form* to answer the B question since it is neither able to accommodate a condition of political equality nor of political bindingness.

Let us first take a look at political equality. As argued by Robert Goodin, the all affected principle is fundamentally egalitarian since it counts all interests equally and equal political power is the cornerstone of democracy.[14] However, it is not clear how it is able to get us from a conception of moral equality in terms of counting all interests equally to political equality in terms of the equal political power that Goodin stresses. For political equality is not *only* premised on the idea that members of a constituency are morally equal and as such have *an* opportunity (secured by a right) to participate in the decision-making to the extent that they are relevantly affected, but more specifically, that they have an *equal* opportunity to do so (i.e. equal decision-making power).

The difference is crucial: the all affected principle allows for a proportional view of affectedness, according to which those who are more affected by a decision should have more influence than those who are less affected.[15] Indeed, supporting proportional influence seems sensible since it is affectedness that *motivates* a right to participate in the decision-making in the first place; it is one of the features that make the principle so attractive from a normative point of view. Consider the alternative, according to which those who are affected should have the same degree of influence. This would draw an indefensible dividing line between those that are not at all affected and those that are very little affected.[16] It would also undermine majority voting as a

---

[14] Goodin, 'Enfranchising All Affected Interests and its Alternatives', p. 50; see also C. Beitz, *Political Equality*. Princeton: Princeton University Press, 1989.

[15] See Gould, *Globalizing Democracy*; T. Macdonald, *Global Stakeholder Democracy*. Oxford: Oxford University Press, 2008; J. Rawls, *A Theory of Justice*. Cambridge, MA: Harvard University Press, 1971.

[16] L. Bergström, 'Democracy and Political Boundaries', in F. Tersman (ed.), *The Viability and Desirability of Global Democracy*. Stockholm: Stockholm University Press, 2007.

justified procedure from the standpoint of democracy, since voting on an issue would generate clear winners and losers in the light of the fact that it will never be the case that people are equally affected.

In a democracy, members are supposed to rule over themselves through a political arrangement that takes numerous decisions on a wide range of social, political, legal and economic issues. To the extent that such arrangements have 'proportional influence' due to 'proportional affectedness', it is at set levels (e.g. local municipality) within a legal-institutional framework that secures *equal* decision-making power on *each* level, and in which the ultimate legal competence derives from the *same* source. In fact, even if we abandoned the idea of political equality by applying the all affected principle within such a framework, such that people had the opportunity to participate in the decision-making to the extent that they were relevantly affected, it is difficult to see how we could justifiably use the principle for setting up this framework and establishing these decision-making structures in the first place (i.e. answering the B question). Hence, while the all affected principle might be used as a justification of democratic borders as part of a moral theory, it is difficult to see how it can constitute part of a democratic theory, equipped to translate by itself its moral egalitarian underpinnings into political equality.

Moving to political bindingness, this condition also seems to pose a problem for the all affected principle, stressing that all those whose interests are affected should have a right (and thus an opportunity) to participate in the decision-making. For no matter how fully implemented, this right is *individual* and does not by itself say anything about *collective* decision-making, that is, about the democratic practice being the result of the *exercise* of this very right. This has nothing to do with whether rights are successfully implemented or not. We can have numerous of fully secured rights (and opportunities) without any democratic rule-making or political action whatsoever.[17] At a minimum,

---

[17] E. Erman, 'Human Rights do not make Global Democracy', *Contemporary Political Theory* 10(4), (2011), 463–81; ibid., 'The Right to Have Rights' to the Rescue: From Human Rights to Global Democracy', in M. Goodale (ed.), *Human Rights at the Crossroads*. Oxford: Oxford University Press, 2012.

'affected persons' must *authorize* the authority (decision-making body) in question by accepting the constitutionalized procedures as valid for this right to have a binding force.

Winding up this section, the first step of the argument pursued here is thus that these two conditions, the answer to the C question, as it were, set the normative and conceptual limits on possible answers to the B question, insofar as we approach the boundary problem with the intent of holding on to democracy as an ideal. Now, of course, one might not agree on the proposed basic conditions of democracy. If we were to answer the C question by construing conditions that made up a thinner notion of democracy, this would certainly give us more options for answering the B question. However, I suspect that whatever suggestion we would come up with that dismissed either political equality or political bindingness, would very likely be controversial and go against strong normative intuitions about what we could possibly mean by democratic rule-making, that is, the ideal of the rule by the people.

Discourse theory and the boundary problem

So far I have tried to expose some of the problems that the all affected principle faces as a candidate for solving the boundary problem *within* democratic theory. In this section the question addressed is whether discourse theory is better equipped to solve the boundary problem. I contend that it is, but not the way it has been theorized by two of its most influential proponents, namely, Habermas and Forst.

One possible explanation for the incompatibility of the all affected principle with the basic conditions of democracy, such as political equality, could be traced to its reliance on a very limited notion of 'democratic politics', which does not seem to capture crucial aspects of the broader established understanding of the concept. The demand for democratic legitimacy does not arise primarily because decisions on separate issues to which people are differently affected must be made, but because people have interdependent interests and therefore are in need of a collective decision-making apparatus to solve common problems in a justified way. On this established view, democratic politics consists of numerous different potential issues and deals among other things precisely with the question of what should count as a political problem in the first place.

That said, this doesn't take away the normative attractiveness of the all affected principle. That people who are affected by a law should have a say in its making is indeed a strong intuition underlying the ideal of democracy. In order to account for this intuition, but at the same time meet the challenges this principle faces, an alternative route to take is to go for another candidate in the debate, namely, the so-called 'all subjected principle'. In its general form, this principle states that all those who are subjected to the laws, that is, those whose actions are governed by them, should have a say in their making.[18] Hence, while people might be (and presumably are) differently affected by a society's laws and regulations, they are still equally subjected to them. Thus, on the standard version of the all subjected principle, the criterion of inclusion is not gradually but *binary* coded such that either one is a legal subject or not.

Habermas's principle of democracy is perhaps the most influential all subjected principle in the contemporary debate. It states, 'only those laws count as legitimate to which all members of the legal community can assent in a discursive process of legislation that has in turn been legally constituted'.[19] In brief, the democratic principle arises from a specific interpretation of Habermas's discourse principle and the legal code (basically a legal community and legal subjects), the latter of which can be neither epistemologically nor normatively justified,

---

[18] Dahl, *Democracy and its Critics*; Habermas, *Between Facts and Norms*; Abizadeh, 'Democratic Theory and Border Coercion'; Lopez-Guerra, 'Should Expatriates Vote?'; D. Owen, 'Transnational Citizenship and the Democratic State', *Critical Review of International Social and Political Philosophy* 14(5), (2011), 641–64; ibid., 'Constituting the polity, constituting the demos'; Erman, 'Human Rights do not make Global Democracy'; ibid., '"The Right to have Rights" to the Rescue'.

[19] Habermas, *Between Facts and Norms*, p. 110.

according to Habermas.[20] While 'assent' on this principle is supposed to be the outcome of legally constituted processes of legislation, a strength of the Habermasian view is that it stresses not only a formal 'track' in terms of *formalized* deliberative decision procedures of will-formation in this regard, but also an interconnected informal 'track' in terms of *informal* deliberative practices of opinion-formation, channelled into these procedures – both secured through a constitutionalized system of rights.[21]

It is clear that Habermas's principle does not offer any guidance concerning the B question, since it has already the democratic boundary built into it in terms of a presupposed legal community, which allegedly can be neither epistemologically nor normatively justified. Still, it has several attractive discourse-theoretical components. Therefore, I suggest a reformulation of the all subjected principle in terms of what I call 'the equal influence principle', which is equipped to accommodate a criterion of justified inclusion and thereby makes the boundaries of the community a justificatory question rather than a premise, as Habermas does. The equal influence principle states that 'all those who are systematically and over time subjected to an authority's (i.e. a decision-making body's) laws, political decisions and rules, in the sense of being governed by them, should systematically and over time have an *equal influence* over its decision-making and in the shaping of its institutions'. 'Influence' is a useful concept for capturing the two basic conditions harboured by the idea of equal decision-making power, expressing equal political status (political equality) and the properties tied to it (such as a set of basic rights) as well as an action-oriented aspect, since you 'bind yourself' to something or 'authorize' it by influencing it (political bindingness). This dual structure is not easily captured by the concept of 'power', which on most accounts a person could possess but not necessarily exercise.

---

[20] Ibid., p. 455.
[21] J. Habermas, 'Reply to Symposium Participants', *Cardozo Law Review* 17(1996c), 1477–557, at p. 1494.

More specifically, 'influence' on the proposed view at a minimum requires a democratic practice in terms of robust participation in both *formal* decision procedures (e.g. through electoral vote) and *informal* processes (e.g. in civil society and the public sphere), in which *a major and not fixed part of the members* takes part.[22] Further, in line with the established view of democratic politics submitted earlier, 'systematically and over time' suggests an institutional approach to democracy, stating that this participation does not concern each and every decision but the complete set of decisions over time.[23] Needless to say, much more fine-grained specifications would have to be made for example concerning how many 'a major part' must consist of, if we were to realize this principle in practice. But at a principled level, we don't have to offer such specifications, as this will vary depending on the context to which the equal influence principle is supposed to be applied.

Now, the sceptic might object that when it comes down to it, the equal influence principle offers as little guidance to the boundary problem as does Habermas's principle of democracy, since it also relies on an authority which makes laws, the only difference being that Habermas's principle explicitly relies on a legal community, whereas the defended principle does so only implicitly. But this is a chimera. In the equal influence principle, 'authority' is a *descriptive* concept, referring to any authority that subjects people to its laws and regulations. It cannot be turned into a normative concept of democratically legitimate authority by other means than by following the principle itself. In Habermas's principle, by contrast, 'legal community' is a *moralized* concept, referring to a horizontal association of individuals, who voluntarily have come together and recognized one another as free and equals, as

---

[22] The 'not fixed' condition is crucial to avoid persistent minorities.

[23] Erman, '"The Right to have Rights" to the Rescue'; In contrast to those who see rights as a protection 'against' democratic rule-makers and democratic authority, my institutional approach, following Habermas, sees a set of rights protecting fundamental interests as an essential part of any reasonable conception of democracy applied under modern conditions, not only for the protection of members but also in large part for non-members, such as short term residents, resident aliens, visitors and people seeking asylum.

well as mutually accorded each other a set of rights.[24] With the collective intention of legitimately regulating their life by means of positive law, they have entered into a common practice that allows them to frame a constitution, the latter of which precisely takes form by adopting and fleshing out these rights in a deliberative and egalitarian fashion.[25] So this legal community is far from empty of normative content.[26]

In other words, the work of justifying the boundaries of a democratic arrangement on the proposed account is made *through* the equal influence principle, which decides who are supposed to have equal rights and equal decision-making power. By contrast, this normative groundwork is already presupposed in Habermas's principle of democracy. The reference to 'all' in Habermas's principle refers to 'all members of the legal community', whilst the reference to 'all' in the equal influence principle refers to all persons, not just to members (citizens), which makes it open *in principle*.

Let me demonstrate some strengths of the defended proposal in comparison with another influential discourse-theoretical view, namely that of Forst. In Forst's view, the common source of all claims of validity in normative space is the principle of equal respect for autonomous agency, from which he derives a basic moral right to justification. This principle requires that we regard others as autonomous sources of normative claims within a justificatory practice such that each person is an 'authority' in the space of reasons, as it were.[27] Justification on this view is understood as a *discursive* process whose primary addressees are those affected in relevant ways.[28] Thus, insofar as we get our normative statuses in practices of giving and asking for reasons, Forst argues, we should have a moral right to justification in those very

---

[24] J. Habermas, 'Paradigms of Law', *Cardozo Law Review* 17(1996b), 771–84, at p. 777.

[25] This constitution-making process is guided by Habermas' discourse principle.

[26] Habermas, 'Reply to Symposium Participants', pp. 1504–5.

[27] R. Brandom, *Making it Explicit*. Cambridge, MA: Harvard University Press, 1994; ibid., 'Some Pragmatist Themes in Hegel's Idealism', *European Journal of Philosophy* 7(2), (1999), 164–89.

[28] Forst, *Right to Justification*, ch. 1; As such, the principle of equal respect for autonomous agency is a 'dialogical' version of the all-affected principle.

practices, that is, a right to be recognized as an agent who can demand acceptable reasons for any institution or structure which claims to be binding upon her or any action that claims to be morally justified.[29]

However, the right to justification does not constitute the criterion of rightness solely in contexts of *moral* justification, on Forst's account, but also the criterion of democratic legitimacy in contexts of *political* justification. Forst's discursive conception of justice as non-domination[30] is seen as inseparable from his conception of democracy, because the moral point of human rights, that is, to have an active status as a justificatory equal, is not only about the *protection* of our agency but also about *expressing* our agency and autonomy in practice as 'norm-givers'. This is by Forst articulated as a human right to democracy in terms of a basic right to democratic participation, viz. a *right to full membership in a democratic community*, which

---

[29] R. Forst, 'The Justification of Human Rights and the Basic Right to Justification: A Reflexive Approach', *Ethics* 120(4), (2010), 711–40. On Forst's account, the right to justification accommodates two criteria, *reciprocity* and *generality*. In moral contexts, the criterion of generality takes the form of *universality* or 'generality in a strict sense' (R. Forst, 'The Rule of Reasons: Three Models of Deliberative Democracy', *Ratio Juris* 14(4), (2001), 345–78, p. 363; Forst, 'The Justification of Human Rights', p. 734), similar to Habermas' universalization principle (J. Habermas, *Moral Consciousness and Communicative Action*, trans. by C. Lenhardt and S. Nicholsen. Cambridge, MA: MIT Press, 1990; J. Habermas, *Justification and Application: Remarks on Discourse Ethics*, trans. by C. Cronin. Cambridge, MA: MIT Press, 1993; J. Habermas, *The Inclusion of the Other*, eds. C. Cronin and P. De Greiff. Cambridge, MA: MIT Press, 1998; J. Habermas, *Truth and Justification*, trans. by B. Fultner. Cambridge, MA: MIT Press, 2003; E. Erman, 'Conflict and Universal Moral Theory: From Reasonableness to Reason-Giving', *Political Theory* 35(5), (2007), 598–623). However, in contrast to pure consent theories of moral justification, the criteria of reciprocity and generality allow for the justifiability of claims even in cases of dissent, because normative claims are justified to the extent that they are not 'reasonably rejectable', viz. as long as no reciprocal and general reasons can be legitimately raised against them. Of course, within this dialogical framework, universalizing a maxim of action is not about an agent asking herself whether her action can be willed generally without contradiction in a monological fashion. Instead, justification is understood as a discursive process whose primary addressees are those *affected in relevant ways*. And disputes about 'relevantly affected' could only be addressed by way of a process of reciprocal and general justification (R. Forst, *The Right to Justification: Elements of a Constructivist Theory of Justice*, trans. by J. Flynn. New York: Columbia University Press, 2012, ch. 1).

[30] R. Forst, 'Radical Justice: On Iris Marion Young's Critique of the "Distributive Paradigm"', *Constellation* 14(2), (2007c), 260–65, at p. 260; ibid., 'First Things First: Redistribution, Recognition and Justification', *European Journal of Political Theory* 6(3), (2007b), 291–304, at pp. 299–300.

realizes for agents the right to justification in the political realm, and thus recognizes their equal right to effective political justification.[31] Hence, rather than limiting the right to democracy by appealing to the principle of collective self-determination, which is a 'recursive' principle according to Forst, the border of the democratic community is to be decided and justified with reference to the right to democracy, viz. the right to democratic participation.[32]

The problem with Forst's proposal is that while *political equality* is a necessary condition for democracy, it cannot alone satisfactorily answer the C question. Hence, the equal right to participation (i.e. the right to justification applied to a political context) cannot constitute a criterion of democratic legitimacy standing by itself, since it doesn't say anything about collective decision-making, which is dependent on a condition of *political bindingness* in order for authorization to take place. To repeat the argument against the all affected principle: universal rights alone (legal *or* moral) cannot substantiate a normative theory of democracy mainly because no matter how fully implemented, universal rights of any kind are *individual* rights, which could be enforced without any *collective* exercise of egalitarian decision-making whatsoever on any level.[33] There are two points of importance here. First, in contrast to basic civil rights, such as freedom of speech, and basic socio-economic rights, such as the right to healthcare, a condition of political rights, at least of those labelled 'democratic rights', is that they depend on being exercised jointly with others. Thus, while I may have a right to vote, I cannot exercise this right anytime I want, but only in an election together with others. Second, if we all had a right to vote in an election but nobody ever did (or, minimally, if we had a moral right to create a constitutional structure, but no one participated in this endeavour), we would not

---

[31] Forst, 'The Justification of Human Rights', pp. 724–35; ibid., 'The Rule of Reasons', p. 362–70.
[32] Forst, 'The Justification of Human Rights', p. 730.
[33] E. Erman, 'Human Rights do not Make Global Democracy'.

fulfil the condition of political bindingness since there would be no authorization involved. Something similar would not be the case if we all had a right to healthcare but never got sick. In other words, what is peculiar about democracy is that individual and collective autonomy are simultaneously at work when democratic legitimacy is generated.

Thus, Forst faces a dilemma pertaining to how a condition of bindingness is to be accommodated by his principle. For even if he wishes to avoid requirements of actual participation in the decision-making, he would at least have to require that an authorization takes place by the subjects involved through which the basic constitutional procedures are accepted as valid. In order to do so, the first option would be to claim that his principle already relies on such an authorization (bindingness), similar to Habermas's principle of democracy, which presupposes a moralized legal community whose constitutional structure is already accepted (authorized) by members who have mutually accorded each other a set of rights. However, in this case Forst's theory becomes impotent for addressing the boundary problem. The other option would be to build a condition of bindingness into the principle itself as a normative criterion, similar to the equal influence principle defended here, in case of which something more must be added to the right to justification so that it can take a collectively binding form.

To sum up, Forst's approach to the boundary problem (answering the B question) is not compatible with the basic conditions of democracy (answering the C question). By defining democracy in terms of the right to justification, Forst is at the most able to offer a theory of *democratization*, according to which processes of democratization are instrumentally justified to the extent that they approximate an *ideal of justice* as non-domination. But however attractive such a theory may be, it does not suffice as an ideal of *democracy*, that is, an ideal about the rule by the people as a form of political arrangement in which people collectively rule over themselves as political equals.

Winding up: The ideal of democracy and different contexts of justification

Let me conclude by specifying the conditions under which the equal influence principle is applicable and how we may approach contexts where democracy is not an applicable normative ideal. Undeniably, we live in a world in which our interests are affected by what people do around the globe. As argued by Goodin, virtually everybody in one way or the other seems affected by everybody else.[34] In a democratic arrangement or polity, however, members' interests are deeply interdependent and connected in multiple ways, such that the realization of nearly all of the fundamental interests of each member is connected with the realization of nearly all fundamental interests of every other member.[35] So, while the call for collective decision-making and common institutions may emerge in other contexts too, there seems to be no reason why collective *democratic* decision-procedures and common *democratic* institutions would emerge if people's interests were not deeply interconnected in this way. Hence, it is under the empirical condition of interdependent interests that the call for democratic decision-making emerges and democracy becomes a applicable ideal. On the proposed account, it is in such contexts that the equal influence principle is applicable.[36]

---

[34] Goodin, 'Enfranchising All Affected Interests and its Alternatives'.

[35] Christiano, 'A Democratic Theory of Territory', p. 97.

[36] In the light of the requirement of interdependent interests, the equal influence principle has several advantages to competing all subjected principles in the debate (Abizadeh, 'Democratic Theory and Border Coercion'; C. Lopez-Guerra, 'Should Expatriates Vote?', *The Journal of Political Philosophy* 13(2), (2005), 216–34; L. Beckman, *The Frontiers of Democracy: The Right to Vote and Its Limits*. Basingstoke: Palgrave Macmillan, 2009; L. Beckman, 'Is Residence Special? Democracy in the Age of Migration and Human Mobility', in L. Beckman and E. Erman (eds), *Territories of Citizenship*. New York: Palgrave Macmillan, 2012). Most importantly, it is equipped to distinguish the businessman who visits a democratic society on a long-term basis from a long-term resident alien. While both are subjected to the laws, the businessman is not likely to be *systematically* subjected to them (even if he is subjected to some of them 'over time') or to have *interdependent interests*. By contrast, this may be the case for the resident alien.

Now, that interdependent interests are normatively relevant empirical facts for the applicability of the ideal of democracy does not take away the fact they are products of morally arbitrary and contingent causes.[37] Moreover, democracy is merely one ideal among several that we strive towards. In fact, it is not even the only ideal that is valuable for elaborating the notion of political legitimacy, since we would also want political authority to be sufficiently just. Contexts of interdependent interests are only *one* context of political justification and we should be able to require that authority is politically legitimate also under circumstances in which people's interests are not interdependent and thus when democracy is not applicable. To address this question and account for its complexity from the standpoint of discourse theory as well as position the proposed equal influence principle in the larger context of justificatory practices among discursive agents in the space of reasons, I find Forst's work particularly valuable since he distinguishes between different contexts of justification.

Following Forst, I consider the right to justification to be the best candidate for a criterion of rightness in both 'contexts of moral justification' and 'contexts of political justification', the difference being that the former concern interpersonal moral conduct, whilst the latter concern legal, political and institutional structures. To these two contexts of justification, however, I have added 'contexts of interdependent interests', which is a specific kind of political context. These contexts are neither mutually exclusive nor mutually constitutive, since a moral context of justification need not be a political context, whereas a context of interdependent interests is always a kind of political context.

The equal respect for autonomous agency forms the normative basis for the evaluation of all three contexts of justification, requiring that our normative considerations be guided by the right to justification. However, the specification of this abstract right varies depending on context. On the proposed account, there is a division

---

[37] Christiano, 'A Democratic Theory of Territory', p. 87.

of labour between the all affected principle and the all subjected principle. In both moral and general political contexts, justification is understood as a discursive process whose primary addressees are those who are *relevantly affected*, in line with Forst. As we have seen, however, the all affected principle is not appropriate for theorizing democratic legitimacy and justified (democratic) inclusion.[38] Instead, in contexts of interdependent interests, a particular version of the all subjected principle is applied, securing the equal influence among those who are systematically and over time *subjected* to the decisions and laws.[39]

To illustrate this, take the nuclear plant Barsebäck located at the south coast of Sweden, very close to Denmark. From the view defended here, Danes should not have an equal influence over the democratic decision-making in Sweden, because they are not systematically and over time subjected to Swedish laws. Neither is the realization of nearly all of their fundamental interests connected with the realization of nearly all fundamental interests of Swedes. However, their fundamental

---

[38] Of course, this does not imply that democracy cannot be instrumentally justified in contexts of political justification generally, for example, as the best practical device for securing our interest in non-domination or the just distribution of primary goods (E. Erman, and A. Follesdal, 'Multiple Citizenship: Normative Ideals and Institutional Challenges', *Critical Review of International Social and Political Philosophy* 15(3), 2012), 279–302. Neither does it imply that there aren't other normative ideals of importance in the space of reasons (G. A. Cohen, 'Facts and Principles', *Philosophy & Public Affairs* 31(3), (2003), 211–45, at pp. 244–45). As with the application of any normative principle, assessments, judgements and trade-offs will inevitably have to be made between ideal conditions against the backdrop of the specific social context in which the action is supposed to take place, specifying which conditions to prioritize and for what reasons (R. Goodin, 'Political Ideals and Political Practice', *British Journal of Political Science* 25(1), (1995), 37–56; I. Kant, 'On the common saying: this may be true in theory, but it does not apply in practice', in H. S. Reiss (ed.), *Kant's Political Writings*. Cambridge: Cambridge University Press, 1970; O. O'Neill, 'Abstraction, idealization and ideology in ethics', in J. D. G. Evans (ed.), *Moral Philosophy and Contemporary Problems*. Cambridge: Cambridge University Press, 1987).

[39] In order to protect the equal respect for autonomous agency in contexts of political justification, I argue, the right to justification requires the fulfilment of two conditions in order for institutions to be *politically* legitimate: first, the *substantive* condition that subjects' fundamental interests be secured through a set of basic rights, including political rights; and second, the *procedural* condition that channels and procedures are established on the basis of and through this set of basic rights, which secure the opportunity for discursive agents *relevantly affected* by the decisions and laws of a political arrangement to demand *acceptable reasons* from it.

interests are still affected in relevant ways by decisions made by the Swedish people concerning Barsebäck. Therefore, some kind of 'say' for Danes concerning this particular issue is called for, so that they have an institutionalized opportunity to require acceptable reasons for the decisions taken (see note 39 for details).

7

Justice and the Basic Right to Justification

Simon Caney
Professor of Political Theory, University of Oxford, UK

Rainer Forst's work on the right to justification represents an important contribution to contemporary theories of justice and democracy.[1] It presents a rich systematic account of justice – one that has an attractive unity.[2] I am sympathetic to many of its themes – its defence of a kind of universalism; its sensitivity to power, exploitation and oppression; its commitment to justification and reason-giving; and its treatment of global justice and injustice. I agree with its response to those who argue that human rights discourse is necessarily guilty of ethnocentrism, and am also in agreement with its analysis of Rawls's *The Law of Peoples*. Moreover, I admire Forst's capacity to discuss and integrate some very different thinkers and traditions of thought. In short: the account developed in *The Right to Justification* is a powerful and appealing one.

As the title suggests, the account that Forst develops and defends has at its heart the concept of a 'right to justification'. My aim in this paper is to explore this concept, and thereby, the theory of justice that Forst develops. To do so, I shall begin by outlining the nature of his account of justice as I understand it (Section I). I would then like to examine two specific features of Forst's account – namely his account of what I

---

[1] All references in the text are to R. Forst, *The Right to Justification: Elements of a Constructivist Theory of Justice*, trans. by J. Flynn. New York: Columbia University Press, 2012.
[2] Although I argue below that we should in fact resist the attractions of this unified account and adopt something that is somewhat less unified but which is, so I argue, a more accurate reflection of our fundamental moral commitments.

shall term the 'nature' of justice and the 'scope' of justice. I begin with the former.

Forst offers an account of justice that is, as he recognizes, 'monistic' in an important sense (p. 195) for it reduces (and subsumes) all justice claims to one core idea (captured by the idea of a Basic Right to Justification). I argue that justice does not have this monistic character, and I seek, in particular, to defend a way of thinking about distributive justice that Forst criticizes. My aim here, though, is not to reject Forst's ideal of a right to justification, but rather to argue that at its most basic and fundamental level justice involves *both* a 'distributive' component as well as the 'procedural' component that Forst defends. Forst accords primacy to what I am calling the 'procedural' component: I think, though, that there are two distinct types of justice and, crucially, that neither is reducible to the other. So, in place of his monism I offer a more pluralistic conception of justice with different types of claim, none of which can be subsumed by each other.

I then turn to Forst's account of the *scope* of the right of justification (Section III) (specifically, when does it apply and who owes a duty of justification to whom?). My suggestion is that Forst's account of the scope of the right of justification is drawn too narrowly.

Forst's account of justice

Let me begin by outlining Forst's account of justice. As I interpret it, Forst's approach contains the following core features.

The Nature of Justice and Injustice: First, he insists that the core idea of justice is avoiding arbitrariness. More specifically, on his view, justice is concerned with avoiding arbitrary *rule*. Thus Forst writes in Chapter 8 that 'the core idea of a just order . . . consists in the idea that its rules and institutions of social life be *free of all forms of arbitrary rule or domination*' (p. 189). In the light of this, Forst argues, justice – the avoidance of such arbitrariness and in particular arbitrary rule – requires what he terms the 'basic right of justification' (hereafter BRJ). Rule would not be arbitrary if its exercise were justified – if the right of the people to justification is met.

The Basic Right of Justification – Reciprocity and Generality. This then poses the question: What does justification involve? Forst's reply to this is that justification must have two features: it must exhibit 'reciprocity' and 'generality'. It is worth unpacking these two notions. Forst understands reciprocity as follows: A participant acts reciprocally when they do not seek simply to advance their own interests, but rather affords a similar status to the interests of others. Participants motivated by a sense of reciprocity accord to others the same benefits and opportunities that they call for themselves. The second feature of the right of justification is 'generality': participants honour this constraint when they include all and do not arbitrarily exclude anyone. In Forst's words:

> The criterion of reciprocity means that none of the parties concerned may claim certain rights or privileges it denies to others and that the relevance and force of the claims at issue are not determined one-sidedly; generality means that all those affected have an equal right to demand justifications. (pp. 129–30)

Scope. We can now ask: What triggers the right of justification? What is the scope of the BRJ? Forst often writes that the BRJ arises when people are 'affected by' social processes of various kinds. He says of the '*basic right to justification*' that '[t]his right expresses the demand that there be no political or social relations of governance that cannot be adequately justified to *those affected by them*' (p. 2: emphasis added). I shall say more about this later but want to turn now to two further implications of Forst's view.

Justification. The first is: Why is *this* the appropriate response? For Forst, I think, the answer has to do with his philosophical anthropology. He affirms a rationalist conception of human nature. We are (exclusively?) reason-giving beings. He often invokes this conception of human nature. The thought then is that to show persons the respect that they are owed political actors is to owe them a duty of justification – not only this, but also they are owed the specific kind of justification described above.

Implications. My next question is: What implications does this Basic Right to Justification have? Forst argues (plausibly in my view) that to realize the BRJ the participants are entitled to (i) rights to individual liberty (civil rights), (ii) the right to take part in politics (political rights) and (iii) the material resources required for persons to enjoy those rights (economic rights) (p. 262). A political order that satisfies these would be, in Forst's terms, a 'minimally just discursive basic structure' (p. 262). He argues that these kinds of rights must be honoured in both domestic contexts and at the international level. The international system must, for example, be structured in such a way that it does not undermine, but rather supports, democratic deliberation within political communities.

Alternatives. If we wish to defend a view, it often helps to know the alternative that the author is rejecting. Forst gives a clear account of *one* of the views he seeks to dislodge in the Introduction.[3] There he contrasts two pictures of justice. According to the first picture, justice is conceived of being as primarily concerned with the fair distribution of burdens and benefits. In Forst's words, it 'concentrates on what individuals are due in terms of a just distribution of goods. This leads to either reasoning in relative terms through a comparison of each person's provision of goods, or it leads to the question of whether individuals have "enough" essential goods irrespective of comparative considerations' (pp. 3–4). This alternative view is also discussed in Chapter 8 where he writes:

> the contemporary discussion seems to suggest that we view justice itself as a largely empty shell, which can only be filled in with substantive values, values that specify the respects in which social institutions are

---

[3] Elsewhere he makes it clear how he differs from others (such as communitarians). I focus on his opposition to those who affirm a 'distributive' approach because I want to defend it.

to be free of arbitrariness. Justice would then be normatively dependent
on this content and these values. I will show how misleading this view
is by briefly going through various notions that are taken to be the basis
for justice: freedom, equality, basic needs, democracy, and recognition.
(p. 189)

Forst finds approaches which identify the core notion of justice as one
centred around the correctness of distribution of resources wholly
unsatisfactory. The distribution of burdens and benefits matters, of
course, for Forst (p. 4), but on his view it is secondary. The primary – or
fundamental – nature of justice is that persons implicated in social and
economic processes have a basic right to justification – to a discursive
process of justification which honours the norms of reciprocity and
generality.

Having given a *very* rough and necessarily brief outline of some of the
key features of Forst's account, I now wish to consider three aspects of
his approach that I think merit further exploration. I begin with Forst's
critique of the 'distributive' approach, and then turn to two features of
his own preferred approach.

What is wrong with the other picture of justice? The 'Two Picture' View

§1. As noted above, Forst contrasts his view with an alternative picture
of justice. My first critical comment is going to be that I don't think that
we have been given enough reason to reject this alternative. Instead,
I suggest, we should endorse a hybrid view that encompasses both
the first picture and Forst's view, *and which treats neither as the sole
fundamental consideration*. In my view, justice is a hybrid concept with
many different components that can pull in different directions. Forst
offers what is in one sense a monistic theory that has a common root –
justice simply is the Basic Right of Justification. He writes in Chapter 10
that 'the question of the justifiability of power, rule, and coercion' is 'the
first question of justice' (p. 239). I think that it is *one* of the questions of

justice but not that it is the only or the first or the most basic question. As I reported at the start, I incline to a more pluralistic view. On this pluralistic view, justice has the following features:

(1) an account of how burdens and benefits should be distributed (Distributive Justice),
(2) an account of the justified exercise of political power (Political Justice or Legitimacy) *and*
(3) neither (1) nor (2) is more basic.

Condition (3) is of critical importance. As noted above, Forst does not deny that justice involves the distribution of burdens and benefits (p. 4) – no one could plausibly deny that – but he denies it primacy. The just distribution of such burdens and benefits, on his view, is not the *root* idea of justice, and it is subordinate to Forst's account of the just exercise of power (what I am referring to as (2) above). What constitutes a just distribution of burdens and benefits simply is that defined by the BRJ. I think, by contrast, that (1) has a separate existence. On my view, the fairest distribution of burdens and benefits is *not* defined by the BRJ but is derived (at least partially) independently of the BRJ. (I say 'at least partially' because I agree that the securing the BRJ has distributive implications. My point is that distributive justice is not *wholly* derived from the BRJ.) On this view, the nature of distributive justice is not reducible to either, (a), what is presupposed by the BRJ (the material conditions that must be realized for people to engage in the necessary dialogue or, (b), what is produced by the BRJ (i.e. the decisions that emerge from the political process).[4] Let us call this the 'Two Picture View'.[5]

§2. Let me explain why we should hold on to the first picture of justice as representing an autonomous part of the concept of justice. I shall do

---

[4] I am thus querying Forst's statement in Chapter 12 that 'it is mistaken to assume that distributive justice and political justice, as freedom from domination, require distinct normative considerations' (p. 258).
[5] See, in this context, Nancy Fraser's 'perspectival dualism' in 'Social Justice in the Age of Identity Politics: Redistribution, Recognition, and Participation', in N. Fraser and A. Honneth *Redistribution or Recognition? A Political-Philosophical Exchange*, trans. by J. Golb, J. Ingram, and C. Wilke. London: Verso, 2003, p. 63ff.

so by Forst's reasons for rejecting it. Forst engages in a critique of it in at least three places – first in the Introduction, then in Chapter 8 ('Social Justice, Justification, and Power') and in his discussion of conceptions of global justice that conform to the first picture in Chapter 11 ('Justice, Morality, and Power in the Global Context'). Let's consider the Introduction first. In a compressed passage Forst indicates four faults in the first picture. Though the passage is lengthy, it is worth quoting in full. Forst writes of the first picture:

> this picture not infrequently ends up cutting out essential dimensions of justice, such as, first, the issue of how the goods to be distributed come "into the world," that is, questions of production and how it should be justly organized. But even more so, second, the political question of who determines structures of production and distribution – and in what way – is thereby ignored, as if there could be a giant distribution machine that would merely have to be programmed correctly. But such a machine is not acceptable not simply because justice would then no longer be understood as an achievement of subjects themselves, which would make subjects into passive recipients; in addition, and this is the third point, this idea neglects the fact that justifiable claims to goods are not simply "given," but can only be established discursively in appropriate procedures of justification. Fourth, a perspective fixated on goods also has the potential to block out the question of injustice, for insofar as it concentrates on a shortage of goods to be rectified, those who suffer from privation as a result of a natural disaster are viewed like those who suffer the same lack of goods from economic or political exploitation. To be sure, these are both rightly viewed as cases in which help is applicable, though in one case as an act of moral solidarity and in the other as an act of justice, the latter differentiated according to one's involvement in conditions of exploitation and injustice and according to the means at one's disposal to change these. If one ignores this difference, one can end up in a dialectic of morality that views an act as generous aid when it is actually required by justice. Autonomous persons are thereby turned from subjects into objects of justice, and then become objects of aid or charity.

For these reasons, precisely when it is a question of distributive justice, it is essential to see the *political* point of justice and free oneself from the false picture, which highlights only the quantity of goods (as important as that surely is). In accord with a second, more appropriate picture, which conveys the fundamental impulse against arbitrariness, justice – which always includes an analysis of injustice – must aim at intersubjective relations and structures, not at a subjective or supposedly objective provision of goods. (p. 4)

Let's consider each of these in turn.

§3. Consider then the first: The first picture is said to neglect 'the issue of how the goods to be distributed come "into the world," that is, questions of production and how it should be justly organized' (p. 4).

In Reply: This might fit what Nozick terms 'end-state' theories of justice, but I don't think it has any force against 'historical' theories.[6] Indeed one of Nozick's central points is that this is what is wrong with certain conceptions of justice, but is amply recognized by his own account. Moreover, I think (contrary to Nozick) that very many theories of justice – including those of Rawls, Dworkin, Sen and Cohen – are concerned with 'how goods come into the world'. Robert van der Veen and Philippe van Parijs brought this out nicely in their 'Entitlement Theories of Justice: From Nozick to Roemer and Beyond' where they persuasively argue that many theories of justice (including Rawls's) have a 'historical' component.[7] Their point carries over to other theories not discussed by them. For luck egalitarians, for example, the historical genesis is very relevant to determining whether a given state of affairs is just or not, for luck egalitarians care whether a given outcome is the product of 'brute luck' or 'option luck'.[8] I also don't think it is fair to

---

[6]   R. Nozick, *Anarchy, State, and Utopia*. New York: Basic Books, 1974, p. 155.

[7]   R. van der Veen and P. van Parijs, 'Entitlement Theories of Justice: From Nozick to Roemer and Beyond', *Economics and Philosophy* 1(1), (1985), 69–81.

[8]   These terms come, of course, from R. Dworkin, *Sovereign Virtue: The Theory and Practice of Equality*. Cambridge, MA: Harvard University Press, 2000, p. 73ff. Note that Dworkin denies that he is a 'luck egalitarian': 'Equality, Luck and Hierarchy', *Philosophy & Public Affairs* 31(2), (2003), 190–8. See, however, Scheffler's persuasive response: S. Scheffler 'Equality as the Virtue of Sovereigns: A Reply to Ronald Dworkin', *Philosophy & Public Affairs* 31(2), (2003), 200.

say that this view need be silent on the just organization of systems of production. Rawlsians will want to design the basic structure – including the workplace and organization of firms – in ways which affirm the 'social bases of self-respect' (which is, of course, one of Rawls's primary goods), and thereby promote the realization of the difference principle.[9] This takes us to the second consideration adduced by Forst.

§4. Forst's second point is that the first picture ignores 'the political question of who determines structures of production and distribution – and in what way' (p. 4).

In Reply: Two points can be made in response to this. The first follows on from the last paragraph. I think that the mainstream theories of distributive justice have the conceptual resources to take into account these questions (and, given their commitments, they must in fact do so). Consider again Rawls's notion of the 'social bases of self-respect'. To further this good will, however, have great implications for the structure of production and distribution. Realizing the Rawlsian ideal is incompatible with just sending everyone a certain package of goods; it requires, for example, among other things a workplace that is organized in such a way as to embody reciprocity and promote the social bases of self-respect.[10]

Second: let us suppose that a wholly distributive approach does neglect this aspect. My second point is that, without further argument, this *cannot* show that we should reject the first picture. It can show only that we need to augment it. This is what my proposed Two Picture View does. It says that there are two questions – (a) what is a fair distribution of burdens and benefits (distributive justice) and (b) who should

---

[9] For the social bases of self-respect, see J. Rawls, *Justice as Fairness: A Restatement*, ed. E. Kelly. Cambridge, MA: Harvard University Press, 2001, p. 59. For good discussion of the implications of the social bases of self-respect for the organization of power in the workplace (and, more generally, for a discussion of how Rawlsian ideals entail a commitment to preventing power and domination in economic life), see M. O'Neill, 'Free (and Fair) Markets without Capitalism: Political Values, Principles of Justice, and Property-Owning Democracy', in ibid. and T. Williamson (eds), *Property Owning Democracy: Rawls and Beyond*. Oxford: Blackwell, 2011, esp. pp. 87–91. See also M. O'Neill, 'Three Rawlsian Routes towards Economic Democracy', *Revue de Philosophie Économique* 8(2), (2008), 29–55.

[10] See again the papers by O'Neill cited in the preceding footnote.

exercise power and how should they do so (political justice/legitimacy). And, it insists, neither can be fully captured by, nor can be subsumed under, the other. Thus someone might answer:

(a) with respect to the first question: I think that justice requires economic equality

(b) with respect to the second question: I think that those who are democratically elected should exercise power and should do so in ways that they can justify to those governed by them.

Moreover, they might then add: we might come up with different answers to the two questions. For example, *I* think that justice requires equality, but I also think that a political actor may be exercising power legitimately even if they do not pursue these egalitarian ideals so long as they can justify their decisions to those they govern (and the system meets certain civil rights and socio-economic standards). In short: the second consideration *logically cannot* give us reason to reject the first picture. Justice does include the question 'who decides?', but it does not include just that.

§5. Consider now the third consideration: the first picture is said to neglect 'the fact that justifiable claims to goods are not simply "given," but can only be established discursively in appropriate procedures of justification' (p. 4).

In Reply: I think we need to be very clear on what we mean by 'justifiable' in this context. Let us distinguish between the justification required for *political legitimacy* (political justification) and the justification required for a view to be *philosophically correct* (philosophical justification). Now the claim that political legitimacy-justification might require a discursive justification through political 'procedures of justification' seems plausible (though not uncontroversial). However, it does not follow from this that my views on justice are only (philosophically) sound and correct if they have gone through the same political process. So – in line with the first picture – one can say that Rawls's or Dworkin's or Nozick's views are justified because they result from a sound philosophical argument, while at the same time agreeing with the second picture – that these may not be enforced through the exercise of political power without some kind of process of political justification. Distributive justice is one thing and political legitimacy is another and, though I think (with Forst) that the second entails some kind of socio-economic preconditions, that does not undermine the fundamental point that they are conceptually distinct (and moreover they might pull us in different directions).

§6. Let us turn now to the fourth consideration. This is a concern that Forst raises both in the Introduction and also in his discussion of global poverty in his chapter on 'Justice, Morality, and Power in the Global Context' (Chapter 11). Forst puts the point like this in his Introduction:

> a perspective fixated on goods also has the potential to block out the question of injustice, for insofar as it concentrates on a shortage of goods to be rectified, those who suffer from privation as a result of a natural disaster are viewed like those who suffer the same lack of goods from economic or political exploitation. To be sure, these are both rightly viewed as cases in which help is applicable, though in one case as an act of moral solidarity and in the other as an act of justice, the latter differentiated according to one's involvement in conditions of exploitation and injustice and according to the means at one's disposal to change these. If one ignores this difference, one can end up in a dialectic of morality that views an act as generous aid when it is actually required by justice. Autonomous persons are thereby turned from subjects into objects of justice, and then become objects of aid or charity. (p. 4)

In short: the distributive view confuses justice with other values like solidarity (and, one might add, compassion and humanity). This might, moreover, have malign effects because by eliding the difference it can transform acts that are 'required by justice' as ones seen as acts of generosity.

Chapter 11 develops the same point at considerable length. It considers those in gruelling poverty. To give it focus it considers the perspective of someone who works at the Serra Pelada goldmine in Brazil. It then considers several different ways of thinking of this person's plight and asking which best captures the normative situation. The possibilities considered are:

(a) a 'humanitarian' approach which emphasizes the duties to meet people's basic needs (pp. 243–4);
(b) a 'humanist' approach which emphasizes a sufficientarian conception of justice (p. 244);
(c) a 'human rights' approach which says that persons have human rights and that the responsibility lies with his or her government (pp. 244–5);
(d) a 'human rights' approach which says that persons have human rights and that the responsibility lies with both national and international actors (p. 245);
(e) an 'egalitarian' approach which takes 'equality' to be the default setting, so to speak, and allows deviations from it only if there is a good reason (p. 246).

Now Forst makes many points against these rival views. Perhaps the central theme, however, is that none of these are adequate because they omit a crucial component – that the people in question are being exploited, that others are the cause of their misery and poverty, that they are powerless and subject to the domination of others. Justice requires that we address this structural inequality and not treat people as passive 'recipient[s]' of benefits but rather as active 'agent[s] of justice' (e.g. pp. 245–6).

In Reply: Two points can be made in response. The first is this: I think that there is a weak and a strong version of Forst's point. The weak version replies: 'any adequate normative account of justice must include the concepts of exploitation, domination and self-government. Any account that omits these is defective'. I wholly agree with this. Given this I think we need to augment accounts (1)–(5) with an account of exploitation, subjugation and oppression. There is, however, a strong version of Forst's argument. This says that the very essence of injustice is exploitation, subjugation and oppression. Exploitation is thus not just one kind of economy injustice: it is a necessary aspect of all economic injustice. This is clearly more controversial and I am not persuaded by this.

This takes me to the second point. Forst often writes that where someone suffers from poverty or malnutrition but that this is not the result of exploitation or subjugation, then there is no injustice. It is morally bad – and we have duties of solidarity and charity to help – but it is not a matter of injustice. I am not sure why we should take this view. There is an established body of thought which takes quite the contrary view. This is, for example, embodied in the Universal Declaration of Human Rights and the United Nations International Covenant on Economic, Social and Cultural Rights. It is the view defended by Henry Shue in *Basic Rights* and many others.[11] It is, for example, affirmed by James Griffin in *On Human Rights* and Amartya Sen in *The Idea of Justice*. Sen, for example, makes it clear that justice is what he terms a 'realization-focused' or 'accomplishment-based' concept – that is, it is concerned with the kinds of 'lives that people can actually live'.[12] David Miller and John Rawls also adopt Shue's approach.[13] I have sought to defend this kind of view in *Justice Beyond Borders* and elsewhere.[14] Given this I don't think we can simply assume that the eradication of poverty that stems wholly from natural causes is necessarily a humanitarian matter as opposed to a matter of justice.

[11] H. Shue, *Basic Rights: Subsistence, Affluence, and U. S. Foreign Policy*, 2nd edition. Princeton: Princeton University Press, 1996.
[12] A. Sen, *The Idea of Justice*. London: Allen Lane, 2009b, pp. 7, 10 and 18.
[13] I include Miller and Rawls because both explicitly endorse Shue's account of basic rights. See D. Miller, *On Nationality*. Oxford: Clarendon Press, 1995, p. 74; and J. Rawls, *The Law of Peoples with 'The Idea of Public Reason Revisited'*. Cambridge, MA: Harvard University Press, 1999c, p. 65.
[14] S. Caney, *Justice Beyond Borders: A Global Political Theory*. Oxford: Oxford University Press, 2005; S. Caney, 'Global Poverty and Human Rights: the Case for Positive Duties', in T. Pogge (ed.), *Freedom from Poverty as a Human Right: Who Owes What to the Very Poor?*. Oxford: Oxford University Press, 2007, pp. 275–302.

Henry Sidgwick tells us in *The Methods of Ethics* that when seeking to define the concept of 'justice' (as well, no doubt, as other moral and political concepts) 'we may, so to speak, clip the ragged edge of common usage, but we must not make excision of any considerable portion'.[15] My worry is that Forst's approach makes an 'excision of [a] considerable portion'. That is, it redefines justice in ways that lose touch with the way in which it is often used.

This last point can be developed further. For someone may quite rightly respond that what I have done so far is challenge Forst's critique of the 'distributive' picture, but I have not given any positive reason to endorse it. This is where Sidgwick's admonition is relevant, for my (positive) suggestion is that wholly subordinating 'distributive' issues to the basic right to justification fails to fit with the ways in which people often think of justice. In many cases, it seems to me, we may want to call a distribution unjust *even if* it arose from a process that was characterized by justification that honoured Forst's norms of reciprocity and generality. The latter, we might say, might give the decision-maker some *legitimacy*, and it may create a reason to obey it. But, in itself, it is insufficient to show that what results is just. If this is right, then it strongly suggests that justice claims do not necessarily conform to Forst's unitary account.

*

It might be helpful to sum up here. I think that Forst's account – a political world in which those who exercise power engage in a process of reciprocal and general dialogue and justification – is a compelling and attractive one. What I am calling into question is the rejection of the other picture of justice – the 'distributive' approach – and the subordination of distributive concerns (the 'distributive' picture, so to speak) to Forst's preferred approach. And, here, my suggestions are that

(1) Forst's account of the first picture may fit some theories, but I don't think that all are vulnerable to his objections. I think that the most

---

[15] H. Sidgwick, *The Methods of Ethics*, 7th edition with a foreword by J. Rawls. Indianapolis: Hackett Publishing Company, 1981, p. 264.

plausible accounts of distributive justice are sensitive to concerns about the nature of the production process and the allocation of power.

(2) Many of Forst's points do not give us reason to reject the first picture. Rather they give us reason to embrace the second picture as well. They are, thus, compatible with what I termed the Two Picture View. Forst, I think, gives us part of the picture, but I am not sure if his view captures the whole of it. Forst's language fits in well with the point that I am making. In the last chapter of the book, he writes, for example, that 'a focus on only distributive justice may be *insufficient*' (p. 258: my emphasis). If this is right, and the 'distributive picture' is on its own 'insufficient', – and I think it is – then the answer is to supplement it. It is not to reject it or to treat it as an aspect of the second picture, but to recognize its autonomy as a normative realm.

Forst may respond that the pluralistic conception must itself appeal to some unifying ideas. It must do so if the 'distributive' and 'procedural' elements that I mention are both to count as being claims of *justice*. This is true. However, it does not establish that the unifying feature is the one that is offered by the *basic right to justification*. We might, for example, say that the common feature that renders them (and other claims) claims of *justice* is simply that they are claims about what *rights* people have. And then we can say that people can have different kinds of rights – some to do with *just decision-making procedures* (a right to justification) and others to do with *just distributions* (a right to a just distribution of burdens and benefits) – rights that may pull us in different directions.

The *scope* of the right to justification

In the remainder of this chapter I want to turn from Forst's critique of other approaches to his outline and defence of his own preferred view.

More specifically I wish to examine what I termed earlier the 'scope' of the basic right of justification (*Who* has the basic right of justification and *against whom* do they hold it? *Who* is the rights-bearer in any given situation? and *Who* has the correlative duty?).

Forst's approach is one of a broad family approaches which affirm the following type of claim:

> All those who stand in a *certain kind of relationship* (**R**) have in virtue of that a certain kind of *entitlement* (**E**).

Many adopt views that have this kind of structure. David Held, for example, writes that 'those whose *life expectancy and life chances are significantly affected by social forces and processes* [the R-component – SC] ought to have *a stake in the determination of the conditions and regulation of these, either directly or indirectly through political representatives* [the E-component – SC]' (words in brackets added by me).[16] And Thomas Pogge writes that 'those *significantly and legitimately affected by a political decision* [the R-component – SC] have a *roughly equal opportunity to influence the making of this decision – directly or through elected delegates or representatives* [the E-component – SC]'.[17] In this section I examine Forst's account of when the basic right of justification is triggered. What kinds of relationship must exist for it to apply?

§1. I have two points to make here. The first is that I am not altogether clear what conditions have to be met for one group of people to have a basic right of justification against others. Forst writes, for example, in Chapter 9 that the basic right of justification 'must include all those affected by actions or norms *in morally relevant ways*' (p. 214: emphasis added). He also writes in Chapter 12 that 'in a given context of justice, all social relations to which one is subject and that can be changed by political action are to be justified reciprocally and generally to all those

---

[16] D. Held, *Global Covenant: The Social Democratic Alternative to the Washington Consensus.* Cambridge: Polity, 2004, p. 100: emphasis added.

[17] T. Pogge, *World Poverty and Human Rights: Cosmopolitan Responsibilities and Reforms,* 2nd edition. Cambridge: Polity, 2008, p. 190: emphasis added. Three footnotes have been omitted.

affected in a relevant way, be they economic relations or relations of political authority' (p. 258: emphasis added). A similar formulation is also given later in Chapter 12: 'the primary context in which this right [the basic right of justification] is situated is the moral context of actions that affect other persons *in a relevant way*' (p. 261: emphasis added). But what are these 'morally relevant ways'? I think that the answer for Forst is: when persons are subjected to economic and political *power, then* they have the BRJ. As noted earlier, Forst writes that justice is essentially concerned with power, rule and domination. This also makes sense of Forst's discussion in Chapter 10 where he argues that the global political and economic context is 'a *context of force and domination*' (p. 234) and hence that the BRJ applies globally. So, I take it that being subject to power triggers the basic right of justification. This, though, raises the question 'what counts as power?' Are we operating with a Foucaultian notion of power (or domination)? Or Dahl's or Lukes's? Or Weber's? Or something else?

§2. Let us suppose that being subject to the power of others generates a right to justification for those who are subjected and a duty of justification on those exercising power. This shows that being subject to power is *sufficient* to grant one a basic right of justification. Forst, however, goes further than this. He appears to hold that being subject to power is both sufficient *and necessary* to trigger the duty of justification. Persons have basic rights of justification only against those who exercise power over them? But why should we hold this? To bring out the issue let us compare two positions.

(a) The systemic view: justice is owed only to co-participants in a system of power.
(b) The humanity-centred view: justice is owed to all persons, in virtue of their humanity.

Forst affirms (a). He does not deny that we may have duties of morality to non-members, but he does not think that we have duties of justice to non-members. Forst is hardly alone in this. Many – such as Thomas

Pogge – affirm (a).[18] (b), however, also has its adherents – including Richard Arneson, Brian Barry, Charles Beitz and David Richards. I too have sought to defend (b).[19]

My question, then, is: why should we endorse (a). I have three comments to make.

§2.1. The first is that I don't think Forst gives a positive defence of (a).

§2.2. The second is that some of the things that Forst does say fit as well (maybe even better) with (b) as they do with (a). For example, Forst appeals on several occasions to a certain conception of human nature to ground his political constructivism. Human beings, he writes, are '*justificatory beings.* They not only have the ability to justify or take responsibility for their beliefs and actions by giving reasons to others, but in certain contexts they see this as a duty and expect that others will do the same' (p. 1). This approach suggests that persons bound together in political and economic governance structures owe others that they affect duties of justification. However – and this is the crucial point – if we think that persons are justificatory beings, then why do we not owe justifications to all persons – whether or not we currently affect them.

Michael Mann once identified a kind of imperialism that he called 'ostracizing imperialism'.[20] This refers to situations where wealthy would-be imperialists eschew contact with a society because they hold that it is not in their interest to conquer them. As Mann puts it, some parts of the world 'are "ostracized" by a capitalism which regards them as too risky for investment and trade'.[21] So such people are disadvantaged

---

[18] Pogge *World Poverty and Human Rights*.

[19] R. J. Arneson, 'Luck Egalitarianism – A Primer', in C. Knight and Z. Stemplowska (eds), *Responsibility and Distributive Justice*. Oxford: Oxford University Press, 2011, pp. 24–50; B. Barry, *Theories of Justice: A Treatise on Social Justice, Volume I*. Hemel Hempstead: Harvester Wheatsheaf, 1989; C. R. Beitz, 'Cosmopolitan Ideals and National Sentiment', *Journal of Philosophy* 80(10), (1983), 591–600; D. A. J. Richards, 'International Distributive Justice', in J. R. Pennock and J. W. Chapman (eds), *Ethics, Economics, and the Law: NOMOS XXIV*. New York: New York University Press, 1982, pp. 275–99. I have also argued along these lines in Caney, *Justice Beyond Borders*, ch. 4.

[20] M. Mann, 'Globalization and September 11', *New Left Review* 12 (November–December 2001), 53.

[21] Mann, 'Globalization and September 11', p. 54.

because they are too poor to colonize. From now on Forst's theory there is no duty of justice to these people because one lacks links with them, but this seems to me questionable. Suppose that they call across the ocean and ask why we do not assist them to overcome the poverty that undermines their capacity to lead autonomous lives. Do we not owe them – as a matter of justice and respect for their common humanity – *any* justification?

§2.3. Consider, finally, a further point that Forst makes. He writes of justice that 'its core meaning is found in its fundamental opposition to arbitrariness' (p. 2). I agree. But (b) can accept this: it simply gives a different interpretation of arbitrariness. It maintains – in line with luck egalitarian thought, but not just luck egalitarian thought – that it is morally arbitrary for some to face such terrible deprivation for the mere fact that they are born in a resource-poor country. So my point then is that (b) fits in with Forst's appeal to our nature as justificatory beings and it fits in with his account of justice-as-opposed-to-arbitrariness. Consider in this light, the research by Jeffrey Sachs,[22] Paul Collier[23] and Ian Morris[24] (among others) on the geographical determinants of people's economic standard of living. It is, I think, arbitrary that some should face much worse opportunities in life merely because they are born in one place rather than another.[25] So (b) can also reflect and accommodate Forst's point that justice stands opposed to arbitrariness. It gives us a different conception of it – but one that I think is compelling – and I am not sure why we should reject this conception and adopt the more narrowly conceived conception that Forst offers us.

[22] J. L. Gallup, J. D. Sachs and A. D. Mellinger, 'Geography and Economic Development', *International Regional Science Review* 22(2), (1999), 179–232; J. L. Gallup and J. D. Sachs, 'The Economic Burden of Malaria', *The American Journal of Tropical Medicine and Hygiene* 64(1) (suppl.), (2001), 85–96.

[23] P. Collier, *The Bottom Billion: Why the Poorest Countries Are Failing and What Can be Done About It*. Oxford: Oxford University Press, 2007.

[24] I. Morris, *Why the West Rules – for Now: The Patterns of History, and What They Reveal About the Future*. London: Profile Books, 2010.

[25] S. Caney, 'Cosmopolitan Justice and Equalizing Opportunities', *Metaphilosophy* 32 (1/2), (2001), 113–34, S. Caney, 'Humanity, Associations and Global Justice: In Defence of Humanity-Centred Cosmopolitan Egalitarianism', *The Monist* 94(4), (2011), 506–34.

Concluding remarks

This brings my analysis to a close. Rainer Forst's *The Right to Justification* raises a number of interesting and important questions. I have focused here on only two of the many questions that one might ask about the key idea of a basic right to justification.[26] The first concerns the very nature of justice. Does Forst give us reason to endorse his monistic account of the nature of justice, and, related to this, do his criticisms of the 'distributive' picture succeed? I have argued that the 'distributive' picture can withstand the objections he levels against it, and, moreover, that we do not have reason to endorse, and have good reason to reject, a single picture of justice of the kind that Forst canvasses. I offer instead a more pluralistic conception.

The second issue concerns the scope. On Forst's view the scope of justice – as expressed by the basic right of justification – is set by certain kinds of socio-economic or political relations. Here I have two concerns. First, it is not clear to me exactly what type of relations generate the BRJ, but it is vital to have a precise account in order to determine who is obligated to engage in justification to whom. Second, it is not clear to me why the scope of the BRJ should be circumscribed in this way.

These disagreements, I hope it is clear, arise within the context of very many shared commitments – commitments to universal values; to freedom, equality and rights; to an opposition to domination and exploitation; and to a commitment to reason and to the importance of justification in contexts of power.

---

[26] A third question that I have not explored here, but which I believe is of fundamental importance is: what exactly *is* justification? Why should we accept Forst's suggestion that it requires reasoning and deliberation characterized by reciprocity and generality?

Part Three

Reply

8

Justifying Justification:
Reply to My Critics

Rainer Forst

The task of replying to the distinguished colleagues gathered here presents an aporia for me. For it is such a great honour and pleasure to have these powerful minds comment on my work that out of sheer gratitude I feel I should applaud everything they say. But at the same time, that would violate the game of giving and asking for reasons that we are playing here – and it would be disrespectful of the marvellous reconstructions and thorough criticisms they have to offer. So I fear I am forced to show my gratitude by a response that explains, defends and refines my often inchoate and muddled views – though not really retracting. But I assume that – knowing me – my dear colleagues also did not quite expect me to go that far.

I also want to express my heartfelt thanks for the completely unde-served privilege of being in the position to reply to these critics – and a special thanks to David Owen who, together with Matt Matravers, organized the wonderful conference at the University of York on my work in June 2011, where a number of these papers (and others which will appear in a second volume) were presented. David was also responsible for organizing a panel at the Annual Meeting of the American Political Science Association in Seattle in September 2011, from which three more papers included here stem.[1] I am deeply indebted to him.

---

[1] There was also a symposium at the American Philosophical Association's Eastern Division Meeting 2012 in Atlanta with comments by Seyla Benhabib, Jeff Flynn and Matthias Fritsch to which I replied; the symposium is forthcoming in *Political Theory*.

From Germany to Scotland – and back

In his excellent piece, Andrea Sangiovanni forces me to clarify my discourse-theoretical constructivism, and I could not think of a better challenge to explain the moral-philosophical 'groundwork' of my Neo-Kantian view. I admire Sangiovanni's work on justice and the relation between morality and politics, and I feel close to his 'practice-dependent' account of justice, though I have some questions about the relation of immanence and transcendence with respect to that.[2] I leave that aside here, as I will have further occasion to comment on my view of practice in replying to some of the other papers.

In a fine instance of Humean-humane empathy and solidarity, Sangiovanni wants to save me from German rationalism and asks me to join the club of what he calls Scottish constructivists, which strikes me as a rather new club, given that constructivism generally holds that the principles of construction are principles of practical reason – implying a notion of practical reason for which Hume had little time. So I think that Sangiovanni's Scotland is already closer to the Continent than is normally the case. Still, according to him, 'rationalist constructivism' cannot stand on its own feet as long as it lacks a good account of moral emotions, like empathy. For him, these 'contingent human sensibilities' present the 'seat of normativity' (58); in other words, only where empathy is coupled with 'deliberative reflection and action' (62) can we find the very ground of morality.

I think I should, in typical dialectical fashion, agree and (mostly, I fear) disagree: Empathy is an important capacity of responsible moral agents, but it can only be such if it is guided by practical reason and indeed a part of practical reason, properly understood. Otherwise, empathy can be partial and thus also be 'morally blind', to use Sangio-vanni's term, to which I will return. In conjunction with norm-guided practical deliberation, empathy is a necessary condition for engaging

---

[2]   See my 'Transnational Justice and Democracy. Overcoming Three Dogmas of Political Theory', in Eva Erman and Sofia Näsström (eds), *Political Equality in Transnational Democracy.* New York: Palgrave Macmillan, 2013d, 41–59.

in moral justification in the right way, but that does not mean that it has a 'grounding' role to play. For the reconstruction of the moral point of view follows another route and presupposes a reconstruction of moral validity claims and criteria for their justification (one notion of 'grounding' I use),[3] and, furthermore, the validity of the fundamental right and the categorical duty of justification cannot be made contingent upon the existence of certain humanitarian motives of persons (another notion of 'grounding'). In a nutshell, that would be to mistake a *justificatory* and an *explanatory* account of moral action and to exchange the standpoint of the first and second person with that of the third person – a mistake easily made by those fully enthralled by Scottish empiricism, as Andrea Sangiovanni is not, I believe.

According to my Kantian view of the autonomy of morality, morality can only be based on *moral* grounds, namely on the respect for every other person as an equal in the normative space of justifications, regardless of how close to or distant one feels from him or her. Moral empathy thus has gone through the filter of justificatory reason, not the other way around, for it recognizes the moral status of others as equals and thereby abstracts from the different ways in which we empathize with others as an empirical and emotional fact. That does not mean that moral respect only regards others as 'generalized others', as Seyla Benhabib once called it[4]; rather, it asks us to respect others as 'concrete', finite and needy, and yet still through a generalizing lens, not giving priority to some persons that could not be justified to all others as equals. As moral persons, we are all equal authorities in the realm of reasons.

But I am leaping ahead. In order to do justice to Sangiovanni's rescue efforts and in order to try to save him from Humeanism in return,

---

[3] For the different ways to understand what it means to 'ground' morality, see my *The Right to Justification*, New York: Columbia University Press, 2012a, 22f. (henceforth *RJ*).

[4] Seyla Benhabib, *Situating the Self. Gender, Community and Postmodernism in Contemporary Ethics*. New York: Routledge, 1992, ch. 5. See also the exchange between Rainer Forst, 'Situations of the Self: Reflections on Seyla Benhabib's Version of Critical Theory', *Philosophy & Social Criticism* 23 (1997), 79–96, and Benhabib, 'On Reconciliation and Respect, Justice and the Good Life: Response to Herta Nagl-Docekal and Rainer Forst', ibid., pp. 97–114.

I will start from the basic tenets of Sangiovanni's fine reconstruction of constructivism. There is much I agree with here, such as the thesis about the 'stance-dependence' of moral claims (31), yet I would emphasize the non-arbitrary, rational character of that stance, being guided by principles of practical reason. (I will come back to my notion of reason and that of Sangiovanni, for there one of our basic disagreements seems to lie.) Sangiovanni is also correct in locating my constructivism in the camp that makes no strong metaphysical investments – I call it a 'practical' and not a 'metaphysical' form of constructivism.[5] That means that the reconstruction of reasonable principles of construction can remain agnostic about whether in following these principles moral reasons are 'produced' or 'discovered'.

In a further important step, Sangiovanni emphasizes that construc-tivists believe that the proper procedure of construction (or justification) generates categorical moral reasons and norms which 'bind us whether or not we desire to be so bound or have an interest in being so bound' (33). As I said above and as Sangiovanni affirms himself (59), this is no small burden for any form of constructivism that aims to settle on Scottish turf.

Furthermore, Sangiovanni rightly stresses, as do I, that Kantian constructivists in particular need to explain the strong normativity of the constraints and principles of the justification procedure. And since this form of normativity obviously cannot be generated through the procedure which it is to ground, Sangiovanni sees a dilemma there: either one refers to an independent set of moral values to justify the procedure and thus includes a heteronomous normative element or one looks for non-moral grounds and then lacks moral reasons to engage in the procedure in the first place. This is indeed a problem that has haunted many discussions of constructivism[6]; and it has led to

---

[5] *RJ*, p. 50.

[6] See, for example, Onora O'Neill, *Constructions of Reason. Explorations of Kant's Practical Philosophy.* Cambridge: Cambridge University Press, 1989, chs 3 and 11. Christine Korsgaard, *The Constitution of Agency. Essays on Practical Reason and Moral Psychology.* Oxford: Oxford University Press, 2008, ch. 10.

different versions of it that Sangiovanni calls – following Susan Street – 'restricted' and 'unrestricted constructivism' (34). In that connection, I have criticized Habermas's constructivist discourse theory for not providing adequate moral grounds for the normativity of the discourse principle.[7] My own suggestion tries to avoid that dilemma by interpreting the principle of justification in moral contexts as a moral principle of practical reason, thus going back to Kant's essential thesis that the categorical imperative is a *moral* principle of practical *reason*. There is no magic involved in such a dilemma-avoiding move, as a Humean would think: for practical reason would be a half-baked faculty if it only told you *how* to justify yourself morally, but not *that* you need to do so. Unpacking this 'that' is not an easy task, as I will explain in a second, but it can be done if we reconstruct the kind of moral responsibility that we have as persons who are always already participants in practical contexts where moral claims are raised by ourselves and others and where the expectation to make good on them is the most natural expectation – an expectation both reasonable and moral. The overarching principle of reason says that you ought to base your actions on reasons proper to justify them, depending on context, and in moral contexts that means that you have a duty of justification to provide morally justifiable – reciprocally and generally non-rejectable – reasons for actions that concern others in a morally relevant way. Thus the dilemma dissolves: there are free-standing moral grounds for the duty and right of justification, yet they do not refer to a set of values distinct from the practice of justification – indeed, the right to justification is the most basic right that moral persons as agents of justification have, and respecting persons as ends in themselves means to respect them as having that right. The practice of justification is a *normative* practice, and to be part of it means to understand the particular kind of normativity relevant to moral contexts (which is a special area of justification). Practical reason is the faculty of engaging in practices of practical justification, and there is no reason why we

---

[7]   *RJ*, pp. 55–7 and 77f.

should truncate that faculty by reducing it to a 'know-how' and cutting the 'know-that' out. In other words, with Kant I believe that practical reason determines the will of reasonable moral persons.

Thus I find Sangiovanni's distinction between the two kinds of constructivism overdrawn. Every form of constructivism has to be restricted in such a way that its very foundations cannot be constructed in the same way as the norms generated in the constructivist procedure, as I argue in my book.[8] But that does not mean that the normativity of the constructivist procedure stems from an arbitrary set of independent values or conventions. I cannot go into the interesting discussion of Rawls and Scanlon that Sangiovanni presents, but would like to emphasize that even in *Political Liberalism* Rawls stresses that only 'principles' and 'ideas' of practical reason are the non-constructed but reconstructed basis of the constructivist procedure – the important 'ideas of reason' being the relevant moral-political conceptions of society and person which 'characterize the agents who reason and specify the context of practical questions'.[9] And in Scanlon's theory, I also find that the 'ideal of justifiability to others'[10] he cites as the reason to be moral expresses the immanent moral normativity of the constructivist procedure that practically reasonable persons accept – thus an ideal of reason, so to speak, not being dependent upon a certain conception of the good, as Sangiovanni thinks (41).

As far as my own account is concerned, it is more modest than a full-blown constitutivist account which implied that in order to be a rational agent or person at all one needs to follow the precepts of morality. I suggest that to be *fully* reasonable in a practical sense, one must be able and willing to provide adequate reasons for one's morally relevant actions – yet I do not think that someone who lacks that capacity is

---

[8] Ibid., pp. 48 and 84 and already Rainer Forst, *Contexts of Justice. Political Philosophy beyond Liberalism and Communitarianism*, trans. J. Farrell. Berkeley and Los Angeles: University of California Press, 2002, ch. IV.2.

[9] John Rawls, *Political Liberalism*. New York: Columbia University Press, 1993, p. 108. See also my discussion of Rawls's constructivism in ch. 4 of *RJ*.

[10] Thomas M. Scanlon, *What We Owe to Each Other*. Cambridge, MA: Harvard University Press, 1998, p. 156.

not capable of acting, deliberating or communicating. He or she is just limited in this ability and violates the norms valid in moral contexts. So I do hold what Sangiovanni calls 'justificatory constitutivism' (44) as far as I think that to orient ourselves in the space of reasons we need to have the capacity and willingness to follow the reasons that are adequate in the contexts in which we move – some theoretical, some practical and of the practical ones some moral, some ethical, some legal, political, professional or what have you (and some mixed, of course). So the moral capacity is not constitutive of the whole game of asking for and giving reasons, only of a particular one. Thus it is a limited constitutivism which I defend. But with respect to moral contexts, I do indeed think that we must, as participants inevitably affecting others, accept the duty of justification. Accepting that duty and also one's right to justification categorically constitutes us as *moral* persons – but we can also be persons and *rational* agents without accepting this duty, just not fully *reasonable* moral persons.

Sangiovanni presents a very illuminating discussion of cases of moral blindness, and as I said above, I agree that a certain form of empathy belongs to being a responsible moral agent – yet I do not see this as separate from practical reason properly understood, nor do I think that this is a grounding issue. For it is misleading to say that only persons with certain abilities and dispositions have moral duties and that thus there are no universal and categorical duties (I am not sure Sangiovanni would say this). Rather, when someone seems to act amorally rather than immorally, we might have to shift our perspective towards him – from the participant's perspective of the first and second person to that of a third person trying to explain what is 'wrong' with someone. But that is an explanatory form of discourse, not a justificatory one. It does not touch the normative question of moral duties in a fundamental way.

I do not deny that there are cases of moral blindness as Sangiovanni describes them. And I also do not doubt that they are connected to a pathological lack of empathy. Yet I would also add cases of moral blindness due to an overflow of empathy, either such that you give – 'unreasonable', as we say – privilege to your own family or people of your age, or such that you forget yourself in a selfless and self-damaging way in helping others. Thus empathy itself is not yet a moral quality of persons, as it can have lots of amoral or immoral results. Sangiovanni is aware of these problems (59) and thus only counts a particular form of empathy among the requirements of morality: to be able to see in others – and in all others – their humanity, that is, 'as bearing the same range of sensibilities, concerns, emotions as we do, and that are typical of all human beings' (58). I would add that another side of moral empathy is also to be sensitive to the ways in which others are *not* like us, but I leave that aside here. What I want to point out is that the quote by Sangiovanni makes it clear that, contrary to what he says, empathy cannot have a grounding role, for it is *only* those aspects of empathy that belong to an impartial form of justificatory morality to which he refers, and thus the grounding relation goes in the other direction: morality asks us to cultivate those forms of empathy that sustain it.

Thus the kind of empathy required for morality is a form of *reasonable* empathy, guided by principles such as treating like cases alike, treating all persons equally and so on. So this is no faculty separate from reason; indeed, it is guided by reason in following the criteria of reciprocity and generality. As Kant remarks, moral emotions cannot give us the criteria of moral justification, but they accompany our interest in acting from the right reasons.[11] The true moral feeling he thought was based on respect for the moral law. I, however, would say that it is based on the respect for others as directed by the moral law that calls us to treat them as justificatory equals. Thus the main 'organ', contrary to what Sangiovanni says, to 'respond to moral reasons' (51) is reason, properly understood, and only through that does the right form of empathy come to the fore. (I sometimes think it is those who criticize rationalism harshly who are the most radical rationalists, since

---

[11]   Immanuel Kant, *Groundwork of the Metaphysics of Morals*, trans. M. Gregor. Cambridge: Cambridge University Press, 1998, p. 64 (Prussian Academy Edition 4:460); Kant, *Critique of Practical Reason*, trans. M. Gregor. Cambridge: Cambridge University Press, 1997, pp. 62–70 (5:72–82).

they purify rationality so much of normative content.) In other words, empathy does not make us 'see' moral reasons (53); rather, reason makes us see them and empathy is an aspect of that seeing. Reason is not just an instrument. The wrong involved in failing to take up the moral point of view is indeed not primarily a type of 'rational inconsistency' (57) – though it is that, too. Basically, it is a failure of the form of moral empathy that we expect of competent reasonable agents, emphasizing the difference between *rationality* and *reason* as Kantians do.

So seeing the humanity in others in the moral context is a particular way of seeing others. It means to respect others as ends in themselves, that is, as justificatory equals who have a right to justification such that I am not free to determine what I can justifiably do to them, or expect of them. Morality is a relation between us, and it is established by way of justification. Regarding the other as 'human' in a 'humane' way means to see him or her as needy and finite and at the same time as an equal authority in the space of reasons. It means to accept and recognize an 'original' form of responsibility not dependent upon contingent circumstances, but on sharing a world together, and with that world we share a number of practices, one of them being called 'morality'. I am not sure whether someone who gives unjustifiable privilege to his kin or to someone else is not a 'normal' person, as Sangiovanni argues (62) – I would just say this persons lacks the moral corrective in his or her emotional set-up that qualifies him or her as a responsible moral person. Yet that we 'cannot but' respond to others' suffering and vulnerability as if it were our own if we are 'normal' is a very strong thesis of Sangiovanni's bordering on what I would call 'Scottish constitutivism'. As I see it, empathy can take many forms, and the form it needs to take in moral contexts we determine by criteria of reasonable justification, not by a criterion of 'normalcy' versus 'pathology'. When Sangiovanni argues on an earlier page that 'the deliberative standpoint from which we either create or discover moral reasons must also model the particular character of our shared human empathy' (56), he seems to agree – and so I think he can be saved from embarking towards the wrong shore.

Power and reason(s)

There are very few contemporary theorists who have thought about power as originally and comprehensively as has Amy Allen.[12] I have learnt from her and keep learning from her, probably more than she thinks I do. That is because, on one view, our positions seem to be strictly at odds, while in other ways, they are very close. Her critique motivates me to make clearer the way in which I take power, justification and reason to be intertwined. With that basic thesis I should not quarrel, only with her critique that my approach cannot account for that intertwinement.

Allen is right to stress that I regard the question of power as the first question of justice – and she is also right to ask me about the theory of power that fits my view. In my work after *The Right to Justification*, I have elaborated on this, but already in that book – as Allen remarks – I argue for a critical theory programme of a 'critique of relations of justification'[13] which analyses not just the lack of acceptable social justifications but also the lack of a language, of social spheres, of individual and collective possibilities and institutions of challenging existing justifications. These are the themes taken up in *Justification and Critique* and in my 'Noumenal Power' essay.[14] Let me explain briefly.

My main ideas with respect to the notion of power are (1) to see it as a normatively neutral phenomenon – assuming that the exercise of power can be good or bad, depending on whether it is justifiable. Amy Allen agrees, as she uses terms like 'domination' or 'subordination' when she talks about negative forms of power. The second idea (2) with which Allen does not quite agree[15] is to locate the phenomenon of

---

[12] See Amy Allen, *The Power of Feminist Theory. Domination, Resistance, Solidarity.* Boulder: Westview, 1999, and *The Politics of Our Selves. Power, Autonomy, and Gender in Contemporary Critical Theory.* New York: Columbia University Press, 2008.

[13] *RJ*, p. 121.

[14] Rainer Forst, *Justification and Critique. Towards a Critical Theory of Politics*, trans. C. Cronin. Cambridge: Polity, 2013, and Forst, 'Noumenal Power', Normative Orders Working Paper 2(2013), (www.normativeorders.net).

[15] See our exchange in 'Power and Reason, Justice and Domination. A Conversation between Amy Allen, Rainer Forst and Mark Haugaard', *Journal of Political Power*, forthcoming.

power primarily in the noumenal space, or less paradoxically sounding, to place power in the space of justifications.[16] So let us define power as *the capacity of A to motivate B to think or do something that B would otherwise not have thought or done.* It is open as to whether this is done for good or bad reasons, for the sake of or contrary to B's interests and by which means. These means can be a 'powerful' speech, a well-founded recommendation, an ideological description of the world, a seduction, a command that is accepted or a threat that is perceived as real. The limiting case is one of pure force, where A moves B purely by way of physical means, by handcuffing him or her or carrying him or her away. At that point, power as a relation between agents turns into physical violence, and the noumenal character vanishes.

Different from the exercise of physical force or violence, a relation of power rests on recognition. This is not necessarily a happy form of recognition, for the threat that is perceived as real is in that very moment also 'recognized' and gives one a reason for action intended by A – but if, as in some cases it happens, the threat by the blackmailer or the kidnapper is no longer seen as serious, their power disappears. They can still use brute force and kill the kidnapped person, but that is rather a sign of having lost power (either over those who are not willing to pay or over the kidnapped person, who refuses to recognize the kidnapper as dominant). Power is what goes on in the head, so to speak, and what goes on is a recognition of a reason (or better and more frequently, various reasons) to act differently than one would have without that reason. This recognition rests on seeing a 'good enough' reason to act; it means to see a *justification* for changing your way, a motivation based on reasons. Power rests on perceived and recognized, accepted justifications – some good, some bad, some in between. A threat can be seen as such a justification, as can a good argument. But power only exists when such an acceptance exists.

Thus the original phenomenon of power is of a noumenal, intellectual nature: *to have power means to be able – and this comes in different*

---

[16] In the following paragraphs, I rely on my 'Noumenal Power'.

degrees – to use, influence, determine, occupy or even to seal the space of reasons for others. This can happen in a singular event – of a powerful speech or a deceit – or in a sequence of events or in a general social situation or structure, where certain social relations are seen as justified, so that a social order comes to be accepted as an *order of justification*. Relations and orders of power are relations and orders of justification; and power arises and persists where justifications arise and persist, especially where they are integrated into certain *narratives of justification*.[17] In their light, social relations and institutions – but also certain ways of acting and thinking – appear legitimate, possibly also as natural or according to God's will. These can be relations of subordination or of equality, political or personal, and the justifications can be well founded and collectively shared with good reasons; they can be merely 'overlapping', or they can be distorted and ideological (i.e. justifying a social situation of asymmetry and subordination with false reasons that could not be shared among free and equal justificatory agents in a discourse free from such asymmetry and distortion).[18] Such a notion of ideology has no strong investment in a notion of 'objective' or 'true interests'. All it implies normatively is a right to justification of normative relations between free and equal persons.

As I see it, a noumenal account of power relations is more 'realistic' than theories that locate power in physical means, be it money or weapons. For it explains all those forms of power that cannot be explained by recourse to such means – the power of speech, of (again: good or bad) arguments, of seduction, of love, of 'acting in concert', of commitments, of religion, of morality, of personal aims, etc. More importantly, it also explains the power of these material means – for money only motivates those who see its use as justified and who have

---

[17] For the notions of orders or narratives of justification, see Rainer Forst and Klaus Günther, 'Die Herausbildung normativer Ordnungen', in Forst and Günther (eds), *Die Herausbildung normativer Ordnungen.* Frankfurt/Main: Campus, 2011, 11–30, and Forst, 'Zum Begriff eines Rechtfertigungsnarrativs', in Andreas Fahrmeir (ed.), *Rechtfertigungsnarrative.* Frankfurt/Main: Campus, 2013, 11–28.

[18] Here I am in agreement with the central insight of Jürgen Habermas' version of critical theory.

aims which make money necessary; and weapons, as I explained above, only serve their function if they are seen as reason-giving. If not, they can still be used to shoot, but then power is transformed into physical violence, and the real intention of using them – being recognized as superior and threatening – might remain unrealized.

So based on that view, I do not think that Allen is right to point out that I use the idea of the power of justification only 'in positive terms' and have no way to explain the use of justification and reasons when it comes to 'legitimate existing relations of domination' (67). My theory of power tries to provide the conceptual tools for exactly this; it is only in understanding the noumenal power of, say, patriarchy, the idea of the free market and other ideological complexes that we understand the power they have over people. So here I agree with Allen in spirit, though not in her critique of my approach.

What I am less sure about is whether I would want to join Allen in saying that 'practical reason' itself is a tool of domination. I believe that many complexes of justifications and hegemonic reasons serve that purpose and that many historical forms of what has been seen as 'reasonable' have been legitimizing domination and oppression.[19] But, as Allen suspects, I would still hold onto the view that reason is the only critical faculty we have to object to such justifications, and so we are back in a dialectical two-worlds-scenario of immanence and transcendence. It is not mysterious or paradoxical to say that many notions of the 'reasonable' have been exclusionary, one-sided, racist, paternalistic, etc. *and* hold onto the idea that a better understanding of what is reciprocally and generally rejectable and what is not is the main means to criticize such forms of domination in the justificatory realm. Indeed, this is unavoidable, and however 'scandalous' or 'impure' (81) social and historical forms of reason have been and as much as we need to critically reflect on the blind spots of our own notions of the 'reasonable', there is no other faculty of seeing through that but the

---

[19] See, for example, Thomas McCarthy, *Race, Empire, and the Idea of Human Development.* Cambridge: Cambridge University Press, 2009.

always imperfect and yet infinitely improvable finite faculty of reason. How could a theory be critical if it did not use that faculty, and indeed, I think that a theory only deserves to be called *critical* if it makes the very principle and practice of rational critique its cornerstone; that is what my idea of a critique of relations of justification does. Reason may always be impure in its finite forms, but that does not mean that we have other ways to overcome its reified and limited forms. I do not see that Allen provides another such faculty. As I will explain below in responding to Kevin Olson, it is a mistake to confound a critical social analysis of given structures of justification with the conceptual and criterial apparatus to do so – an apparatus, to be sure, that constantly directs its criticism also to itself, as any Kantian view would do.[20]

In that connection, I want to respond to a number of the critical claims Allen makes and that relate to the opposition she constructs between her contextualist approach and my discourse theory. First, there is the question of foundationalism. I am happy to be a 'foundationalist' when it comes to the reconstruction of the moral point of view of practical reason, for two reasons. First, it is not a metaphysical foundation I point to, but one we arrive at through proper reflection – it reconstructs the conditions of the possibility of acting with appropriate moral justification. Allen asks why that is not an 'arbitrary' (72) exercise if it is a mere reconstruction. Yet it seems to me that to ask the question in that way reveals a foundationalist desire for a metaphysical security we cannot have. All we have is the best account of the principles of the practice we call the use of reason, and there is no God or eternal truth that dictates that to us. If someone wants to call that 'nonfoundationalist', that is fine with me, too. Yet you can also call it 'transcendental'.

Second, as I explained above in my response to Sangiovanni, if we reconstruct morality properly and the place it has in human life, we

---

[20] See the famous quote from the *Critique of Pure Reason*, trans. P. Guyer and A. Wood. Cambridge: Cambridge University Press, 1998, p. 643 (A 738/B 766) I cite in *RJ*, p. 13: 'Reason must subject itself to critique in all its undertakings, and cannot restrict the freedom of critique through any prohibition without damaging itself and drawing upon itself a disadvantageous suspicion.'

can (and should) look sceptically at what at a given time counts as 'moral' or 'immoral', but we cannot bracket the validity of morality in a contextualist manner. Why not? Why should we not declare the basic moral respect of others as justificatory equals as something not strictly binding or a mere cultural invention of Western or Christian cultures? Because this is to mix up genealogy and validity, and it is morally, historically and sociologically questionable. In a moral and conceptual perspective, it seems contradictory to call the right to, and power of, justification a 'weapon of the weak' (as Allen does) and also to say that the basic claim of being respected morally is only valid within a particular ethical-cultural horizon 'of European Enlightenment modernity', as Allen's communitarian view suggests (77f.). It is contradictory since the critical claims against racism and sexism rest on precisely such a moral ground, as I do not think that for Allen, racism and sexism do not exist in non-European cultures. The validity restriction for which she argues would mean that people in non-European societies in the past or the present have no justifiable claim to be respected as moral equals, or at least that they speak a foreign, 'Western' moral language when they make such claims. The result would be to exclude those who struggle for emancipation in such societies from the realm of justifications; it would disenfranchise them morally, for they would be seen to have the wrong, non-European passport to properly speak the language of 'European' morality. In my work on human rights[21] I have tried to show the ideological implications of such a normative inversion.

The contextualist view is also historically problematic, for it does not appreciate how radical the critique of Christian and other justification narratives had to be in *establishing* notions of human rights or basic moral respect. As I try to show in my *Toleration in Conflict* – whether we refer to the Levellers who argued that the king is not the divinely ordained father of the subjects but their employee based on a contract, or to Pierre Bayle who argued for the moral faculties of atheists – the critics within European history had *no* socially recognized 'ethical notion of

---

[21] *RJ*, ch. 9 and *Justification and Critique*, ch. 2.

the good' on which to rely and *no* 'particular form of life' established – rather, they were revolutionary forerunners in *creating* such a life form. I am not denying that the form it took is historically situated, of course, but I am denying the conservative view that only certain forms of life generate productive developments by way of immanent critique such that radical critique and innovation would not be possible. It would be better in critical theory to remind ourselves of the possibilities of *radically* transcending certain ethical life forms rather than tying our imagination to them and only see the recurrence of the same. Surely, every form of social criticism uses the material that is there, but the way it (re)forms this material can be truly innovative and will then be seen as 'unreasonable' by most people, as the fate of radical critics such as Bayle and Spinoza attests.[22] But beyond and above all that material, or rather deep inside of it, the structure of asking for better justifications and ultimately for ones that could gain assent by all as free and equal is an essential part of every such struggle if it is a struggle for emancipation. It is a 'deep grammar' of social conflict and emancipatory aims – and as such, it 'belongs' to no particular culture, history or life form. The language of emancipation and of no longer wanting to be denied one's right to be a participatory equal is a universal language spoken in many tongues. It is spoken, and that is why contextualism is also sociologically wrong, where people engage in struggles for emancipation, wherever that takes place. It does not determine their substantive language and their interests to form their society as they see justified, so it does not limit but *express* their autonomy. The claim to that kind of autonomy, to be an equal justificatory authority in the normative order of which you are a part, is the basic human rights claim persons can raise.

The question of socialization that Amy Allen brings up is distinct from the question of historical contextualism, though she relates them convincingly in pointing to the fact that human beings always grow up by being initiated into concrete forms and practices of justification

---

[22] See, for example, Jonathan Israel, *Radical Enlightenment. Philosophy and the Making of Modernity 1650–1750.* Oxford: Oxford University Press, 2001.

that make them into subjects of justification – thus raising the question how they can generate the critical power to transcend these forms and practices. I am not an expert on theories of socialization, much less so than Allen, and so I hesitate to dabble in this field. But since I do not see power as a negative phenomenon (and think we agree on that), I do not find the idea that 'power relations are constitutive of subjectivity' (82) wrong or surprising. I also find that a social power analysis is necessary which can show how many forms of dominating or oppressive power constitute subjects and produce 'docile bodies', as Foucault says.[23] So I am not sure where to disagree – up to the point maybe where Allen wants to say that because of the inextricable relation between (dominating) power and subjectivity and reason we should be less confident 'in the ability that reason itself gives us to distinguish between legitimate and illegitimate forms of power and dependency' (82). I am torn here, as these judgements, especially when it comes to personal relations but also with respect to larger social ones, are indeed hard to make, but I take that to be a challenge for practical reason to try and see clearer despite its imperfection, and I do not see the conceptual problem this seems to raise for Allen. I also cannot resist questioning the necessary role of sanctions in moral education, for it seems what is essential for the child is to internalize that morality needs to be followed for the sake of the other, without reward, not for the sake of avoiding sanctions. In the Nietzschean and Freudian tradition, there is the dominant idea of morality being based on the internalization of sanctions, but maybe it is time to overcome the *Obrigkeitsstaat* in our conception of socialization.

But I do not want to avoid the central problem that Amy Allen puts her finger on: If we always already are socialized into certain life forms, how can we attain the critical distance required to identify them as ideological, oppressive or patriarchal, as the case may be? And if we do so, how can we be sure that our critical standards are free from

---

[23] Michel Foucault, *Discipline and Punish. The Birth of the Prison*, trans. A Sheridan. New York: Random House, 1977, p. 136.

other forms of ideology and domination – and so on? The danger of a vertigo of arbitrariness seems to loom large here: not seeing the plank in one's own eye. In response, I should stress that I am not committed to the metaphysical claim that in every form of life and development of subjectivity there is a 'conatus' that resists domination. Yet I believe that socialization is not to be seen as a one-dimensional process of adapting to certain forms of power. If socialization allows for some form of autonomy, this is an achievement of the internalization of social norms as well as of the internalization of the normative possibility to question given norms and to reflect on their justificatory quality. This in itself strikes me neither as a particularly modern nor 'Western' idea; cultures and societies generally develop 'cracks' used and sometimes created by critics (in different ways), and each culture and society tries to develop forms of justificatory power to close these cracks discursively or to seal them by ideological means. Socialization processes are located within these processes, navigating the space for individuality within sociality.[24] No subjectivity is 'free from power', but it is also not simply a 'product' of arbitrary power – rather, in learning to understand oneself as a justificatory being, one can also learn to use that capacity critically. Again, there is no metaphysical guarantee for that, yet there is also no reason to assume that the space of reasons is generally sealed and closed by forms of domination inherited through socialization. The 'ground' of reflexively transcending those forms is the self-awareness of being a justificatory agent, nothing more and nothing less. Social critical theory has the task of analysing the social conditions under which such awareness can develop.

Finally, a word on 'applied ethics'. Following Raymond Geuss,[25] it is a common critique of types of 'ideal theory' to point to their abstraction from the real world and their blindness to 'real politics'. I share this critique to some extent, especially when it comes to institutional

---

[24] Jürgen Habermas, 'Individualization Through Socialization: On George Herbert Mead's Theory of Subjectivity', in his *Postmetaphysical Thinking*. Cambridge, MA: MIT, 1992.

[25] Raymond Geuss, *Outside Ethics*. Princeton: Princeton University Press, 2005, and *Philosophy and Real Politics*. Princeton: Princeton University Press, 2008.

ideals of justice that do not take into account the structural social contexts of domination and exploitation to which they are supposed to 'apply', but still I do not agree with the 'realist' critics' ideas of what is 'real' or what the grounds of critique can be.[26] It should, however, be obvious that discourse theory cannot be the subject of such critique. For discourse theory rests on the very idea that the authors of norms and social orders ought to be the subjected or affected *themselves*, and so there are no abstract normative ideals constructed that then are 'applied' by someone (the philosopher king?) to a 'non-ideal' world. The assumption that a discourse theory operates in an ideal or applied ethics mode overlooks the main point of discursive autonomy. So as I will explain below in responding to Kevin Olson, we do start within social practices, but we require normative and sociological tools to orient ourselves critically within them. Some of these tools will be moral concepts, and we situate them when we criticize false justifications and argue for proper structures of justification to oppose the structures of domination there are – yet all that is far from what can be called 'applied ethics'.

The universality and reflexivity of the right to justification

Kevin Olson also engages with my arguments for a basic right to justification, in a way related to some of Amy Allen's critique but also quite distinct. He questions the idealizing implications that he thinks are entailed in my version of the linguistic turn in political philosophy and that blind me to the social stratification in contemporary societies. I deny, however, that I make these idealizing moves. Here is why.

When we engage in political philosophy, we need an anchor, or, less metaphorically, a starting point. With Kevin, I think that such a starting

---

[26] See my introduction to *Justification and Critique*.

point should be our social *practice*, and what else could it be, since philosophy's task is to rationally reconstruct our practices of thinking and acting? But which practice shall that be if we are interested in questions of justice, for example? Some, like Olson (and Allen), say it ought to be practices of power and domination, the 'messy world' (100) of social differentiation, recognition as well as disrespect – and not an idealized world of reciprocal justification. Contrary to what he thinks, I completely agree,[27] as it cannot be otherwise for a critical theory of our actual social practices. But at this point, it is important to be clear about what we mean by 'practices of power'. As I just explained, I suggest that we see power as a *noumenal phenomenon*: having power is having the capacity to influence, determine, maybe even to dominate the space of justifications for others. So if we are interested in power, we should be interested in the structures of justification that lie at the bottom of social and political relations – and then we may want to ask whether the justifications given for certain relations are good justifications (and we need a standard for that), and we ask whether the existing practices of justification, including those that are institutionalized, are adequate for the purpose of generating generally binding and acceptable justifications, which brings us to the programme of critical theory that (as I said above) I call a *critique of the relations of justification*.

Note that I started with a brief reflection on power and then moved to a view of our social practices as practices of justification – some democratic, some ideological, some riddled with asymmetry and false assumptions, some being practices of critique.[28] So a justificatory view like mine does not start from an idealized picture of us as purely noumenal beings engaged in free and equal discourse; rather, it starts from a reconstruction of the various practices of justification we are engaged in, as *social* noumenal beings. We have to see society as a

---

[27] For that argument, see esp. ch. 12 of *RJ*.

[28] I cannot go into the similarities and differences here with the rich social theory of justification provided by Luc Boltanski and Laurent Thévenot in *On Justification*, trans. C. Porter. Princeton: Princeton University Press, 2006.

'normative order' in the sense of an 'order of justification(s)' of very different kinds (to use the Frankfurt Research Cluster terminology).[29]

Among these practices of justification, two have a special character that is important in our context. The first is the practice of *critique*, of saying 'no' (or, one step prior, 'why?') to given and possibly long-established narratives of justification and to the structures generating them, and I am interested in the normative power that is entailed by such critique: What exactly is it that is claimed when someone doubts one-sided justifications, unjustifiable distributions or political institutions that are unjust? Many things, to be sure, but fundamental among them is one basic claim: Not to be disregarded as an authority in the social space of justifications that we all share and where we ought to be equals when it comes to rules or norms that bind us all. So our view of justificatory practices has to be *threefold*: there is the realm of given social justifications, and with Olson I believe that many of them have to be analysed in Bourdieuian terms as practices of exclusion and power; but then there are also practices of mutual justification, though never 'pure', where we reflect on what good and defensible justification is. Then there is the 'third world' of critique, where we raise concrete critical claims, and, reflexively speaking, the most basic one is to be a subject with the right to demand and deliver justifications for the norms that bind one in the first place.

There is also a more abstract dimension involved here, and this is what Olson focuses on. We can look at *morality* as a practice of justification, the second peculiar practice, and in order to reconstruct it, we start from the validity claims that would have to be made good for moral norms to be strictly, reciprocally and generally valid and binding. These criteria of validity are then transformed into criteria of justification, expressed by the duty to present reciprocally and generally non-rejectable reasons for reciprocally and generally binding norms. Why a duty? Because – as I tried to explain in answering Andrea Sangiovanni and Amy Allen – the practice of morality is a game unlike

---

[29] See Forst and Günther, 'Die Herausbildung normativer Ordnungen'.

others. It is a game that humans cannot opt out of without violating a basic moral demand, namely that of treating others as autonomous 'ends in themselves', that is, as beings with a right to justification with respect to how one treats them. The insight relevant here is an insight of reason and morality at the same time: you see the other as like and as unlike you; like you, he or she can use and in any case[30] deserves reasons in moral contexts of action; unlike you, he or she might have justifiable claims and reasons you did not recognize and at first may not understand. So my moral 'outlook' is not 'humanist' in the sense that I project one form of recognition onto all others; what I mean is that morality is a particular practice of respect, and it involves not essentializing or idealizing others, but seeing them as reason-giving and reason-deserving autonomous and yet vulnerable beings.

In analysing practices of justification, we must not mix philosophical and sociological categories: in reconstructing the practice of morality, neither do I say that this practice is an empirical sociological fact to be ascertained in purity (not even Kant thought that) nor do I say that such a practice is the dominant one in contemporary society. Rather, I reconstruct the logic or normative grammar, if you like, of a practical context, that of morality, and extrapolate and abstract (though not idealize) the kind of recognition that is specific to this context. Nowhere do I say that such an outlook 'characterizes the practices of contemporary societies' (93) or that this 'actually characterize[s] the norms and attitudes of the real people around us' (ibid.). That would be an impermissible idealization.

I also think that the interesting difference between a constructivist and a reconstructive account of morality that Olson suggests is overdrawn. When we reconstruct the practice of morality, we give the best account of it that is possible for finite beings like us who reflect on what we do and should do. The practice of morality takes place in the empirical *and* the noumenal realms; if things go well, we strive for justifiable ways of acting, yet oftentimes, we fail. As I said, I do

---

[30] That is: even if unable to use his or her capacity of reasoning.

not think that the moral form of recognition is the only normative or dominant one. In my *Contexts of Justice*, I distinguished between a number of different contexts of recognition. But the moral dimension is one that critically cuts through the others – in the case in which the other forms (ethical or political, for example) are criticized as morally unacceptable and when one reclaims one's basic right to justification. In the absence of such a dimension, I do not see where Olson, in his version of reconstruction, would otherwise gain a normative foothold in the 'ways that people actually recognize one another' (101). For a critique of such forms, whether Bourdieuian or Foucauldian, one needs a normative basis that the principle of justification provides – as a principle immanent to and at the same time transcending social practice. This is not an intellectualist or overly rationalist construction – reason-giving comes in a myriad of forms, and when critique goes well, it shows that some forms of justification fail and exclude certain voices. Such critique must be performed in a mode of justification, even if it consists of holding up signs or pictures of missing persons in a public square.

So I agree that we need a differentiated epistemology of justification and of justifications. I also believe that the main medium of power is justification, and that can be good or bad, depending on the justifications given. I do try to avoid an idealized picture of such practices – yet at the same time we cannot do without the three worlds of *actual* justifications, of *better* ones and of the world of *critique* moving between them. In political philosophy, it is a mistake to conflate these worlds and fancy yourself into a world of glorious justificatory practices that has nothing to do with reality. But if we reflect on the justificatory qualities of our social world critically, then we do gain access to another practice of justification, and that is how we attain critical distance here and now. The practice of critique itself is norm-governed, but these are norms against any reification of norms. Critique is a reflexive practice, as Kevin Olson himself affirms in his own important work on democratic theory.[31]

---

[31] Kevin Olson, *Reflexive Democracy: Political Equality and the Welfare State*. Cambridge, MA: MIT Press, 2006.

He also raises an important point highlighted in the Marxist tradition, that of reflecting on one's own possibly class-based bias in theory production. For a Frankfurter, this is not an unfamiliar theme. Clearly, certain evaluations of the high standard and importance of particular forms of discourse can reproduce class bias and have exclusionary implications. But the critique as put forth by Olson might itself reproduce a class bias in reducing the meaning of discourse to elaborate argument only, which I do not intend, and in arguing that discursive practice is an elite practice as the public use of reasons for social groups may be a 'less intuitive practice, and perhaps worse, one at which they perceive themselves as less competent' (97). As critical theorists, I believe, we should not just be wary of a confusion of conceptual and sociological arguments but also be careful not to restrict discursive competence to the seminar room. That would indeed be a form of 'cultural imperialism' (98), and I fear Olson is coming close to reproducing it. But that is not what he intends. Rather, we both agree, I believe, that many different forms of critical discourse have been and are valid and powerful in politics, and that they need not be intellectualistic in order to be so. I also think – and tried to show in my *Toleration in Conflict* – that the demand for justification is a strong motivating force in historical struggles for recognition[32] and emancipation, and that this is no business restricted to intellectual elites, but to protesters in the street or in other public or non-public settings.

In critical theory, it is important, and here I take a point of Olson's on board, to always be aware of the different worlds one is part of and thus use at least two different versions of normativity: the normativity of the (noumenal) power structures that surround us that fix and 'normalize' identities and that determine what can be said and what

---

[32] On that point, see my '"To tolerate means to insult": Toleration, recognition, and emancipation', in Bert van den Brink and David Owen (eds), *Recognition and Power*. Cambridge: Cambridge University Press, 2007, pp. 215–37, (reprinted in *Justification and Critique*, ch. 6) and Axel Honneth's 'Rejoinder' in the same volume, esp. pp. 363f.

not; and the normativity of critique directed against such reifications, essentially claiming a right to justification and the right to construct a normative order on the basis of (more) acceptable reasons.[33] These two normativities are always intertwined, but we must not lose track of their conceptual distinction.

Justification – political, but not in the wrong way

I am immensely honoured and pleased that Tony Laden has dedicated his marvellous piece to my work and thus continues a discussion on justice that goes back to our time together at Harvard in the early 1990s when we both were thinking about ways to 'radicalize' Rawls by connecting his insights with those of discursive and deliberative democracy, as Laden did admirably in his *Reasonably Radical*[34] and as I tried to do in *Contexts of Justice*.

Like my previous critics, Laden wants to save me from an overly foundationalist stance with respect to the grounding of my theory and gently invites me to follow his more practical understanding of what political philosophy can and ought to do – namely to provide no more and also no less than a justification that is 'intersubjective all the way down' (123) without any impersonal or transcendental banisters of thought. His way of thinking is so close to mine that I am tempted to accept that kind invitation, but I fear I should resist, as I find that between the notion of an independent and impersonal philosophical justification and Laden's idea of intersubjective practical justification we need to take into account the *moral* dimension of justification and of basic questions of justice and insert that between 'philosophical' and 'practical-political' justification. If we fail to do that, intersubjective

---

[33] I have developed this in my 'Towards a Critique of Justificatory Reason', German version forthcoming in my *Normativität und Macht*. Berlin: Suhrkamp.

[34] Anthony Simon Laden, *Reasonably Radical: Deliberative Liberalism and the Politics of Identity*. Ithaca: Cornell University Press, 2001.

justification could become 'political in the wrong way', to use a phrase of Rawls which he used in a (only slightly) different context.[35] Let me explain.

Laden reconstructs the relational, practical conception of justice we both share in an attractive way. Like him – as I spell out more fully in the longer piece on the 'Two Pictures of Justice' that is reprinted here – I believe that justice is essentially about how we relate to one another, not primarily about the goods we have or receive. 'How we relate to one another' refers not only to the legal and institutional status persons have but also to the *practice* of recognizing one another and treating one another as social equals. Justification, as I conceive of it, is indeed the essential practice of constructing justice. As I argue in the Introduction to *Justification and Critique*, we need to make philosophy 'practical' by reflexively understanding the principle of justification as a practical imperative, thus liberating political philosophy from an authoritarian slumber.

I also agree with Laden that we need to pay close attention to the kind of arbitrariness that a conception of justice aims to overcome or prevent; and as I argue in 'Two Pictures', I think that priority needs to be given to social and political forms of arbitrariness, that is, to forms of rule without proper justification and – again reflexively speaking – without proper procedures and possibilities for justification in place. I am not sure I 'occlude' (107) this in *The Right to Justification*, but in any case I say more about it in the full version of the argument reprinted here.

The two conceptions (or 'pictures') of justification Laden distinguishes bring us to the heart of his argument – and to his own elaborate view of reasoning as a demanding social art and virtue as laid out in his recent book *Reasoning*.[36] In his view, an 'impersonal' justification possesses an independent warrant of truth that authorizes reasons, whereas an 'intersubjective' justification is truly addressed to others and aims at consensus between them (I take it). Yet as important as this distinction

<hr />

[35] John Rawls, *Political Liberalism*, pp. 39f., 142.
[36] Anthony Simon Laden, *Reasoning. A Social Picture*. Oxford: Oxford University Press, 2012.

is, I fear it might be overdrawn. For if intersubjective justification is a form of justification that generates valid norms, it aims at *reasonable* acceptance, not merely at any form of acceptance, as Rawls, to whom Laden refers here, also stresses throughout both his earlier and his later works. If 'reasonable' were not put in as a qualifier (itself to be concretized), how could such justification overcome arbitrariness and be a practice of reason(ing)? So for Laden, too, as he explains in his book much more fully,[37] reasoning is a norm-governed practice of free and equal exchange of arguments with certain criteria for reasonable or unreasonable acceptance or rejection – provided that these criteria do not lead to reification but are open enough to allow for normative innovation by discursive challenge and reorientation. So in any practice we call intersubjective justification, I think some 'impersonal' or 'transpersonal' aspect needs to be present, as the game of justification is not owned by me, you or even us as a particular (and potentially exclusive) community. So when Laden says that the egalitarian practice of justification implies that the participants are 'prepared to offer justifications to one another and . . . take themselves to be bound by the uptake or rejection that their justifications meet' (113), I would add the tiny but important word 'reasonable' before 'uptake and rejection' – as Laden expects me to do. This is because justification in normative contexts is about something – call it justice – that even general acceptance, if based on improper reasons, can fail to achieve. Thus to reject such improper reasons is also a demand of justice and justification and a form of showing respect – towards those who would suffer if those bad reasons were followed, but also towards those whose reasons one rejects. For by seriously engaging in discourse, we show respect by saying 'yes' *or* 'no' to the statements of others provided we try to offer good reasons. Rejecting someone's arguments is no sign of misrecognition; rather, rejecting someone as a person and as an author of potentially valid claims is a severe form of disrespect. These two dimensions of recognition must not be confused. It is no sign of

---

[37] See ibid., Part II.

misrecognition to reject homophobic or racist positions; rather, it is a demand of justification and recognition to do so. When we situate discourses on justice socially, we also have to situate them in contexts of severe injustice and of views that support such injustice. Otherwise, our theory of justice is not critical enough and idealizes in a problematic way (as I explained in my previous reply to Olson). Justification in real life often is a polemic rather than a peaceful form of discursive exchange; and for such polemic, we need criteria beyond consensus – criteria of the justifiable or unjustifiable rejectability of claims. Does Laden disagree?

Let's see. In a beautiful passage, he asks me to follow him into the land of completely intersubjective justification. I hear the sirene's song, yet I should hold onto the mast. But I think he should not go there, too, and here is why. I still remember how baffled Rawls was when Habermas criticized him for not sufficiently placing the method of discursive justification at the centre of his theory, and Rawls strongly affirmed in his reply that in his theory 'there are no experts'.[38] So it is an elegant dialectical move by Laden to, in turn, criticize Habermas and myself for giving too much room to transcendental expertise. Like Laden, I criticize experts like 'Jeremy' (118) for whom politics eventually seems to reduce to social engineering realizing the right principles of justice – think, for example, of the idea of the 'distributor' as a political figure in G. A. Cohen's thought.[39] I also agree with the critique of 'Ronnie', though that is a more difficult matter which I will leave aside for now. But then there is the philosophical expert called 'Jürgen' who lays out 'the boundaries of public reason or the structure of genuine moral discourse' (118f.) or – possibly – the expert 'Rainer' who even argues for a 'right to justification'. This addition might be adequate since Habermas rejects that deontological notion of a basic right.[40]

---

[38] John Rawls, 'Reply to Habermas', *The Journal of Philosophy* 92 (1995), p. 140.

[39] G. A. Cohen, *On the Currency of Egalitarian Justice, and Other Essays in Political Philosophy*. Princeton: Princeton University Press, 2011, p. 61.

[40] See Jürgen Habermas, 'Reply to My Critics', in James Gordon Finlayson and Fabian Freyenhagen (eds), *Habermas and Rawls: Disputing the Political*. New York and London: Routledge, 2011, pp. 295–8.

Laden is right in saying that the discourse-theoretical 'expert' does not lay out a theory of just institutions or distributions but restricts himself to more formal and criterial arguments. Yet I go – again departing from Habermas, who has no room for a theory of justice between his theories of morality and of democracy – even further and say that on the basis of a conception of the right to justification we can construct a theory of 'fundamental justice' which includes the principles of a fundamentally just basic structure of justification which is required if further democratic constructions of justice are to get off the ground. The main consideration here is a *reflexive* and a *moral* one: without such a basic structure of justification in place, a fundamental moral demand is violated. Laden neglects this moral argument, I fear – though only explicitly, while implicitly he uses it. And that argument makes no one a paternalist expert – it just points out what any participant in a justice discourse accepts who understands the term in the correct – non-arbitrary – way. So the kernel of truth in 'impersonal' justification is deeply 'personal', stressing the importance of egalitarian respect.

The reason why I think that Laden uses this reflection implicitly is that I think he is much closer to 'experts' such as 'Jürgen' or even 'John' (Rawls) than to 'Richard' (Rorty), though he comes at times close to a Rortian view of groundless dialogical justification. But only close, not really to it. Because Laden's notion of intersubjective justification 'all the way down', to my mind, is still *norm-governed all the way down*. The intersubjective justification implements 'shared ideas about how to live together' (119, my emphasis) – so there is the norm of *shareability*. Furthermore, no one concerned is to be excluded from such discourse – so there is the norm of *full inclusion* (and the question of how many forms exclusion can take – legal, social, political, economic, etc.). There is also the norm of '*equality* and *reciprocity*' (109, my emphasis), and we might add others such as deliberative *autonomy, sincerity,* etc.[41] And how could it be otherwise as long as the practice of justification is the

---

[41] See, again, Laden, *Reasoning*, chs 4–6.

paradigm of the non-arbitrary practice of constructing justice, as we both think it is?

So as Laden anticipates, I would say that his 'rules of the game' do indeed 'look a whole lot like Forst's criteria of accountability, reciprocity and generality' (112), since 'certain basic rules and norms of justification must be observed'. But this does not make us 'experts' in a problematic way because what we both do is reconstruct the implicit knowledge of *participants* in such a justification exercise, yet I would add that we thereby also need to reconstruct the *moral* perspective and duties of participants in such discourses. It would be a rather pale view of intersubjective justification not to see this moral dimension of it. Participating in the practice of justification, we do not just 'invite' (124) others to see things our way; sometimes, for the sake of ourselves or others, we need to make it clear that others are wrong and unjust. That is how I would interpret Gandhi's idea of 'being the change we want to see in the world' (125). So I don't know whether the difference between the two of us comes down to a difference between a Kantian versus a more contextual philosophical temperament; that is possible, but if so, it is because a Kantian sees himself or herself bound by an imperative not to leave certain things 'up for grabs' when it comes to basic questions of justice (124) and as I said, given the normative frame of Laden's own view, I don't think we disagree over much here.

A reflexive, autonomy- and discourse-based philosophy that opts for a certain normative 'ground' claims no super-political authority, as Laden fears; it only reconstructs the immanent structure of justice discourse and unveils its normative core. So it is not from the standpoint of 'philosophy' alone but also from a contextual, participant's perspective that there is a transcending quality to justification – the question of what 'could' be accepted will not go away, and no Rortian (or other) contextualism can ever dissolve it. It remains with every protester who says 'no' to a given system of justifications and institutions. The world of *acceptance* is always accompanied by the world of *acceptability*, and reason is the – finite and fallible – faculty to move between the two. Otherwise, no critical thinking or theory is possible – as Bernard

Williams saw following Habermas in stating 'that the acceptance of a justification does not count if the acceptance itself is produced by the coercive power which is supposedly being justified'.[42] This 'critical theory principle' clearly rests on the idea of a basic right to justification, as I would argue, but here I leave that aside.[43]

Laden agrees (on 122), I think, when he argues that no justification that violates basic discourse norms can be acceptable – even if it were accepted. We need to recursively reflect on every form of acceptance and ask whether a superior form of acceptability is thinkable, and for that we need no elaborate notion of 'false consciousness'. We only need a recursive notion of the criteria of justification. In no way will this make, as Laden fears, 'the actual offering of justifications' (121) unimportant – for neither can empirical consensus claim the dignity of full justification if it is based on reciprocally rejectable reasons nor can we know the reasons and claims persons really have in complete abstraction from real discourse. But apart from that epistemic point (often stressed by Habermas) for actual discourse: to be the author of valid claims is a basic *moral* right of autonomous persons and it implies the right to *participate* in *actual* discourses as much as it implies the right not to be overpowered by actual discourses that lack justification. There is no contradiction here, as these are only two sides of the same coin of discursive autonomy. As justificatory equals, we need to be able to speak here and now, but we also have the (noumenal) power to transcend what is and has been spoken. The imperative of reciprocal and general justification, by recursively inquiring into the quality of its procedures as well as its products, never takes away the voices of justificatory equals but implies that their voices must not be silenced by domination or false agreements. It is an imperative immanent to, and at the same time transcending, the practice of justification. Taking this into account means to look at justification as intersubjective all the way down – and all the way up.

---

[42] Bernard Williams, *In the Beginning Was the Deed. Realism and Moralism in Political Argument.* Princeton: Princeton University Press, 2005, p. 6.

[43] Williams himself affirms that the 'basic legitimation demand' of general justification is a moral principle 'inherent in there being such a thing as politics' (ibid., p. 5).

Locating political contexts of (in-)justice

Eva Erman is a kindred spirit with whom I share many basic assumptions and ideas. Her work on a discourse theory of human rights and of democracy marks an extremely important development and refinement of the approach we both value.[44] Yet the landscape of discourse theory is large, especially when it comes to the issue Erman presses me on, the 'boundary problem' with respect to conceptualizing a democratic community of justification. In her view, I do not properly take the question of the 'conditions of democracy' into account in the way I locate political contexts of justice, especially when it comes to transnational justice and democracy. Criticizing my version of the 'all subjected' principle – which says that all those who are subject to norms and institutions of political and/or social rule or domination have to be seen as political subjects with a right to co-determine these norms or institutions – Erman argues for what she calls the 'equal influence' principle which she situates in thicker contexts of 'interdependent interests' (143) within a political people as a democratic collective. I fear I have to disagree, however, for I think that she uses the wrong kind of empirical precondition for locating political contexts of justification properly, restricting them to already existing and functioning democratic collectives. This connects empirical and normative considerations in the wrong way and excludes justifiable claims of persons or groups to be included in democratic practices of justice, practices that first and foremost address existing injustice and thus 'track', as it were, relations of rule and domination. Let me explain.

According to the principle of justification as I interpret it, in contexts of political and social justice which are guided by norms, rules and institutions that claim to be valid and binding for all subjected to them, the right to justification is not just a right that such rules

---

[44] Eva Erman, *Human Rights and Democracy: Discourse Theory and Global Rights Institutions.* Aldershot: Ashgate, 2005; idem., 'Human Rights Do Not Make Global Democracy', *Contemporary Political Theory* 10 (2011), 463–81.

and norms are justifiable to all as equals; it also requires that a basic structure of justification (what I call 'fundamental justice') is in place in which justificatory practices exist such that those subjected can be the co-authors of these rules and norms. That is why, in my view, democracy is *the* political practice of justice grounded in the right to justification. So democracy in my view is not 'instrumental' to justice; it is what justice demands. I am not sure Erman and I disagree here.

The basic right to justification is a non-domination right, as Erman rightly says. But it is a version of non-domination which does not use a negative, neo-republican notion of liberty as freedom of choice secure from the possibility of arbitrary interference; rather, domination I call any kind of arbitrary rule without proper justification and without proper possibilities of justification in place, and the basic liberty *and* justice claim to non-domination is the claim to be respected as a justificatory equal.[45] So a context of political and social *justice* exists where there is a context of social or political *rule* (in German *Herrschaft*), whether formal legal or informal social or economic rule, and also where a context of *domination* (*Beherrschung*) exists (i.e. a form of unjustified and unjustifiable rule, formal or informal). These are the structures of power which generate duties of justice and of justification – the first duty of justice being to establish relations of justification that overcome or avoid relations of domination. Justice is a reflexive term: the first duty of justice is to establish normative authorship (and structures of justification) where rule or domination resides such that justice can become an autonomous achievement of those subjected to power in these two forms.

So in my view, justice 'tracks' power as rule or domination. Hence a *demos* – or better: a political community of justification – exists where a context of rule or domination exists, and such contexts are often not coextensive with established political communities. In my work on a critical theory of transnational justice, I speak of contexts of 'force

---

[45] I explain the difference to Philip Pettit's view in my 'A Kantian Republican Conception of Justice as Non-Domination', in Andreas Niederberger and Philipp Schink (eds), *Republican Democracy*. Edinburgh: Edinburgh University Press, 2013, 281–92.

and domination'[46] in the plural, as contexts of 'multiple domination', from the local to the global level, connecting people's lives primarily not by positively established and legitimate forms of rule, but by a plethora of forms of domination. So the proper *empirical* as well as *normative* condition of locating a political context of justification is the existence of contexts of rule or domination. There are many such contexts, some national, regional, transnational or international; I stress the transnational dimension because complexes of political, legal and economic power in today's world transcend classic boundaries and form a system of interdependence that we could only very euphemistically call a system of 'cooperation'.[47] Rather, it is a system of asymmetrical burdens and benefits that all too often serves to reproduce these asymmetries. This is what a 'realistic' conception of transnational justice has to start from being confronted with the (difficult) task of finding the right connection between these different power structures.[48]

Erman holds a different view. For her, the B-question of who may decide democratically over whom needs to be connected to – and essentially depends on – the C-question of what the basic conditions of democracy are. And since these conditions are the two of political equality and political 'bindingness', a context of democratic justification can only be located where an already functioning and established democratic community exists in which there is not just the possibility of exercising equal political influence guaranteed by a scheme of rights and institutions but also where there is a 'democratic practice' (131) in place in which those subjected recognize the good of exercising their political power together as a collective. So Erman's view of where a democratic context can exist is substantive: only where 'political bindingness' (in the sense of citizens seeing themselves bound to others politically) is in place can there be a democratic community. Thus, to

---

[46] *RJ*, 256f.

[47] See, for example, Deborah D. Avant, Martha Finnemore, and Susan K. Sell (eds), *Who Governs the Globe?* Cambridge: Cambridge University Press, 2010.

[48] On this, see my 'Transnational Justice and Democracy', supra note 2.

my mind, the C-question basically answers the B-question in Erman's argument. As she emphasizes, the 'deep' form of interdependence within a 'people' is not just an objective fact but also a subjective fact of seeing one another connected in that way, of regarding oneself 'bound' by collective decisions. From that substantive empirical presupposition of a democratic community, a moral-political argument for locating a context of democratic justice where domination needs to be corrected such that those subjected *can become* co-authors looks like a pale construct because of the lack of the ethical-political bindingness condition.

I think that is a problematic view. For it gives priority to certain social contexts that can be described as a common *positive* world of bindingness and political recognition, but then *negative* social contexts of domination, exploitation or contexts of rule and structures of governance beyond borders fall out of the democratic picture. All that remains for these relations is a form of political justification that need not be democratic according to Erman (143f.). That view gives such a high premium on already existing democratic communities that justifiable claims of groups that are ruled by or dominated by such communities can only be dealt with in a reduced political way. But for a world in which 'postcolonial' is an all too euphemistic term to describe relations of 'interdependence' as what they really are, namely relations of rule and/or domination, this is insufficient. It replaces the proper empirical question – that is, which contexts of rule and/or domination exist transnationally speaking – with the wrong question – that is, where do collectives exist which are deeply socially interconnected and in which there is general acceptance of binding political structures and decisions?

In that connection, a remark on Erman's 'equal influence' principle may be appropriate. It seems to me that this is a misleading term, for what we are looking for is a *criterion* of 'affectedness' that is more concrete than merely general 'affectedness' to determine contexts of political justification. The principle Erman suggests says that 'all those who are systematically and over time subjected to an authority's . . . laws, political decisions and rules . . . should . . . have an equal influence over its decision-making' (137). But then 'influence' is not the criterion we look for, rather, being *subjected* in a particular way is. Equal influence describes what those subjected can claim; it is not the criterion we required as an answer to the boundary question. Thus this answer does not move beyond the 'all subjected' principle. Yet it is in further argumentative steps that Erman presents not just a substantive argument about the kind of influence one can claim but also about its preconditions, namely 'robust participation in both formal decision procedures . . . and informal processes . . .' (138). It is at this point that the idea of 'conditions' of democracy actually leads to a different notion of the criterion of being affected in the relevant way: as already being a member of a self-governing collective which demonstrates a certain quality of democracy. If that interpretation is correct, I think it is her and not Habermas – whom she criticizes for that – who fixes the notion of democracy to an already existing political or legal community.

Furthermore, I think that in her reconstruction of my approach to the B-question, Erman overlooks the point I make of tracking relations of rule and/or domination.[49] But more than that, if she were right that 'a condition of political rights . . . is that they depend on being exercised jointly with others' (141), and if this refers to the B-question (as I take her to argue), nobody who is excluded from such a joint exercise could claim a right to be included, as disenfranchised groups in the past did and do in the present. So I take her to say that the proper 'exercise' of that right depends on the existence of a democratic practice, rather than that having such a right presupposes that practice. Otherwise, that would reduce to the tautology that only those would possess rights who already have well-functioning rights. But her formulations are ambivalent, which is why I fear that Erman connects in a problematic way an empirical thought about a functioning democracy with the normative argument about who has

---

[49] I stress this in 'Transnational Justice and Democracy'.

which rights to democratic participation (and, more importantly, to participation in a practice of *establishing* proper procedures and institutions of justification).

So, to sum up, rather than focusing on the C-question, I would focus on what we can call the D-question: Who dominates whom? *That* defines where the borders of a context of justice as justification lie. To analyse the relevant contexts of rule and/or domination, and on that basis to think of practices of critique and democratization to establish relations of justification, is a difficult task. But we cannot cut this path short by giving priority to the democratic contexts that exist, as they are implicated in relations of domination in so many ways.

The unity of justice

I am grateful to Simon Caney, with whom I share many philosophical and political convictions, for addressing head-on the issues that divide us despite these similarities. I have been benefiting from engaging with Caney's work for a long time, ever since we both worked on the debate between liberals and communitarians. In my own attempts to work out a conception of justice he is a vital and constant dialogue partner.[50] When – if you permit, for a moment – I muse over our differences in a genealogical perspective, I am reminded of his teacher Jerry Cohen's remark about the difference between 'Harvard people' and 'Oxford people': according to Cohen, the former seek to unify the plurality of values and principles by way of spurious constructivist methods, while the latter have more tolerance for moral pluralism and possible tensions, following the 'sovereignty' of individual judgements about ultimate values.[51] I am not sure about this characterization and shall not comment upon it, except for saying that seen in this light Caney is

---

[50] See, especially, his path-breaking *Justice Beyond Borders. A Global Political Theory.* Oxford: Oxford University Press, 2005.
[51] G. A. Cohen, *Rescuing Justice and Equality.* Cambridge, MA: Harvard University Press, 2008, p. 4.

an 'Oxford man' indeed, while a 'Frankfurt man' like me shares enough Kantian constructivism to find himself on the Harvard side, but would essentially differ from both by the notion of discursive autonomy at the core of a discourse-theoretical view. I think that the role played in my theory by this very notion of autonomy as being the author of the norms to which you are subject, both methodologically and substantively, lies at the heart of the disagreement between Simon Caney and myself.

Caney addresses a number of points and raises many important questions to which I better have an answer. But before I come to the issue of the two pictures of justice, or that of the 'nature of justice', let me try to answer the question of scope to clarify the 'all-affected/ all-subjected to what' difference. I will be brief here, as this already played a role in Eva Erman's paper and in my reply to it. Caney rightly points to formulations of mine, some of which are very broad, where I say that the right to justification is triggered wherever persons are 'affected' by other's actions in *morally* relevant ways, and to formulations which are more narrow in which I say that the right to justification is triggered in contexts of social and political *justice* where persons are subject to other persons' power in the form of rule or domination. These different formulations are no accident, but I should have been more explicit about them. I believe that the basic right to justification is a general *moral* right which every person has and can claim whenever others' actions affect him or her morally (which needs to be determined with the help of the criteria of reciprocity and generality). I call that a *moral context* of individual action and responsibility. But contexts of political and social *justice* are more specific: they are contexts in which persons stand in particular relations of rule and/or domination to one another. So when it comes to the right to justification generally, I do indeed hold what Caney calls a 'humanity-centred view' (163), such that we always have *moral* duties of justification towards others (relevantly) affected by us. But when it comes to political and social *justice*, I hold something like the 'systemic view', as he calls it. For justice is a part of (social and political) morality, but a special one. We do owe justifications to all persons morally, regardless of 'systemic' relations, and, for example, a denial of help if you could help others in need is something that cannot be justified to those concerned. So if in Caney's imagined case,[52] there were people in a dire situation with whom we have had no relations in the past and still do not have any (and yet we know about them), then we would have duties of moral solidarity towards them to help them out of their misery if we can, on the basis of respect for their humanity. We would have no good reason not to help (if we could), given that we are always in a justificatory community with them, that is, the moral community of all persons, the dignity of whom has to be respected.[53] So I agree that we have moral duties towards these people based on the 'respect for their common humanity' (165) – but I would not call them duties of justice, as Caney does, for I do not think it useful to elide the difference between the moral duties you have to help others in need and the duties not to dominate or exploit others – and I think the term 'justice' properly applies to the latter. There surely are cases in between which we need to sort out – such as profiting from an arbitrary distribution of natural resources, which is a justice issue if the profiting establishes unfair and asymmetrical relations between the parties. And I should also add the important 'natural duty of justice', to use Rawls's term[54] in a different way, to help those who suffer from injustice by others dominating them, even though we have no relation to either group but possess the means to help. Not assisting those who suffer from injustice in such a case makes you the accomplice of the injustice being done. But this does not change my main point, namely that we need a moral grammar to distinguish cases of helping others in need from cases of stopping an injustice as something *committed* by humans.

This brings me to the central issue of debate between us. Briefly put, Caney thinks I narrow the concept of justice too much, while I think he broadens it such that it encompasses too much of morality's other

---

[52] I simplify this case here, as Mann's example of an 'ostracized' society is very special and might well be a case of justice, depending on the general context in which this takes place and the relations already established.

[53] See Forst, *Contexts of Justice*, chs 4 and 5. See also ch. 4 of *Justification and Critique*.

[54] John Rawls, *A Theory of Justice*, rev. edn. Cambridge, MA: Harvard University Press, 1999, p. 99.

departments and loses both its specificity and its underlying unity. To be sure, he recognizes the conceptual and normative challenge of a general and unifying use of the term 'justice' – yet I think he gives us two different answers to that question. The one answer says that what possibly unifies proper justice talk is that this always refers to rights claims (161). But I don't think that helps much, as justice is what *grounds* rights claims of a certain kind – and so when we inquire into those grounds we need a different, maybe 'deeper' answer. Implicitly, I think, Caney gives us such an answer, namely when he – in agreement with me – says that the basic opposing term to that of justice is arbitrariness (165). But then we differ as to the forms of arbitrariness we think justice ought to address. As I argue in 'Two Pictures', justice to my mind addresses *social* forms of arbitrariness, that is, those that lead to domination, exploitation and relational asymmetry. Many 'natural'[55] contingencies play a role in constituting such arbitrary relations, but they only are a matter of justice once they do have certain relational implications. If justice were a term that did not refer to social *arbitrariness* of particular kinds, but generally to all kinds of *contingencies* relevant for human beings and their 'luck', then I think we entered the realm of the metaphysical and left the social behind. For then 'nature' itself – and not the human beings that use it for unjustifiable purposes – is turned into an agent that is 'unjust', and justice is seen as a supernatural force to create a new world overcoming a great number of personal or positional differences between human beings – from their looks to their talents or other characteristics. But that is a matter for the gods, I fear. This does not mean that we ought to be fatalistic and accept contingencies as given and unalterable, but we should have a moral grammar that distinguishes between the cases in which there is no moral reason to overcome a difference between persons from cases in which moral solidarity for people in need is called for, and from

---

[55] I use bracket quotes here since the distribution of natural resources in today's world is hardly a natural fact as so much depends on the use of these resources and the relational power goods they are turned into.

the cases in which justice calls upon us to avoid or stop relations of domination and the improper 'use' of persons by others. Injustice is an evil that is *done*, not a malady that is 'there'.

So unlike Caney (157f.), I hold on to the distinction between humanitarian duties and duties of justice, and I think it makes a huge difference whether states, for example, recognize that they have to help others on the basis of humanitarian grounds *or* on the basis of justice reasons. In our world, exchanging these grammars comes at a huge ideological cost, for all too often those states that benefit from a gravely unjust international system 'generously' offer 'help' to those who suffer most from that systemic injustice. Thus contrary to Caney (159), I believe that his elision of the difference in moral grammar is in danger of making a huge 'excision' (Sidgwick) of an essential portion of our moral vocabulary. To say it in a nutshell, giving up the distinction I hold on to not only loses the positive vocabulary of justice as something specific but also takes away our vocabulary of being able to identify phenomena of *injustice* (a point to which I will return).

With these short remarks on what we could call the 'metaphysics of justice', I have already approached the important topic of the 'nature of justice' that Caney raises. He takes issue with my distinction between two pictures of justice, elaborated (and addressing some of Caney's concerns) in the piece that precedes this exchange with my critics. Of the two ways to think about justice I distinguish, one is centred on *outcomes* and desirable states of affairs to be brought about by a distribution of certain goods. Here, the focus is on the recipient side, that is, on the quality and quantity of goods and on the kind of life thus made possible. The other way to think about justice is *relational* in the sense I explained above, namely that it asks in which relation persons stand to one another, what their social status is and whether relations of rule or domination are in place. I call both of these ways of thinking 'pictures' of justice as they are more general than conceptions or particular theories of justice. I should emphasize – as I do in my Two Pictures paper – that I think that a number of theories are not easy to classify with respect to these pictures and often are ambivalent – as is Rawls's, for example, though I think he is closer to the second picture.[56]

As I argue, one of these two pictures – the goods- and recipient-focused one – holds our thinking about justice captive. Caney agrees at least in part, for he believes that a purely distribution-oriented view is one-sided; but on the other hand, he believes that justice is a 'hybrid' (151) concept, essentially combining a distributive and a political side. There are a number of hugely important issues here, and I shall try and address them.

To start with, I do not deny that political justice and distributive or social justice are important and to some extent distinct *aspects* of a just basic structure. But I do not think that these are two distinct 'types' (148) of justice conceptually and normatively, as they both go back to the basic concept of justice as demanding political and social relations free from arbitrary rule (i.e. domination, in all politically and socially relevant spheres of social life). So contrary to Caney's interpretation (151f.), I do not argue that political justice is more basic or primary, if political justice merely refers to the way a political system is ordered. Rather, I say that justice essentially refers to the standing of persons as justificatory equals – in the political domain of justifying legal norms *as well as* in the contexts of social and economic life more generally. The right to justification is not just a right to political participation and representation but more fundamentally a right to be a justificatory equal in all relevant 'spheres' of justice.[57]

Thus in my view, the just distribution of social benefits and burdens cannot be determined independently from the implications of the right to justification. Which implications are these? Caney believes that the right to justification applies mainly to the question of the legitimate exercise of political power and thus has only few distributive

---

[56] See my 'Two Pictures of Justice', above pp. 17–20.
[57] On this point, see my debate with Nancy Fraser in Rainer Forst, 'First Things First. Redistribution, Recognition and Justification', *European Journal of Political Theory* 6 (2007), pp. 291–304, and Nancy Fraser, 'Identity, Exclusion, and Critique: A Response to Four Critics', ibid., pp. 305–38.

implications. But I would not want to restrict my view of social justice like that. I distinguish between *fundamental* and *full* justice – earlier called 'minimal' and 'maximal', but that is misleading and sounds too 'minimalist'. When it comes to fundamental justice, a 'basic structure of justification' needs to be in place in which social status and social and political power of citizens are equal to the extent that discursive justice can be set in motion as an autonomous political enterprise. Such discursive justice then applies to *all* relevant distributions of goods and to the sphere of production itself, such that based on this kind of *background justice* (to use Rawls's term) every important social scheme of production and distribution of goods is the subject of discursive distributive justification. In these discourses, when it comes to basic questions of social standing, the 'worst off' have what Rawls (in the revised edition) called a 'veto'.[58] Hence I interpret the difference principle as a discursive principle.[59] Discursive social justice understood in that way not only calls for a certain plateau of basic rights, but also demands distributive justice all the way down, as resulting from an autonomous discursive practice of equals. And it is here, by the way, that my view is more pluralist than Caney's – since contrary to him, I would leave the concrete determination of distributive justice in the single spheres to the participants themselves who will (on the basis of fundamental justice, to be sure) have to find ways to identify the right criterion and determination of justice when it comes to questions of the organization of the market, institutions of education, health provision, etc. Here is where the unity of justice allows for a plurality of criteria and perspectives.[60]

Given my interpretation of the difference principle as providing the 'worst off' with a veto, Caney and I may not differ much in our generally egalitarian approach to social justice, but we differ in our account of how to think about distributive justice. I think about it in political and discursive terms, while Caney believes there is an independent

---

[58] Rawls, *A Theory of Justice*, p. 131.
[59] See *RJ*, pp. 115 and 197.
[60] See *RJ*, p. 197f. et passim.

moral truth as to the right end-state of distributive justice. Yet absent an omniscient (an epistemic point) and authorized (a moral-political point) 'egalitarian distributor' (Cohen as cited above), we *must* leave the determination of forms of full justice to those who have to live in that system for precisely these epistemic and moral-political reasons. Justice is an *autonomous* achievement under certain conditions, not an independent ideal to be realized, as Caney argues.

What exactly is at stake here? Caney takes issue with the four critiques I level against the first picture of justice, and I want to briefly respond to his careful analysis and critique.

(1) When it comes to questions of production, I agree that 'very many' (154) theories have a historical component – yet I would add that it has to be an *appropriate* one and not one of a Nozickian or luck egalitarian kind. The first is a libertarian fantasy, while the latter (to some extent, a cousin of libertarianism in stressing individual responsibility) also has a story to tell, but one so abstract that it can hardly be applied to complex social circumstances. And if it is applied, I agree with Anderson,[61] for example, that it would be unjust and demeaning. When it comes to a relevant and realistic understanding of the genesis of injustice, I would use words such as exploitation or oppression, not descriptions of 'brute' or 'option luck'. This seems to me to look in the wrong direction. Rawlsians, however, and here I agree with Caney, can and should have an adequate story, but as I said, I do not count Rawls as primarily belonging to the first picture camp. So I don't think Caney can count Rawls in his team. As I argue in my book,[62] my view of social and distributive justice is much in agreement with Rawls's thorough critique of the allocative justice of 'welfare-state capitalism' and with his relational rationale for 'pure background procedural justice' in the form of a 'property-owning democracy', for example, the point being to establish a system of social cooperation that is precisely not in need of goods-redistribution to passive recipients.

---

[61] Elisabeth Anderson, 'What is the Point of Equality?', *Ethics* 109 (1999), pp. 287–337.
[62] *RJ*, p. 199.

(2) In separating distributive from political justice, Caney argues that 'a political actor may be exercising power legitimately even if they do not pursue . . . egalitarian ideals so long as they can justify their decisions to those they govern' (156). At this point, he uses a notion of 'legitimacy' which I am not sure I know how exactly to relate to 'political justice'. On p. 152 he calls the question of the 'justified exercise of political power' the question of 'political justice or legitimacy', but I am not sure he would identify the two terms. Caney seems to be ambivalent between a strong and a weak reading of legitimacy – the strong reading connects it to reciprocal and general justification (160), the weak reading merely gives subjects reasons to 'obey' the political authority as long as there is some public justification, even if rejectable from a justice point of view (156). Conceptually, I take the notion of legitimacy indeed to be malleable and not at the same level as that of justice, for normatively speaking it is considerations of basic justice that determine what counts as legitimate. In my justice-based view, contrary to the weak reading of Caney's notion of legitimacy, the exercise of power cannot be justifiable and thus cannot be politically just if it violates reciprocally non-rejectable demands of egalitarian distributions, that is, fundamental justice. Things look different with disagreements over full justice, but I take Caney's critique to be referring to issues of fundamental justice. In that connection, one at times gains the impression that he counts a core of political justice plus some of its distributive implications (socio-economic basic rights) among the essentials of justice, while relegating disputes among 'ideals' (156) of distributive justice to a realm of reasonable philosophical disagreement, as if these ideals (his own egalitarian one among them) were mere 'comprehensive doctrines' in a Rawlsian sense. I think that would be a very unfortunate move, lowering the normative validity of distributive claims and conceptions too much.

(3) This leads to Caney's completely apt question of what 'justifiable' means. He suggests an important distinction between 'justification required for political legitimacy (political justification)' and 'philoso-phically correct' justification (156). Again, I see a weaker and a stronger reading of what a 'correct' philosophical justification is. The weaker

reading calls it 'sound' (157) and counts Rawls, Dworkin or Nozick as candidates, the stronger reading would reserve 'correct' for the conception Caney thinks right. I believe he intends the weaker version, but even for the stronger one I think he would, as he does, argue that it 'may not be enforced through the exercise of political power without some kind of process of political justification' (157). To me, this sounds like a priority argument in favour of the discursive dimension of justice, which Caney tries to refute, but I leave that aside here.

Rather, I want to develop further the discourse-theoretical notion of justification already discussed in my reply to Tony Laden. There I defended the independence of philosophical justification in a certain way; here I need to stress the interdependence of philosophical and moral and political justification (again adding the moral between 'philosophical' and 'political'). For even though I believe that the reconstruction of the principle of justification is epistemically and philosophically correct and true, and even though I think that on that basis one can construct a substantive moral argument for a conception of fundamental justice, I still believe that the determination of the right – and generally and reciprocally justifiable – kind of distribution should be a matter of discursive justice as an *autonomous practice* within a basic structure of justification that rules out unjustifiable power relations dominating discourse. That does not mean that we lose our autonomous philosophical plus moral judgements about justice and hand them over to a collective; but it means that the first task of justice is to aim for forms of political justification that are not deaf to morally justifiable claims of those subjected and possibly marginalized or overlooked. A society aiming for justice moves towards closing the – never to be fully closed – gap between philosophical, moral and political justification by way of discursive and contestatory practice.

Philosophically at issue here, of course, is the question of the role or place of practical reason in philosophy, morality and in politics – or in older terms, the relation between theory and emancipatory practice. I cannot go into that further here, but this refers to what I had in mind when I spoke about the peculiar type called a 'Frankfurt person'. If justification can become a *practice*, it does not cease to be a transcending *idea* at the same time, but is not a mere *ideal* opposing reality. In a process of enlightenment, Habermas says, 'there can only be participants'.[63] Ultimately, in the reflexive form in which I defend it, the philosophical justification of a conception of justice calls for the realization of practices of justification among justificatory equals that would aim at discursively constructing justice for those subject to it.

(4) With regard to the illuminating way in which Caney distinguishes between a weak version of my emphasis on the importance of domination and a strong one which says that the 'very essence of injustice is exploitation, subjugation and oppression' (159), that is, forms of domination, I go – given what I said above – for the strong version. I believe that justice is a man-made Goddess invented for a particular purpose: to make things right that have gone wrong between human beings. Her task is not to create a completely new world with new human beings; rather, she aims at a world free from domination that exists between them. The task of justice is the eradication of the humiliation of persons and of the denial of their dignity, and that denial is a human act.

Limits

The cover of *The Right to Justification* shows a beautiful picture by Paul Klee from 1927 called 'Grenzen des Verstandes' – the limits of understanding or rationality. These limits play a role in my theory in many ways, such as when I speak about reasonable disagreement with respect to ethical or metaphysical views which reason can neither prove wrong nor right, or when I stress the finitude of our attempts at philosophical or practical justification, calling for recursive self-correction. But now, at the end of this attempt to respond to the many challenges my dear critics and friends have posed to me, this

---

[63] Jürgen Habermas, *Theory and Practice*. Boston: Beacon Press, 1974, p. 40.

picture gains a different meaning. It reminds me how limited my understanding of the issues we are discussing is. But if I ever make some progress, it is by gaining a better understanding of these limits, and that is due to the privilege I have in being read and criticized by such great minds as these six to whom I had the honour of replying. I will be forever in their debt.

Bibliography

Abizadeh, A. (2008), 'Democratic Theory and Border Coercion: No Right to Unilaterally Control your Own Borders', *Political Theory* 36(1): 37–65.

—(2010), 'Democratic Legitimacy and State Coercion: A Reply to David Miller', *Political Theory* 38(1): 121–30.

Allen, A. (1999), *The Power of Feminist Theory: Domination, Resistance, Solidarity.* Boulder: Westview.

—(2008), *The Politics of Our Selves: Power, Autonomy, and Gender in Contemporary Critical Theory.* New York: Columbia University Press.

—(2013), 'The Unforced Force of the Better Argument: Reason and Power in Habermas' Political Theory', *Constellations* 19(3): 353–68, September 2012.

Allen, A., R. Forst, and M. Haugaard (forthcoming), 'Power, Reason, Justice, Domination: A Dialogue between Amy Allen, Rainer Forst and Mark Haugaard', *Journal of Power.*

Allen, D. (2004), *Talking to Strangers.* Chicago: University of Chicago Press.

Anderson, E. (1999), 'What Is the Point of Equality?', *Ethics* 109(2): 287–337.

Aniskiewicz, A. S. (1979), 'Autonomic Components of Vicarious Conditioning and Psychopathy', *Journal of Clinical Psychology* 35: 60–7.

Archibugi, D. (1998), 'Principles of Cosmopolitan Democracy', in D. Archibugi, D. Held and M. Köhler (eds), *Re-imagining Political Community: Studies in Cosmopolitan Democracy.* Cambridge: Polity Press.

Arneson, R. (2001), 'Luck and Equality', *Proceedings of the Aristotelian Society* supp. vol: 73–90.

—(2004), 'Luck Egalitarianism: An Interpretation and Defense', *Philosophical Topics* 32(1/2): 1–20.

—(2011), 'Luck Egalitarianism – A Primer', in C. l. Knight and Z. Stemplowska (eds), *Responsibility and Distributive Justice.* Oxford: Oxford University Press.

Arrhenius, G. (2005), 'The Boundary Problem in Democratic Theory', in F. Tersman (ed.), *Democracy Unbound.* Stockholm: Stockholm University Press.

Avant, D. D., M. Finnemore, and S. K. Sell (eds) (2010), *Who Governs the Globe?.* Cambridge: Cambridge University Press.

Ayers, A. J. (1952), *Language, Truth, and Logic*, 2nd edition. New York: Dover.

Azmanova, A. (2012), *The Scandal of Reason: Toward a Critical Theory of Political Judgment*. New York: Columbia University Press.

Bagnoli, C. 'Constructivism in Metaethics', *Stanford Encyclopedia of Philosophy*, published 27 September 2011 at http://plato.stanford.edu/entries/constructivism-metaethics/, accessed 19 January 2012.

Baron-Cohen, S. (1995), *Mindblindness: An Essay on Autism and Theory of Mind*. Cambridge, MA: MIT Press.

Baron-Cohen, S. and S. Wheelwright (2004), 'The Empathy Quotient: An Investigation of Adults with Asperger Syndrome or High Functioning Autism, and Normal Sex Differences', *Journal of Autism and Developmental Disorders* 34: 163–75.

Baron-Cohen, S., A. M. Leslie, and U. Frith (1985), 'Does the Autistic Child Have a "Theory of Mind"?', *Cognition* 21: 37–46.

Barry, B. (1989), *Theories of Justice: A Treatise on Social Justice, Volume I*. Hemel Hempstead: Harvester Wheatsheaf.

Beckman, L. (2009), *The Frontiers of Democracy: The Right to Vote and Its Limits*. Basingstoke: Palgrave Macmillan.

—(2012), 'Is Residence Special? Democracy in the Age of Migration and Human Mobility', in L. Beckman and E. Erman (eds), *Territories of Citizenship*. New York: Palgrave Macmillan.

Beitz, C. (1983), 'Cosmopolitan Ideals and National Sentiment', *Journal of Philosophy* 80(10): 591–600.

—(1989), *Political Equality*. Princeton: Princeton University Press.

Benhabib, S. (1992), *Situating the Self. Gender, Community and Postmodernism in Contemporary Ethics*. New York: Routledge.

—(1997), 'On Reconciliation and Respect, Justice and the Good Life: Response to Herta Nagl-Docekal and Rainer Forst', *Philosophy & Social Criticism* 23: 97–114.

—(2004), *The Rights of Others: Aliens, Residents and Citizens*. Cambridge: Cambridge University Press.

Bergström, L. (2007), 'Democracy and Political Boundaries', in F. Tersman (ed.), *The Viability and Desirability of Global Democracy*. Stockholm: Stockholm University.

Berlin, I. (1981), *Concepts and Categories*. Harmondsworth: Penguin.

Blair, R. (2005), 'Responding to the Emotions of Others: Dissociating Forms of Empathy through the Study of Typical and Psychiatric Populations', *Consciousness and Cognition* 14: 698–718.

Blair, R., L. Jones, F. Clark, and M. Smith (1995), 'Is the Psychopath "Morally Insane"?', *Personality and Individual Differences* 19: 741–52.

—(1997), 'The Psychopathic Individual: A Lack of Responsiveness to Distress Cues?', *Psychophysiology* 34: 192–8.

Boltanski, L. and L. Thévenot (2006), *On Justification*, trans. by C. Porter. Princeton: Princeton University Press.

Bourdieu, P. (1977), *Outline of a Theory of Practice*. Cambridge: Cambridge University Press.

—(1984), *Distinction: A Social Critique of the Judgement of Taste*, trans. by R. Nice. Cambridge, MA: Harvard University Press.

—(1988), *Homo Academicus*. Stanford: Stanford University Press.

—(1991a), 'Distinction Revisited: Introduction to an East German Reading', *Poetics Today* 12(4): 639–41.

—(1991b), 'Social Space and Symbolic Space: Introduction to a Japanese Reading of Distinction', *Poetics Today* 12(4): 627–38.

—(1991c), *Language and Symbolic Power*. Cambridge, MA: Harvard University Press.

—(1998), *Practical Reason: On the Theory of Action*. Cambridge: Polity.

—(2000), *Pascalian Meditations*. Stanford: Stanford University Press.

Brandom, R. (1994), *Making it Explicit*. Cambridge, MA: Harvard University Press.

—(1999), 'Some Pragmatist Themes in Hegel's Idealism', *European Journal of Philosophy* 7(2): 164–89.

Brighouse, H. and A. Swift (2006), 'Equality, Priority, and Positional Goods', *Ethics* 116: 471–97.

Brighouse, H. and I. Robeyns (eds) (2010), *Measuring Justice: Primary Goods and Capabilities*. Cambridge: Cambridge University Press.

Caney, S. (2001), 'Cosmopolitan Justice and Equalizing Opportunities', *Metaphilosophy* 32(1/2): 113–34.

—(2005), *Justice Beyond Borders: A Global Political Theory*. Oxford: Oxford University Press.

—(2007), 'Global Poverty and Human Rights: The Case for Positive Duties', in T. Pogge (ed.), *Freedom from Poverty as a Human Right: Who Owes What to the Very Poor?* Oxford: Oxford University Press, pp. 275–302.

—(2011), 'Humanity, Associations and Global Justice: In Defence of Humanity-Centred Cosmopolitan Egalitarianism', *The Monist* 94(4): 506–34.

Carens, J. (2009), 'Fear vs. Fairness: Migration, Citizenship and the Transformation of Political Community', in K. Lippert-Rasmussen, N. Holtug, and S. Laegaard (eds), *Nationalism and Multiculturalism in a World of Immigration*. Houndmills: Palgrave Macmillan.

—(2010), 'Aliens and Citizens: The Case for Open Borders', in R. Bellamy and A. Palumbo (eds), *Citizenship*. Aldershot: Ashgate Publishing.

Christiano, T. (2006), 'A Democratic Theory of Territory and Some Puzzles about Global Democracy', *Journal of Social Philosophy* 37(1): 81–107.

—(2009), 'Debate: Estlund on Democratic Authority', *The Journal of Political Philosophy* 17(2): 228–40.

Cohen, G. A. (1993), 'Equality of What: On Welfare, Goods and Capabilities', in M. Nussbaum and A. Sen (eds), *The Quality of Life*. Oxford: Oxford University Press.

—(1997), 'Where the Action Is: On the Site of Distributive Justice', *Philosophy and Public Affairs* 26(1): 3–30.

—(2003), 'Facts and Principles', *Philosophy & Public Affairs* 31(3): 211–45.

—(2008), *Rescuing Justice and Equality*. Cambridge, MA: Harvard University Press.

—(2011), *On the Currency of Egalitarian Justice and Other Essays in Political Philosophy*, ed. by M. Otsuka. Princeton: Princeton University Press.

Cohen, J. (1989), 'Democratic Equality', *Ethics* 99(4): 727–51.

Collier, P. (2007), *The Bottom Billion: Why the Poorest Countries Are Failing and What Can be Done About It*. Oxford: Oxford University Press.

Cook, C. (ed.) (1994), *Constitutional Predicament*. Montréal: McGill-Queen's University Press.

Crisp, R. (2003), 'Equality, Priority, and Compassion', *Ethics* 113(4): 745–63.

Curtis, D. E. and J. Resnik (1987), 'Images of Justice', *Yale Law Journal* 96: 1727–72.

Dahl, R. (1989), *Democracy and Its Critics*. New Haven: Yale University Press.

Dworkin, R. (2000), *Sovereign Virtue: The Theory and Practice of Equality*. Cambridge, MA: Harvard University Press.

—(2003), 'Equality, Luck and Hierarchy', *Philosophy & Public Affairs* 31(2): 190–8.

Enoch, D. (2006), 'Agency, Shmagency: Why Normativity Won't Come from What Is Constitutive of Action', *The Philosophical Review* 115: 169–98.

Erman, E. (2005), *Human Rights and Democracy: Discourse Theory and Global Rights Institutions.* Aldershot: Ashgate.

—(2007), 'Conflict and Universal Moral Theory: From Reasonableness to Reason-Giving', *Political Theory* 35(5): 598–623.

—(2011), 'Human Rights Do not Make Global Democracy', *Contemporary Political Theory* 10(4): 463–81.

—(2012), '"The Right to have Rights" to the Rescue: From Human Rights to Global Democracy', in M. Goodale (ed.), *Human Rights at the Crossroads.* Oxford: Oxford University Press, pp. 72–83.

—(2013), 'In Search for Democratic Agency in Deliberative Governance', *European Journal of International Relations* 19(4): 847–68.

Erman, E. and A. Follesdal (2012), 'Multiple Citizenship: Normative Ideals and Institutional Challenges', *Critical Review of International Social and Political Philosophy* 15(3): 279–302.

Erman, E. and N. Möller (2013), 'Three Failed Charges Against Ideal Theory', *Social Theory & Practice* 39(1): 19–44.

Fanon, F. (2008), *Black Skin, White Masks,* trans. by R. Philcox. New York: Grove Press.

Ferrero, L. (2008), 'Constitutivism and the Inescapability of Agency', in R. Shafer-Landau (ed.), *Oxford Studies in Metaethics.* Oxford: Oxford University Press.

Forst, R. (1997), 'Situations of the Self: Reflections on Seyla Benhabib's Version of Critical Theory', *Philosophy & Social Criticism* 23: 79–96.

—(2001), 'The Rule of Reasons: Three Models of Deliberative Democracy', *Ratio Juris* 14(4): 345–78.

—(2002), *Contexts of Justice: Political Philosophy Beyond Liberalism and Communitarianism,* trans. by J. M. M. Farrell. Berkeley: University of California Press.

—(2007a), *Das Recht auf Rechtfertigung: Elemente einer konstruktivistischen Theorie der Gerechtigkeit.* Frankfurt am Main: Suhrkamp.

—(2007b), 'First Things First: Redistribution, Recognition and Justification', *European Journal of Political Theory* 6(3): 291–304.

—(2007c), 'Radical Justice: On Iris Marion Young's Critique of the Distributive Paradigm', *Constellations* 14(2): 260–5.

—(2007d), '"To tolerate means to insult": Toleration, Recognition, and Emancipation', in B. van den Brink and D. Owen (eds), *Recognition and Power*. Cambridge: Cambridge University Press, 215–37.

—(2010), 'The Justification of Human Rights and the Basic Right to Justification: A Reflexive Approach', *Ethics* 120(4): 711–40.

—(2011), *Kritik der Rechtfertigungsverhältnisse: Perspektiven einer kritischen Theorie der Politik*. Berlin: Suhrkamp.

—(2012), *The Right to Justification: Elements of a Constructivist Theory of Justice*, trans. by J. Flynn. New York: Columbia University Press.

—(2013a), *Toleration in Conflict*, trans. by C. Cronin. Cambridge: Cambridge University Press.

—(2013b), *Justification and Critique. Towards a Critical Theory of Politics*, trans. by C. Cronin. Cambridge: Polity.

—(2013c), 'A Kantian Republican Conception of Justice as Non-Domination', in A. Niederberger and P. Schink (eds), *Republican Democracy*. Edinburgh: Edinburgh University Press, 154–68.

—(2013d), 'Noumenal Power', *Normative Orders Working Paper* 2. Electronic: http://www.normativeorders.net/en/publikationen/working-paper-series.

—(2013e), 'Transnational Justice and Democracy. Overcoming Three Dogmas of Political Theory', in E. Erman and S. Näsström (eds), *Political Equality in Transnational Democracy*. New York: Palgrave Macmillan, 41–59.

—(2013f), 'Zum Begriff eines Rechtfertigungsnarrativs', in A. Fahrmeir (ed.), *Rechtfertigungsnarrative*. Frankfurt am Main: Campus, 11–28.

Forst, R. and K. Günther (eds) (2011), *Die Herausbildung normativer Ordnungen*. Frankfurt am Main: Campus.

Forst, R., M. Hartmann, R. Jaeggi, and M. Saar (2009), *Sozialphilosophie und Kritik. Festschrift for Axel Honneth*. Frankfurt am Main: Suhrkamp Verlag.

Foucault, M. (1977), *Discipline and Punish. The Birth of the Prison*, trans. by A. Sheridan. New York: Random House.

—(2000), 'Space, Knowledge, and Power', in J. Faubion (ed.), *Essential Works of Michel Foucault, volume 3: Power*. New York: The New Press.

Frankfurt, H. (1988), *The Importance of What we Care About*. Cambridge: Cambridge University Press.

—(1999), *Necessity, Volition, and Love*. Cambridge: Cambridge University Press.

Fraser, N. (2007), 'Identity, Exclusion, and Critique: A Response to Four Critics', *European Journal of Political Theory* 6: 305–38.

Fraser, N. and A. Honneth (2003), *Redistribution or Recognition? A Political-Philosophical Exchange*, trans. by J. Golb, J. Ingram, and C. Wilke. London: Verso.

Freyenhagen, F. and J. Schaub (2010), 'Hat hier jemand gesagt, der Kaiser sei nackt? Eine Verteidigung der Geussschen Kritik an Rawls' idealtheoretischem Ansatz', *Deutsche Zeitschrift für Philosophie* 58(3): 457–77.

Gaita, R. (2000), *A Common Humanity*. New York: Routledge.

Gallup, J. L. and J. D. Sachs (2001), 'The Economic Burden of Malaria', *The American Journal of Tropical Medicine and Hygiene* 64(1) (suppl.): 85–96.

Gallup, J. L., J. D. Sachs and A. D. Mellinger (1999), 'Geography and Economic Development', *International Regional Science Review* 22(2): 179–232.

Geuss, R. (2005), *Outside Ethics*. Princeton: Princeton University Press.

—(2008), *Philosophy and Real Politics*. Princeton: Princeton University Press.

Goodin, R. (1995), 'Political Ideals and Political Practice', *British Journal of Political Science* 25(1): 37–56.

—(2007), 'Enfranchising All Affected Interests and Its Alternatives', *Philosophy & Public Affairs* 35(1): 40–68.

Gosepath, S. (2004), *Gleiche Gerechtigkeit*. Frankfurt am Main: Suhrkamp.

Gould, C. (2004), *Globalizing Democracy and Human Rights*. Cambridge: Cambridge University Press.

Habermas, J. (1979), *Communication and the Evolution of Society*, trans. by T. McCarthy. Boston: Beacon Press.

—(1984), *The Theory of Communicative Action, volume 1: Reason and the Rationalization of Society*, trans. T. McCarthy. Boston: Beacon Press.

—(1990), *Moral Consciousness and Communicative Action*, trans. by C. Lenhardt and S. Nicholsen. Cambridge, MA: MIT Press.

—(1993), *Justification and Application: Remarks on Discourse Ethics*, trans. by C. Cronin. Cambridge, MA: MIT Press.

—(1996a), *Between Facts and Norms: Contributions to a Discourse Theory of Law and Democracy*, trans. by W. Rehg. Cambridge, MA: MIT Press.

—(1996b), 'Paradigms of Law', *Cardozo Law Review* 17: 771–84.

—(1996c), 'Reply to Symposium Participants', *Cardozo Law Review* 17: 1477–557.

—(1998), *The Inclusion of the Other*, ed. by C. Cronin and P. De Greiff. Cambridge, MA: MIT Press.

—(2003), *Truth and Justification*, trans. by B. Fultner. Cambridge, MA: MIT Press.

—(2011), 'Reply to My Critics', in J. G. Finlayson and F. Freyenhagen (eds), *Habermas and Rawls: Disputing the Political*. New York and London: Routledge.

Hare, R. D. (1991), *The Hare Psychopathy Checklist – Revised*. Toronto: Multi-Health Systems.

Hayward, C. R. (2004), 'Doxa and Deliberation', *Critical Review of International Social and Political Philosophy* 7(1): 1–24.

Heidegger, M. (2010), *Being and Time*, trans. by J. Stambaugh, ed. and rev. by D. Schmidt. Albany, NY: SUNY Press.

Held, D. (1995), *Democracy and the Global Order*. Cambridge: Cambridge University Press.

—(2004), *Global Covenant: The Social Democratic Alternative to the Washington Consensus*. Cambridge: Polity.

Hinsch, W. (2002), *Gerechtfertigte Ungleichheiten*. Berlin: de Gruyter.

Honderich, T. (ed.) (1988), Morality and Objectivity. London: Routledge.

Honneth, A. (2011), *Das Recht der Freiheit: Grundriß einer demokratischen Sittlichkeit*. Frankfurt am Main: Suhrkamp.

Horkheimer, M. and T. Adorno (2002), *Dialectic of Enlightenment: Philosophical Fragments*, trans. E. Jephcott. Stanford: Stanford University Press.

Huffer, L. (2010), *Mad for Foucault: Rethinking the Foundations of Queer Theory*. New York: Columbia University Press.

Hume, D. (1978), *A Treatise of Human Nature*, ed. L. A. Selby-Bigge. Oxford: Oxford University Press.

—(1998), *An Enquiry Concerning the Principles of Morals*, ed. T. L. Beauchamp. Oxford: Oxford University Press.

Israel, J. (2001), *Radical Enlightenment. Philosophy and the Making of Modernity 1650–1750*. Oxford: Oxford University Press.

James, R. and R. Blair (1996), 'Brief Report: Morality in the Autistic Child', *Journal of Autism and Developmental Disorders* 26: 571–9.

Jones, L. (ed.) (2005), *Encyclopedia of Religion*, 2nd edition. Detroit, MI: Macmillan Reference.

Kant, I. (1970), 'On the Common Saying: This May Be True in Theory, but it Does not Apply in Practice', in H. S. Reiss (ed.), *Kant's Political Writings*. Cambridge: Cambridge University Press.

—(1988), *Critique of Pure Reason*, trans. by P. Guyer and A. Wood. Cambridge: Cambridge University Press.

—(1997), *Critique of Practical Reason*, trans. by M. Gregor. Cambridge: Cambridge University Press.

—(1998), *Groundwork of the Metaphysics of Morals*, trans. by M. Gregor. Cambridge: Cambridge University Press.

—(2009), *The Metaphysics of Morals*, ed. and trans. by M. J. Gregor. Cambridge: Cambridge University Press.

Karlsson Schaffer, J. 'The Boundaries of Transnational Democracy: Alternatives to the All-affected Principle', *Review of International Studies*, available on CJO 2011 doi: 10.1017/S0260210510001749.

Kennett, J. (2002), 'Autism, Empathy and Moral Agency', *The Philosophical Quarterly* 52: 340–57.

Kissel, O. R. (1984), *Die Justitia: Reflexionen über ein Symbol und seine Darstellung in der bildenden Kunst*. Munich: Beck.

Korsgaard, C. (1983), 'Two Distinctions in Goodness', *Philosophical Review* 92: 169–95.

—(1996), *Constructing the Kingdom of Ends*. Cambridge: Cambridge University Press.

—(2008), *The Constitution of Agency. Essays on Practical Reason and Moral Psychology*. Oxford: Oxford University Press.

—(2009), *Self-Constitution: Agency, Identity, and Integrity*. Oxford: Oxford University Press.

Krebs, A. (ed.) (2000), *Gleichheit oder Gerechtigkeit*. Frankfurt am Main: Suhrkamp.

Laden, A. S. (2000), 'Outline of a Theory of Reasonable Deliberation', *Canadian Journal of Philosophy* 30: 551–80.

—(2001), *Reasonably Radical: Deliberative Liberalism and the Politics of Identity*. Ithaca: Cornell University Press.

—(2007), 'Negotiation, Deliberation, and Claims of Politics', in A. S. Laden and D. Owen (eds), *Multiculturalism and Political Theory*. Cambridge: Cambridge University Press.

—(2010), 'The Justice of Justification', in F. Frayenhagen and J. G. Finlayson (eds), *Debating the Political: Rawls and Habermas in Dialogue*. New York: Routledge, pp. 135–52.

—(2012), *Reasoning: A Social Picture*. Oxford: Oxford University Press.

—(2013), 'Learning to be Equal: Just Schools and Schools of Justice', in D. S. Allen and R. Reich (eds), *Education, Democracy and Justice*. Chicago: University of Chicago Press.

—(2013), 'Ideals of justice: goals vs. constraints', *Critical Review of International Social and Political Philosophy* 16(2): 205–19.

Laden, A. S. and D. Owen (eds) (2007), *Multiculturalism and Political Theory*. Cambridge: Cambridge University Press.

Lloyd, G. (1993), *The Man of Reason: 'Male' and 'Female' in Western Philosophy*, 2nd edition. Chicago: University of Chicago Press.

Lopez-Guerra, C. (2005), 'Should Expatriates Vote?', *The Journal of Political Philosophy* 13(2): 216–34.

Macdonald, T. (2008), *Global Stakeholder Democracy*. Oxford: Oxford University Press.

MacKinnon, C. (1987), *Feminism Unmodified*, Cambridge, MA: Harvard University Press.

—(2006), *Are Women Human?* Cambridge, MA: Harvard University Press.

Mann, M. (2001), 'Globalization and September 11', *New Left Review* 12 (November–December): 51–72.

Marx, K. and F. Engels (1970), *The German Ideology*. New York: International Publishers.

McCarthy, T. (1994), 'Kantian Constructivism and Reconstructivism: Rawls and Habermas in Dialogue', *Ethics* 105(1): 44–63.

—(2009), *Race, Empire, and the Idea of Human Development*. Cambridge: Cambridge University Press.

McDowell, J. (1988), 'Values and Secondary Qualities', in T. Honderich (ed.), *Morality and Objectivity*. London: Routledge, pp. 110–29.

Miller, D. (1995), *On Nationality*. Oxford: Clarendon Press.

—(2010), 'Why Immigration Controls Are Not Coercive: A Reply to Arash Abizadeh', *Political Theory* 38(1): 111–20.

Milo, R. (1995), 'Contractarian Constructivism', *The Journal of Philosophy* 92: 181–204.

Morris, I. (2010), *Why the West Rules – for Now: The Patterns of History, and What They Reveal About the Future*. London: Profile Books.

Näsström, S. (2011), 'The Challenge of the All affected Principle', *Political Studies* 59(1): 116–34.

Nozick, R. (1974), *Anarchy, State, and Utopia*. New York: Basic Books.

Nussbaum, M. (2006), *Frontiers of Justice: Disability, Nationality, Species Membership*. Cambridge, MA: Harvard University Press.

O'Neill, M. (2008), 'Three Rawlsian Routes towards Economic Democracy', *Revue de Philosophie Économique* 8(2): 29–55.

—(2011), 'Free (and Fair) Markets without Capitalism: Political Values, Principles of Justice, and Property Owning Democracy', in M. O'Neill and T. Williamson (eds), *Property Owning Democracy: Rawls and Beyond*. Oxford: Blackwell.

O'Neill, O. (1987), 'Abstraction, Idealization and Ideology in Ethics', in J. D. G. Evans (ed.), *Moral Philosophy and Contemporary Problems*. Cambridge: Cambridge University Press.

—(1989), *Constructions of Reason. Explorations of Kant's Practical Philosophy*. Cambridge: Cambridge University Press.

Olson, K. (2006), *Reflexive Democracy: Political Equality and the Welfare State*. Cambridge, MA: MIT Press.

—(2011), 'Legitimate Speech and Hegemonic Idiom: The Limits of Deliberative Democracy in the Diversity of its Voices', *Political Studies* 59(3): 527–46.

Owen, D. (2002), 'Criticism and Captivity: On Genealogy and Critical Theory', *European Journal of Philosophy* 10(2): 216–30.

—(2011), 'Transnational Citizenship and the Democratic State', *Critical Review of International Social and Political Philosophy* 14(5): 641–64.

—(2012), 'Constituting the Polity, Constituting the Demos: on the Place of the All affected Interests Principle in Democratic Theory and in Resolving the Democratic Boundary Problem', *Ethics & Global Politics* 5(3): 129–52.

Parfit, D. (2002), 'Equality or Priority?', in M. Clayton. and A. Williams (eds), *The Ideal of Equality*. Houndsmill: Macmillan.

—(2003), 'Justifiability to Each Person', *Ratio* 16: 368–90.

Patrick, C. J. (1994), 'Emotion and Psychopathy: Startling New Insights', *Psychophysiology* 31: 319–30.

Pitkin, H. F. (1972), *Wittgenstein and Justice*. Berkeley: University of California Press.

Pogge, T. (2004), 'The Incoherence Between Rawls's Theories of Justice', *Fordham Law Review* 72(5): 1739–59.

—(2008), *World Poverty and Human Rights: Cosmopolitan Responsibilities and Reforms,* second edition. Cambridge: Polity.

Rawls, J. (1971), *A Theory of Justice*. Cambridge, MA: Harvard University Press.

—(1980), 'Kantian Constructivism in Moral Theory', *Journal of Philosophy* 77: 515–72.

—(1993), *Political Liberalism*. New York: Columbia University Press.

—(1995), 'Reply to Habermas', *The Journal of Philosophy* 92: 132–80.

—(1999a), *A Theory of Justice*, rev. edn. Cambridge, MA: Harvard University Press.

—(1999b), *Collected Papers*. Cambridge, MA: Harvard University Press.

—(1999c), *The Law of Peoples with 'The Idea of Public Reason Revisited'*. Cambridge, MA: Harvard University Press.

—(2001), *Justice as Fairness: A Restatement*, ed. by E. Kelly. Cambridge, MA: Harvard University Press.

Raz, J. (1986), *The Morality of Freedom*. Oxford: Clarendon Press.

Richards, D. A. J. (1982), 'International Distributive Justice', in J. R. Pennock and J. W. Chapman (eds), *Ethics, Economics, and the Law: NOMOS XXIV*. New York: New York University Press, pp. 275–99.

Scanlon, T. M. (1982), 'Contractualism and Utilitarianism', in B. Williams and A. Sen (eds), *Utilitarianism and Beyond*. Cambridge: Cambridge University Press.

—(1998), *What We Owe to Each Other*. Cambridge, MA: Harvard University Press.

—(2003), 'Replies', *Ratio* 16: 424–39.

Scheffler, S. (2003), 'Equality as the Virtue of Sovereigns: A Reply to Ronald Dworkin', *Philosophy & Public Affairs* 31(2): 199–206.

—(2010), *Equality and Tradition: Questions of Value in Moral and Political Theory*. Oxford: Oxford University Press.

Sen, A. (1992), *Inequality Reexamined*. Cambridge, MA: Harvard University Press.

—(2000), 'Consequential Evaluation and Practical Reason', *Journal of Philosophy* 97(9): 477–502.

—(2009), *The Idea of Justice*. Cambridge, MA: Harvard University Press.

Shafer-Landau, R. (2003), *Moral Realism: A Defence*. Oxford: Clarendon.

Shapiro, I. (1999), *Democratic Justice*. New Haven: Yale University Press.

Shue, H. (1996), *Basic Rights: Subsistence, Affluence, and U. S. Foreign Policy*, second edition with a new afterword. Princeton: Princeton University Press.

Sidgwick, H. (1981), *The Methods of Ethics*, 7th edition with a foreword by J. Rawls. Indianapolis: Hackett Publishing Company.

Simmons, J. (2010), 'Ideal and Nonideal Theory', *Philosophy & Public Affairs* 38: 5–36.

Street, S. (2008), 'Constructivism About Reasons', in R. Shafer-Landau (ed.), *Oxford Studies in Metaethics*. Oxford: Oxford University Press, pp. 207–45.

—(2010), 'What Is Constructivism in Ethics and Metaethics?', *Philosophy Compass* 5: 363–84.

Swift, A. (2008), 'The Value of Philosophy in Non-Ideal Circumstances', *Social Theory and Practice* 34(3): 363–88.

Taylor, C. (1989), *Sources of the Self*. Cambridge, MA: Harvard University Press.

Timmons, M. (2003), 'The Limits of Moral Constructivism', *Ratio* 16: 391–423.

Topper, K. (2001), 'Not So Trifling Nuances: Pierre Bourdieu, Symbolic Violence, and the Perversions of Democracy', *Constellations* 8(1): 30–56.

—(2011), 'Arendt and Bourdieu between Word and Deed', *Political Theory*: 39: 352–77.

Tugendhat, E. (1993), *Vorlesungen über Ethik*. Frankfurt am Main: Suhrkamp.

Tully, J. (1994), 'Diversity's Gambit Declined', in C. Cook (ed.), *Constitutional Predicament*. Montréal: McGill-Queen's University Press.

—(2008), *Public Philosophy in a New Key*. Cambridge: Cambridge University Press.

Valentini, L. (2009), 'On the Apparent Paradox of Ideal Theory', *Journal of Political Philosophy* 17: 332–5.

Van der Veen, R. and P. van Parijs (1985), 'Entitlement Theories of Justice: From Nozick to Roemer and Beyond', *Economics and Philosophy* 1(1): 69–81.

Walzer, M. (1983), *Spheres of Justice*. New York: Basic Books.

Walzer, M. and D. Miller (eds) (1995), *Pluralism, Justice, and Equality*. Oxford: Oxford University Press.

Whelan, F. G. (1983), 'Democratic Theory and the Boundary Problem', in J. R. Pennock and J. W. Chapman (eds), *Liberal Democracy*. New York: New York University Press.

Wiggins, D. (1987), *Needs, Values, Truth: Essays in the Philosophy of Value*. Oxford: Oxford University Press.

Williams, B. (2005), *In the Beginning Was the Deed. Realism and Moralism in Political Argument*. Princeton: Princeton University Press.

Wittgenstein, L. (1922), *Tractatus Logico-Philosophicus*, trans. by C. K. Ogden. London: Routledge.

—(1968), *Philosophical Investigations*, trans. by G. E. M. Anscombe. Oxford: Basil Blackwell.

Young, I. M. (1990), *Justice and the Politics of Difference*. Princeton: Princeton University Press.

—(2007), 'Structural Injustice and the Politics of Difference', in A. S. Laden and D. Owen (eds), *Multiculturalism and Political Theory*. Cambridge: Cambridge University Press, pp. 60–88.

Ypi, L. (2010), 'On the Confusion between Ideal and Non-ideal in Recent Debates on Global Justice', *Political Studies* 58: 536–55.

Zimmerman, M. (2001), *The Nature of Intrinsic Value*. Lanham: Rowman and Littlefield.

Author Index

Subject Index